Whole Language:
Literature, Learning, and Literacy

WHOLE LANGUAGE: LITERATURE, LEARNING, AND LITERACY

A WORKSHOP IN PRINT

by

Lou Willett Stanek

The H. W. Wilson Company
Bronx, NY 1993

Library of Congress Cataloging-in-Publication Data

Stanek, Lou Willett.
Whole language : literature, learning, and literacy : a workshop
in print / Lou Willett Stanek.
p. cm.   Includes bibliographical references and index.
ISBN 0-8242-0837-4
1. Language experience approach in education—United States.
I. Title.
LB1576.S753   1992
372.6'0973—dc20   92-29691

For my sister
Loann Willett Hulskotter,
who has always understood
whole kids and their language

CONTENTS

PART II. PRACTICES

PART III. IMPLEMENTATION

PART IV. WHOLE LANGUAGE SUCCESS STORIES

FOREWORD

Lou Stanek and I met many years ago at the Chicago high school where she was teaching students considered "gifted" in English. The school librarian had suggested that I talk about that then-new phenomenon, young adult books. Lou's students had been reading adult books of high quality and were clearly dubious (at first) about "kid stuff." Lou was more broad-minded. That meeting, and our subsequent friendship, were a good example of collaboration between teachers and librarians. At that time many librarians and some teachers were advocating the advantages of trade books replacing textbooks; a very few private schools used only trade books—and "whole language" was a term yet to be coined.

The term has never been clearly and fully defined, although many aspects of its principles, techniques, resources, and methods have been described at length. What Lou Stanek achieves in this book is a convincing argument for its efficacy, a program for implementing and evaluating the use of the whole language approach in the classroom. While it is possible that some aspects of the program may in time diminish in popularity, there is little question that a focus on reading enjoyable books, and on readers' response and participation within the language arts, has already made an impact. While the book often addresses teachers, it recognizes that the librarian is not a clerk but has an important role. One hopes that *Whole Language* will bring the two professional groups together as collegial equals, since each has separate skills to contribute to the common goal of expediting the learning of reading and fostering its lifelong enjoyment.

Zena Sutherland
former Professor
The University of Chicago
Graduate Library School

I. THEORY

Introduction

"Reading to learn," "Teaching to learn," "Learning skills in context," "Writing before they can write," "Integrating the disciplines," "Spelling creatively," "Thinking like a writer," "Building children's self-esteem," "Whole language for whole kids," and "Real literature for real kids," are all part of what all the fuss and excitement is about.

Educators can hardly ignore whole language, a philosophical approach to language, learning, and literacy spreading through American schools at the speed of a loping Australian kangaroo. Teachers and librarians who discovered the theory, tried and tested practices at their own pace, and had success have became strong believers, especially when they work as teams. The problem arises when states or districts mandate the implementation of whole language in the schools without offering training or support. Accepting a learning theory, like a religious or social philosophy, comes from understanding and faith.

Even for the dedicated, defining the theory can present more difficulty than putting the concepts into practice. You could fill a library shelf with recent books explaining what whole language is *not*, an approach as helpful as telling you what ingredients not to use to make fudge.

Reviewing the current literature could also leave you with the impression whole language theory only applies to younger children who are just beginning to learn to read and write. Not at all! Although the new approach to language acquisition starts with a reading-for-meaning theory and is especially important when children's attitudes toward learning are being shaped, I cannot imagine anything more discouraging or disappointing to a child than to have gone K-3 in a whole language classroom and library only to go back to a traditional approach for the remainder of her education. *Whole language—a point of view about learning and the learner—works for all ages.*

However, if you haven't taken a course, had in-service training, or read all the books, you still won't have to change careers. Unlike the new math or computer science which intimidated us all, whole language, primarily an *attitude* about language and learning that developed in New Zealand and Australia in the early eighties, encompasses the new and the not so new. As it operates in a workshop environment, the focus is on learning, not teaching. You could already be doing more of it than you realize. Most teachers and librarians speak not of theatrical overnight conversions but of gradually "becoming" whole language educators by first trying one of the practices like modeled writing, then adding literature focus groups or linking library story hour to classroom activities until finally the basals, the textbooks, and the workbooks were in storage and they were operating a whole language classroom or library. However, they are apt to become more dramatic, even have a gleam in their eye, when describing how much more they and their students now enjoy their work.

Since the approach is a philosophy, not a method, you won't find a model. Whole language classrooms and libraries never look the same, except they are inundated with print—every kind of print imaginable—practical print necessary to function in life: newspapers, magazines, *TV Guides*, signs, posters, charts, play stores stocked with empty food boxes, road maps, letters, as well as student writing, and BOOKS—as many as possible from every available source with reading levels ranging from four to forty. Whole language teachers borrow from the school and public library; they encourage book clubs. Children work together in large groups, in small groups, in pairs, or individually, but are not grouped according to ability. All kids read all day long, instead of in short segments with little groups of birds of a feather.

The children write as much as they read. Paper, pencils, crayons, labels, rulers, and staplers are easily accessible in close proximity to the writing corner. You'll find a class mailbox. They write notes and letters to each other and to the teacher.

Whole language jargon is growing faster than a family of hamsters, but don't be intimidated by educationese like "constructivism," "graphophonic," "predictable cloze," and "syntactic system." If acronyms remind you of the army or Wall Street marauders, you can adopt the viewpoint without labeling yourself a TAWL (Teachers Applying Whole Language), but you might want to become part of the loop. Hundreds of TAWL groups around the country are exchanging ideas. The international organization unifying these hundreds of TAWL groups is called The Whole Language Umbrella.

A Workshop in Print

This book, designed to present *a workshop in print* for those who have not had in-service training and those who have but want to know more, offers definitions in words you can pronounce and plans you can implement in the library, classroom, community and home. You will find suggestions for activities to use with all ages from little kids to adults in literacy, continuing education, and college programs, and for you, the teachers and librarians, to try yourselves.

What exactly is a workshop in print? It's an idea usurped from a whole language classroom activity. When children are beginning to write, it often makes the experience easier or more fun if they imagine they are writing for actual readers like their cousins or the sixth graders down the hall and then have a chance to talk about how having a particular audience affected their style and what they said.

While writing this book, I too, imagined a live audience—you: teachers, librarians, parents, administrators—sitting around with me in a workshop setting. You became so real I could see the young woman wearing jeans and a George Booth, bull terrier sweatshirt; a man with long legs in khakis; a woman in a dress with red poppies. I talked to you. You were writing down what I said, except when your attention wandered. Sharing anecdotes from my life as a writer and teacher, testing whole language theories against my experience, I asked you to do the same. When I suggested themes integrating the disciplines like books about the environment, turning points, the homeless, and brother-sister relationships, I imagined you adding books you knew to the list, including writing activities that had worked in the past. The workshop-in-print idea is to test another whole language belief that integrating learning with our own backgrounds and experience is when that information becomes meaningful and what makes it stick. In this workshop in print, we are carrying on a dialectic in my head, and I assume you're talking back to me as the children talk back to the authors of the stories they read.

Many schools have used *modeling*, another whole language practice, as a means of introducing whole language to their staffs. Such demonstration is an effective but expensive way to enlighten. In the section offering suggestions for implementing whole language, I have often assumed the voice of the teacher speaking directly to the students, as if I were modeling the practice in your class or library. I would be surprised if you followed my suggestions exactly. You will want to adopt or modify to start where your children are, add your good ideas, quality books you love, stop when your kids lose interest.

WHOLE LANGUAGE THEORY

Stripped to the bare, clean bones whole language is:

- a point of view about language, literacy, and learning.
- a theory that has to do with acquiring language based on the assumption that the acquisition of language is what makes people literate.
- an approach to language that moves from "whole" to "part"— whole books, whole paragraphs, whole sentences, whole words.
- an assumption that people learn differently and should be given the opportunity to acquire knowledge in many different ways through visual, oral, global stimuli that include games and dramatic play.
- a set of beliefs about how children gain language to make meaning of things and to accomplish purposes.

Whole Language Beliefs

The basic beliefs in whole language are:

- Children learn language by using it to express their ideas and accomplish meaningful tasks, like finding out what a story is about, not by practicing separate skills, like looking for vowels or memorizing definitions of parts of speech. Words, sentences, poems, stories are left whole. Children learn, as adults do, by making connections. *Children are not learning to read, but reading to learn.*

- The approach to reading and writing is based in the oral tradition where everyone learns to talk. In a classroom or library, educators try to the greatest extent possible to duplicate these conditions for learning to read and to write. If a child isn't learning to read, there is something wrong with the approach or the environment, not the child.

- Reading is "constructing meaning" from many clues, including the reader's purpose, rather than "getting words" which assumes words have constant meanings. Imagine what kind of monster a child, who did not pick up contextual clues, might make of computer bites. Or how about this line from *Fortune* magazine, "The stars tell how they're playing it now." Predictability is the solution to such confusions. Instead of stars that talk as well as twinkle, frolicking in the sky, the photograph shows a man with a five o'clock shadow and another with too many teeth talking about making money.

- Kids respond when reading and writing for real reasons like wanting to know if Joe, Fred, and Sam in *Knights of the Kitchen Table* by Jon Scieszka (Viking, 1991) get back home, or by learning to spell the words they want to use in their stories or notes to each other, rather than doing spelling bees or drills, where being the first to go down does not improve anyone's self-image. In the beginning they might spell creatively—toa for toe—rather than letting one word block the flow of their writing. When reading, they might skip an unfamiliar word, predicting its meaning from the context of the sentence or the paragraph.

- Handwriting has a meaningful purpose like signing a picture, writing a note, telling a story. It is taught as a means of accomplishing a task, not as a separate skill.

- Building a child's *self-esteem* is the most essential ingredient and the place to begin the process. For children or adults who have already faced failure, *revaluing* themselves as language learners is essential. Whole language teachers believe everyone can become literate. The challenge is to convince the learner that the method she has experienced failed, not the student.

- The teacher's and librarian's role is that of *facilitator*. The focal point is learning, not teaching.
- The concentration should be on the *process* rather than the product. If the process is right, the product will be also.
- Teachers and librarians with strong self-esteem are more effective in encouraging children to learn and to develop a strong sense of self. Individuals owe it to themselves and the children to work on strengthening their self perceptions. In-service training programs are also a good idea.

Holistic Theory

Holistic theory assumes that the whole is greater than the sum of the parts—children, words, sentences, literature, language arts, the disciplines, the staff in a school, the community:

- It starts with the child, the whole child, with what she brings to school—her experience, advantages, detriments—as well as what she hopes to receive. Whole language, a child-centered curriculum, strives to be as flexible as Silly Putty, based on the idea of building from where the child is rather than trying to fit her into a prefab course of study. Readers are encouraged to write and talk about their pets, families, troubles, and triumphs, as well as relate to historical figures and storybook characters' lives.
- Whole language *integrates the language arts* as well. Reading, writing, listening, speaking, singing, and acting are presented as a related whole, rather than approached as separate skills. Writing activities, drawing pictures, making oral presentations, acting out plots, impersonating characters, talking for puppets, composing and singing rhymes grow out of the stories children read and tasks they wish to accomplish.
- Language art skills are acquired and practiced for a purpose, across the curriculum in history, art, science, math, and music.

These skills are neither the exclusive property nor sole responsibility of the language arts teachers. Students write math, such as a complete sentence telling how many books with red covers they counted on the book shelves, an essay explaining how the size of a football field affects the rules and the score, or why baseball is played on diamonds. They act out the roles of historical characters like Paul Revere, Dolley Madison, Martin Luther King, Jr., and Sitting Bull.

- Whole language uses a *thematic* approach integrating the disciplines to present a complete body of knowledge. The entire faculty and the librarians work as a team to develop and enrich themes. When children read stories with an ocean setting, if everyone puts their heads together, they can do salt water experiments, measure depths, study animal life, explore maps and raise their consciousness about the environment.

Curriculum-based, whole language relies heavily on *literature*— whole poems, books, stories—rather than textbooks or materials designed specifically to teach reading. Stories work best when kids can recognize real-life situations, can relate to the language, and when the illustrations correspond to the text, such as Tana Hoban's *I Read Signs*; *I Read Symbols*; *I Walk and Read* (all Morrow, 1987), Tomie Ungerer's *No Kiss for Mother* (Delacorte, 1991), Lou Kassem's *Middle School Blues* (Avon, 1987). Older kids identify with S.E. Hinton's *The Outsiders* (Dell, 1967), Paula Fox's *The Moonlight Man* (Bradbury Press, 1986), John Knowles' *A Separate Peace* (Random House, 1960), and Avi's *Nothing But the Truth* (Orchard, 1991). Then there are the treasures that work for all ages like Katherine Paterson's *Bridge to Terabithia* (Thomas Crowell, 1977) and *The Great Gilly Hopkins* (HarperCollins, 1987), E.B. White's *Charlotte's Web* (Harper & Row, 1974), Virginia Hamilton's *Cousins* (Philomel, 1990), Vera Williams' *"More, More, More" Said the Baby* (Greenwillow Books, 1991).

To improve their reading comprehension and their writing, children are encouraged to:

- predict, pretend, retell, and rewrite.
- learn about the author.

- respond in a journal to stories they read (talking back to the author).
- read, write, and think like a writer.
- rehearse, draft, and revise.
- share their work with their peers.
- edit their writing and their classmates'.
- do research, starting in kindergarten.
- publish their writing on bulletin boards, in classroom collections and newspapers or binders (go public with a real audience).
- read self-selected literature that is not taught in the classroom or library.
- follow interests aroused by the stories, like geographical or historical studies of settings.

As facilitators of learning, teachers, librarians, and parents are encouraged to:

- *model writing* in front of the students and talk about the process as each student works on the product. Modeling behavior, like independent reading or accomplishing tasks, such as taking attendance and making lists, also have a positive effect on learners.
- *give mini-lessons* on skills such as punctuation, capitalization, and spelling, or on form and style of different genres such as reports, essays, letters, stories.
- *kid-watch*, Yetta Goodman's invented term for directly and informally monitoring and recording the progress of individual children, as an alternative to testing. Kid-watching alerts a teacher early to unique difficulties, giving her an opportunity to change the prescription if necessary. It also alerts the teacher or librarian when she is overworking a book, poem or story beyond the child's interest level.

STANDARDS

Do not be put off by whole language detractors who contend standards are being lowered. Creative spelling is only the first leg of the journey to acquiring language art skills. The difference is when, how, and in what context they are acquired. Kids in whole language classrooms are not in boot camp working hard to pass a test. Ask yourself what is the basis for "the standards" so often bandied about? This country does not have a national standard to lower. Obtaining realistic data that tell how children are doing, how schools are functioning is almost impossible. For example, we are often told that 64 percent of fourth graders in a certain district function at or above grade level. Few realize there are no norms to measure against when determining grade level. It has nothing whatsoever to do with what a well-educated fourth grader ought to know and be able to do. To the contrary, it simply indicates the performance of the average fourth grade student on this particular test, regardless of whether that performance is good, bad, or mediocre.

Setting rigid standards and teaching only to pass the exams, as the British once did, is not an answer according to novelist, journalist, and critic George Orwell: "Over a period of two or three years, the scholarship boys were crammed with learning as cynically as a goose is crammed for Christmas. And with what learning! This business of making a gifted boy's career depend on a competitive examination, taken when he is only twelve or thirteen is an evil thing at best" (from "Such, Such Were the Joys. . . .").

In addition to Orwell's memories, there is much evidence to suggest that lack of standards is not the culprit. In 1991, when Educational Testing Service conducted a study comparing nine- and thirteen-year-old American children's math and science test scores to school children's from fourteen countries, with the exception of 10 percent, U.S. students made a near-bottom-of-the-barrel showing. The high-scoring 10 percent had three things in common that set them apart from the low-scoring 90 percent:

- They spent more time doing homework.
- They watched less television.
- Their parents showed an interest in what the students were learning.

The whole language point of view—that students will do more homework and watch less TV if the work is meaningful, has a purpose, and if their parents encourage them—is borne out at New York City's Stuyvesant High School. From 1942, when Westinghouse began its prestigious national science competition, to 1991, Stuyvesant has turned out eighty winners. Instead of the usual five, the students take research biology ten periods a week with five of those periods in a lab for work on classical and original experiments. The best are paired with professional scientists at universities and spend scores of additional hours after school and on weekends working on their projects. In interviews, the Westinghouse winners talked about their parents' involvement, like one who said when he was little, instead of encouraging him to push around little cars, his parents encouraged him to take them apart.

THE BOTTOM LINE

It is equally important not to be fooled by egregious publishers pasting 'whole language' tags on backlist materials designed to deal with reading and writing as separate entities. When I urge you not to be threatened by the whole language phenomenon, I do not intend to imply anyone should be blasé. In a capitalistic country like ours, when an idea affects the bottom line, it's Big News and can alter careers, as well as the way a child acquires skills and knowledge. Changing the book orders in thousands of American schools commands everyone's attention. No one has suggested burning basal readers, literature anthologies, spelling, grammar, and math workbooks, or materials compiled to teach writing, but whole language teachers are reversing their strategies and are more apt to spend their book budget on children's literature. All publishers want to tap into this lucrative market.

Euphoric trade publishers vying for teachers' attention provide seminars, catalogues, study guides, and advertisements to promote their lists. The new practice not only affects the budget, but educators' roles. Where teachers used to rely more on the librarian to keep up on what literature was available, they are becoming better informed themselves. No one could quibble with having more knowledgeable teachers, but to avoid becoming only order clerks, librarians will want to join the whole language team to be in on the curriculum planning.

Teachers, not wanting to waste a valuable resource, will welcome the help.

TEACHER/LIBRARIAN RELATIONSHIPS

Book-oriented librarians become concerned when they feel quality might be sacrificed to satisfy need. A kindergarten teacher who submits a request for *all* books related to the four food groups, without reading them or at least asking the librarian to help him sort out the clunkers is indeed teaching thematically, but hardly following the whole language philosophy of offering real literature to kids.

In the best of all possible situations, teachers and librarians have time to brainstorm, plan, and exchange ideas. A librarian will gladly pull good books to support an ocean theme, but as Kate McClelland, head of Children's Services at Perrot Memorial Library in Old Greenwich, Connecticut, said, she would also like to have a chance to tell the teacher about good books she has discovered that could lead to another interesting theme, to suggest follow-up for stories children hear in story hour.

When they help teachers satisfy curriculum needs, librarians also appreciate feedback. Knowing what worked helps them to improve the services they offer. They also appreciate advance notice. The teacher who double-parks while he flies into the library asking for every dinosaur title isn't apt to win teacher of the year votes from the library.

LEARNING FOR A PURPOSE

Literacy is the major purpose of whole language. A student has to be literate to learn to be a plumber, a physician, a policeman, a poet, a professor, or a programmer. Before some face discouragement, humiliation, or defeat, every child wants to learn to read and to write for his own purposes. With whole language, we have a non-elitist approach to education, that—with a little luck and open-minded educators— can work for all classes. If we could eschew political issues rumored to have wrecked The Open Classroom, stick to the theory, educate and involve the parents, stand by the beliefs, and put whole language into practice without distortions, we should not only crush illiteracy, but improve the quality of all our lives.

Stop for a moment to test the theory in your own experience. One added value for whole language is what works for kids works for adults also. Remember when you opened the carton containing your VCR. Think how carefully you read, word for word, the installation instructions. You had a purpose. No matter who dropped in, where you had to go, you were never going to miss "Nova" again. If your directions were written like mine, four hours later, you would have given your left thumb for the opportunity to try to teach every technical writer on the globe to use language to make meaning.

Children who grow up to write technical instructions, medical reports, diplomatic dispatches, financial statements, internal-revenue policy, insurance coverage, news stories—language that affects us all in formidable ways—do not learn to use words with precision by underlining the subject once, the predicate twice or by reading *Silas Marner* because it's a great book and the school has thirty copies stashed in the bookroom.

Remembering his education, cynic H. L. Mencken said, "Schooldays, I believe, are the unhappiest in the whole span of human existence. They are full of dull, unintelligible tasks, new and unpleasant ordinances, brutal violations of common sense and common decency. It doesn't take a reasonably bright boy long to discover that most of what is rammed into him is nonsense, and that no one really cares very much whether he learns it or not." (From *A Mencken Chrestomathy*, Pantheon, 1982.)

Meaningful Learning

One would like to think that young Mencken with his love for words and a desire to express his skeptical ideas would not have found a whole language classroom an unhappy place.

When the whole language approach to learning clicks, it adds pizzazz to life, no matter what the learner's age or purpose. For over a year, I've been meeting with ten people, from twenty-five to fifty years of age, who originally signed up for a course, "So You Want To Write

A Novel," initially scheduled to meet for four Saturdays. There's an actress, a gay clinical psychologist who used to be a minister, a bartender, a lawyer, an accountant, a New Jersey housewife and mother of four grown children, a young Southerner whose characters say "how you?", a professor with a Ph.D. in Latin, a jock. Was central casting playing a bad joke? No. The writers are only as diverse a group as the kids who show up in your class or library every day, as different as the siblings in your family, as dissimilar as your staff or coworkers. Why have they stuck together? They have in common a passionate desire to write a novel. What they learn in the class and from each other is *meaningful*; it serves a purpose.

Meaningful learning is the key to whole language. All of us had someone try valiantly to teach us grammar. Remember memorizing "a participle is the 'ing' form of a verb having the qualities of both verb and adjective"? I remember because I stuffed that definition down the throats of hundreds of my Chicago students. They had to pass the skills tests didn't they, and what about their SAT scores?

Fade to the writers' group. This is not a digression. One Saturday, after having read many chapters of their novels where most of the sentences began with a simple subject, I said, "What do you all have against participles, infinitives, prepositional phrases, subordinate clauses?" If rotten eggs had been available, I would have had to take a shower and shampoo my hair. Only the woman with the Ph.D. in Latin didn't look as if she were in pain.

But when I took lines from the writers' stories—just as teachers of all ages of children in whole language classrooms do—suggesting they begin this sentence with "When John entered the room . . ."; "Running down the street, John . . ."; "In the beginning, John . . ."; "To stop the bleeding, John . . .", facial expressions started to thaw. Epiphanies brightened the room. "Oh, I get it," played in refrain, as they started to reconstruct their work for variety and interest.

Hopefully, their children and grandchildren in whole language classrooms are "getting it" every day, as they apply their skills to something that makes sense to them. Students in whole language classrooms do acquire skills. The main difference is that they acquire them in a meaningful way by using the skills to accomplish a purpose they care about.

Higher education has also begun to pay attention to the whole language philosophy. Millikin University professors, Marilyn Kok and Leah Schietinger wrote *Building College Writing* (Harcourt, 1991) to meet the needs of their undergraduate students in Millikin's Writing Center, basing it on the premise that you don't need to memorize punctuation rules, instead you can learn to punctuate your own writing.

THE AIM OF THIS BOOK

Following the theory of meaningful learning for a purpose, my intent is to present whole language to teachers, librarians, administrators, parents, and interested community members in a manner that makes sense, to show a reason for adopting the philosophy, and to offer practical suggestions on how to do it.

Accepting the whole language point of view is a starting point. Anything new requires change. Change can be difficult, especially if there is subconscious resistance. Since research shows a correlation between effective learning for students and educators' self-esteem, I encourage you to approach switching to whole language, not as if what you have been doing in the past was wrong, but with the idea something more effective has come along. Cooking a hunk of meat over an open fire wasn't wrong, but it sure is a heck of a lot easier to stick it in the oven.

Attention will also be paid to how professional roles and relationships are altered among colleagues, educators, children, parents, the school, and the community.

The major portion of this book is designed to offer a potpourri of suggestions for putting the theory into practice for learners of all ages, even the educators. Whole language librarians and teachers *teach to learn*. I propose books, themes, classroom and library activities, means of involving the parents in their children's learning, ways to use the community as a resource. Some of these ideas have worked in schools around the country. Others could.

Self-Esteem

Educators did not need a new theory to tell them children learn better when the kids and the significant adults in their lives think they can. Whole language simply shifts the emphasis.

Building a child's self-esteem until he has the confidence of the Little Engine that Could is the highest priority. Finding his place in history, identifying with the character in the story, learning more about the author, receiving encouragement for his own writing from his peers as well as his teacher or librarian, involving his family in his learning are some of the many ways a child builds faith in his own abilities.

Rest assured "self-centered" and "self-esteem" are not even kissing cousins. The child who feels good about himself won't always have to be the one to make the basket, dominate the discussion, show off his possessions, or blame others. Speaking at the California Conference on Self-Esteem in February, 1989, Nathanial Brandon said self-esteem was the quiet confidence one has in oneself. Creating an environment where a child has achievable goals, can exercise his values without pretense or fear, can focus on his strengths and take responsibility for his decisions raises his self-respect. *Roots* author Alex Haley said you can never enslave somebody who knows who he is. Whole language advocates would add, "or whom he can become."

Families plant the earliest seeds of self in their offspring, but young children also reflect the attitudes of themselves as perceived by their teachers and librarians. I was concerned when my kid sister, who was having a dreadful time saying her "S's", started to school. I still remember the day she proudly announced to the family she was the only little girl in the first grade who would get to go to the speech correctionist. Today she is a confident woman, who can pronounce her "S's" with the precision of a bingo caller, and I'm still grateful to the first grade teacher who made her feel good about herself while she tackled the problem.

In the beginning, when school is so new and confusing, saving a child from the other kids' laughter can be viewed by the victim as an act of heroism. Once during the holidays, observing one of my University of Chicago practice teachers in a first-grade class, I saw one of those heroic rescues. The young teacher had asked the children to draw a picture depicting the season. She had praised renditions of Christmas trees, the babe in the manger, Santa Claus, Stars of David, when she stopped at Bradley's desk to look at a fat little man with a round body and a feather in his hat.

"And who is this, Bradley?"

"Round John Virgin," he said proudly. "You know, Round John Virgin, Mother and Child."

Before the others could even begin to hoot, the teacher told Bradley about her own experience learning the Pledge of Allegiance, when she thought her teacher had said "one nation, in a dirigible, under God". In a moment, instead of laughing at Bradley's blooper, the other children were eagerly trying to get in on the act to tell their own or make up new ones. The quick thinking teacher not only saved Bradley from ridicule, but used the incident to expand the children's vocabulary by introducing spoonerisms, a term named after an English minister, W.A. Spooner who made slips—the accidental interchange of the initial sound of words. The kids especially liked "a well-boiled icicle" for "well-oiled bicycle".

Just when we think Peggy Parish's Amelia Bedelia has told us everything we need to know about perception, a Bradley reminds us—teachers, librarians, parents—to be alert to how children see, hear, and interpret what we say and how we say it.

TRUST AND RESPECT

No one has come up with fancy new terms to describe it better than trust and respect, but what happens personally between you and a child is as important in building her self-esteem as the best academic exercise. If Daisy tells you she absolutely hates Suzy and you say, "That's nice, Mary," Daisy can't feel very important, even if Mary is her sister who went to your school last year. Remembering to listen,

really listen, even when you have thirteen things to do in five minutes, can make a child feel more valuable than the gold star you were
cutting out while Daisy tried to talk to you.

For children to be the stars, our expectations must remain high for
all of them, not just the one with the clean face whose parents read to
him every night, but the one who could use a bath, a friend, and a lot
of encouragement. In 1991, The Bureau of Labor Statistics reported
thirteen million American children living in poverty. These young
people will have to be literate to improve their condition. The whole
language approach strives to make learning more engaging, but never
simplistic. Nay-sayers wrongly interpret the approach as lowering
standards and expectations. They are concerned about the switch
from phonetics to teaching words in context, about the lack of traditional grammar lessons, about accepting creative spelling in the early
stages of a child's language development. Whole language programs
aspire to literacy, appreciation, and competency, only the means of
attaining the target has changed.

Children learn about capitalization and punctuation, for example,
when they are writing their own stories or letters and really have a
need to know how it's done. Since critics most often seem to attack
inventive spelling, remember it is a starting point, to encourage children to write earlier, not the destination. Whole language educators
believe being able to spell the words he needs to communicate his
ideas will empower a child, but they also believe that in the beginning
the emphasis should be on encouraging him to express his ideas.
Children learn to write by writing, but when their first efforts have
more red circles than a face with the measles, they are less apt to try
again.

I also suggest giving honest feedback, and that's not a contradiction
in terms. When you praise what is good and create a warm, supportive
atmosphere in the classroom, library, or home, a child will also expect
you to point out what needs to be improved. She will want to have
goals, assume she will have to stretch. If we tell her jumbled, unintelligible work is fine because we don't want to hurt her feelings, we have
not only hurt her chances for a future, but damaged her sense of self,
sending a message that we don't think she is capable of doing well.

Teachers and librarians with hearts of gold have let a child's race,
skin color, neighborhood, even clothes lower the level of the bar.

Every child wants the skills to make sense of his world, even the sullen or angry one sprawled in the back of the room. If we don't arm him with the power to read, write, speak, and think, he is apt to arm himself. NBC News recently reported on a New York inner city school where six out of ten kids packed "heat"—that's a gun.

We have all read the staggering statistics about "babies having babies." Organizations like Planned Parenthood tell us why. Young women whose families and schools have failed to make them feel loved, worthwhile, and have given them no hope for a meaningful career, choose to have a baby whom they assume will naturally love, respect, and need them. Most are not girls like those in Ann Head's *Mr. and Mrs. Bo Jo Jones* (Putnam, 1967), or Paul Zindel's *My Darling, My Hamburger* (Harper & Row, 1969) who "make a mistake" or "get caught." They have children without partners or means on purpose, to improve their sense of self-worth.

Easy to build self-esteem in all children, even if they got a bad start? Of course not. Missionary zeal, exceptional skills, meaningful lessons, books, affection, respect and the students' pitching in might do it. Kids are more apt to obey rules when they help to set them and feel important for having been asked. If the classroom or library is noisy, ask the children to analyze the problem and to offer suggestions. Since everyone wants to be heard when they read or tell a story, you can bet they will suggest that when anyone is speaking to the group, everyone else listens.

Children certainly are more apt to get caught up in, and take pride in an assignment that has something to do with the world they live in. Writing an essay on "What I Did on My Summer Vacation" would seem pretty silly to a child who didn't have one, or one who can't go outside to play in her dangerous neighborhood. "Where I Travel in My Imagination" or "The Story Book Character I Would Most Like to Visit" could work for all members of a group. Walter Mitty isn't the only one who had superman fantasies. Most of us, especially children, dream of saving the world. Activities to protect our endangered planet or neighborhoods, like recycling, planting trees, cleaning up litter, conserving water and paper make children feel worthwhile.

Entitlement is a respectable word well-intentioned educators have coated with enough verbiage to gum-up its power, but it's good to remember all kids are entitled to strive to reach the highest level of achievement, and it helps them build their self-esteem when we expect them to make it. Young people have built-in radar detectors programmed to pick up condescension, even from the noblest of motives, as well as danger in the street. Low expectations from adults puts a sneer on their faces and bravado in their swaggers.

HOPE

I favor the view of building self-esteem as giving a child hope. In his *Autobiography* (Harcourt, 1968), Lincoln Steffens said even when he was past his prime, drawing on youthful memories, he still approached a basketball hoop with hope while more reasonable adult tasks squashed him before he tried.

Test Steffens' theory against your own experience. It works for me. When a plumbing pipe bursts, I panic. Nothing in my life has prepared me to deal with problems requiring mechanical skills. My father fixed my bike, wagon, broken saddle girth. I have no hope to stop the flood. Yet, I approached writing this book, which must be harder than shutting off a valve, thinking I could do it because generous people helped me to take pride in my communication skills, even though in the beginning, I was one of the more creative spellers in the Southern Illinois school system. I strongly believe nothing motivates learning more than hope.

Librarians are in the hope business. As a New Yorker, while doing the research for this book, I had access to two college libraries and the entire New York City Branch System, but it was the Vandalia (Illinois) Public Library in my home town that gave me hope that I could find all the books, all the information I would need. The town has 5,000 people. The library has 30,000 volumes. But it also has library coordinator Fran Rickman and computerized access to The Cumberland Trail Library System. Try finding Jerry Spinelli's *Maniac Magee* (Little, Brown, 1990) and Ken Goodman's *What's Whole in Whole Language* (Heinemann, 1986) and Lincoln Steffens' *Autobiography*, in the same New York library. Not only did Fran have them in three days, but she came in early to call me because she knew I was in a bind and alerted me to Judith Rovenger's interesting review of Avi's *Nothing But the Truth* (Orchard, 1991) in the *New York Times Book Review.* For me, hope-peddling librarians are not "unsung heroes," and even though their computer networks aren't as romantic as the chunky bookmobile from my childhood, they have opened the world of books and scholarship to all of us.

Hope is the glue in the American Dream. People don't turn it in with their locker key when they leave school. For empirical evidence, check the burgeoning self-help section of your local bookstore. Aren't people really buying hope to improve their sense of self? One of the reasons I place faith in the whole language approach is because it encourages lifelong learning. Many adults practice the whole language theory unaware.

Take Gloria Steinem, who will surely go down in history for her achievements in the feminist movement. This intelligent woman who, among many other things, made us realize "dumb blonde" wasn't a compound word and established the use of the term "Ms.," attracted our attention a second time when she wrote *Revolution from Within, A Book of Self-Esteem* (Little, Brown, 1991).

Ms. Steinem isn't a conscious proponent of the movement to sell the whole language viewpoint to educators, but her book indicates she would "get it" immediately. She writes that she believes there is a quiet revolution of self-worth going on, with an emphasis on nurturing the damaged self, and the fight today should be to oppose any system that demeans us. Steinem is writing to and about women, but the media constantly pelts us with alarming statistics about eating disorders, suicide, satanic cults, ferocious gang fights for turf, and alcohol and drug abuse, that alert us to the growing numbers of male and female adolescents who have damaged selves.

Unfortunately, as they grow older, many children, especially girls, look outward rather than inward for self-esteem, and the values in our culture advertised on billboards, magazines, movies, and television make them feel inadequate. Brandeis University psychology professors Jennifer Brenner and Joseph Cunningham found in a study comparing male and female fashion models in New York to Brandeis students that female models were 9 percent taller and 16 percent thinner than the average Brandeis student who was five feet four inches and weighed 126.2 pounds.

The Brandeis study would seem to have little significance if research linking self-esteem to academic, occupational and social success did not abound. Statistics tell us that of the 643,910 cosmetic-surgery procedures performed in 1990, 109,080 were liposuction (to siphon away fat) and according to a 1985 *Psychology Today* survey 33 percent of the men and 45 percent of the women were dissatisfied enough with themselves to want to have corrective surgery (Lena Williams, "Image in a Mirror: Who Defines What a Woman Sees or the Reaction to It?" *The New York Times*, 6 Feb. 1992).

I remember a feminist speaker in the seventies asking a crowded room of women how many would ever consider a face lift. When most raised their hands, she said, "I would too. I wonder why youth and beauty is so important to us, we will literally cut our throats to obtain or keep it?"

Farfetched as it is, the plot of Avi's *The True Confessions of Charlotte Doyle* (Orchard, 1990) at least sends the right message. When, to save the day, Charlotte, who long ago has abandoned her white gloves and petticoats, hacks off the hair she herself has been praising throughout the story, those of us rooting for inwardly strong women cheer.

In 1992, Southern Illinois University in Carbondale held a series of conferences called "Expanding Your Horizons in Math and Science" for seventh- through ninth-grade girls. Linda Herrold, a professor in SIUC's medical school, said girls become oriented to how they look, what they're wearing, and to the stereotype of not doing better than boys. The culture also dictates that girls don't belong in the sciences and math. And most disturbing, girls more frequently equate the failure of experiments with personal failure while boys see it as a challenge. Consequently, only 16 percent of American scientists and mathematicians and 7 percent of engineers are women (Shera Gross, AP, "Seminar Pushes Girls To Pursue Math, Science Careers," *Decatur Herald and Review*, 11 Mar. 1992).

California has seen people's lack of self-worth as a serious enough problem to set up The California Task Force to Promote Self-Esteem and Personal and Social Responsibility.

People who don't feel good about themselves as youths don't stop trying to build their self-esteem when they grow up. Some quests can be downright dangerous. While doing research for my dissertation, I stumbled across a disturbing survey indicating that the majority of psychiatrists chose their careers not out of love for the discipline, but because they had not been able to form a meaningful relationship with the significant people in their lives. No wonder so many people spend so much money and so much time in analysis which doesn't always improve their lot.

It is difficult to give what you don't have, as we see with educators and parents who have low self-esteem. We have all observed teachers, librarians, mothers, and fathers who are reluctant to encourage their young charges to become independent because the adult enjoys being needed. Gloria Naylor's Mattie in *The Women of Brewster Place* (Penguin, 1982) expressed it best when describing the irresponsible thirty-year-old son who had financially ruined her. Speaking ironically, she said she had accomplished what she had set out to do: raise a little boy who would always need her.

By striving to strengthen children's self-esteem, do I think the whole language approach to learning will alleviate poverty, make every teenage girl think she is thin enough, stop all boys from drinking beer, smoking a joint, shooting someone for his sneakers or leather coat? Of course not. I'm an optimist, but not a zealot. I do believe the concentration on building a child's self-confidence is exactly the right place to begin to produce literate, productive people. Bruce Brooks' hero Jerome Foxworthy (*Moves Make the Man*, Harper, 1984) was cocky with confidence because he believed "the moves made the man," and he knew the moves. I am convinced kids have a better chance to learn the moves in a whole language classroom.

Integration

A child-centered curriculum forms the foundation. *Make integration the keystone.* Integrating a child's life experience with his academic experience is crucial. Sixteen- and sixty-year-old learners will not want to check their lives in the coatroom either.

Remember the thrill the first time you read a story and thought: that is exactly how I felt when my grandmother died, the cat ran away, my boyfriend quit me, I lost the game, the other kids laughed, my best friend didn't stand up for me, or my parents got a divorce? If you didn't get to share the connection you had made with your own life, you probably also remember the disappointment. Even worse, you might have thought, I could write a story like that about my grandmother. But the class was learning how to compose expository themes and you had chosen "How To Change A Bike Tire."

When I was training to be a teacher, a wise University of Chicago psychology professor, who thought teaching and learning had mostly to do with egos, said, "Until you can show me the me in Hamlet, don't expect me to appreciate him just because you know a lot about him."

Testing his theory with a Chicago high-school class of reluctant Shakespeare readers, before they read the play I retold *Hamlet* this way:

Imagine after graduation you go downstate to The University of Illinois, majoring in business so you can take over your father's string of gas stations. First your father dies, but when you come home, your mother has already married your despised uncle. She is making a fool of herself with him, and he is running the business. Then your girlfriend not only sets you up, but also lets your uncle and her father read your love letters. Your two best friends spy on you for your uncle, who might have murdered your dad and who definitely is spreading the

25

rumor you've gone bonkers. What would you do? Everyone in the class had felt betrayed by someone. Primed by empathy from a lively discussion about their own experiences, many tears were shed in that class when Horatio called upon flights of angels to sing Hamlet to his rest.

Feeling down in the dumps in middle school is as natural as wanting the new jeans all the other kids are wearing. Reading Lou Kassem's *Middle School Blues* (Avon, 1986) will open a dike of similar stories that must be told or written.

It's impossible to imagine that there is even a little kid who hasn't lost something he loved. They will *have* to tell you about it after they have read Beverly and David Fiday's *Time to Go* (Harcourt, 1990) about a small farm boy who is losing the home he loves.

INTEGRATING THE DISCIPLINES

After considering the child's life experience, integrating the disciplines is the next step. Integrating the disciplines means going beyond writing across the curriculum to present knowledge in a broader, more cohesive sense, showing the interrelationships between art and science. Our educational system has been plagued by producing students who could either do math and science or the humanities, but had too few common skills and interests.

Writer and critic Marguerite Yourcenar, the first woman accepted in the prestigious French Academy, confesses, "I wasn't good at arithmetic. The problems seemed stupid to me: How much fruit will you have if you fill a basket with three-quarters of a pound of apples, an eighth of a pound of apricots, and two ounces of something else? I didn't see the problem. I just asked myself why anyone would choose to arrange a basket in such a manner. So there was no answer." (From *With Open Eyes*, Beacon Press, 1984.)

Today, Yourcenar would find teachers connecting math to real life and to other subjects. Finding that most of her students were interested in money, St. Louis junior-high teacher Ann Brenner did a unit on the stock market, tying math to economics, literature, and the history of the Great Depression.

Whole language educators, realizing that some children have failed at both science and art, are not only changing the materials, but are building a child-centered curriculum to take the whole child—his life and level of competence as well as his school training—into consideration. The attempt is to start where the student has a level of comfort, rather than to have her experience doubt or defeat before she has a chance to begin learning.

The goal is to educate articulate scientists and writers who can explain a rainbow as well as describe it. In the past, too often, we chopped the body of knowledge into little pieces, keeping our expertise stored in our separate domains. The whole language approach puts it back together, giving a student, and us, the "whole" picture.

Take the War Between the States. The historian knows what happened when Americans fought the Civil War. The literature teacher knows stories and biographies that tell how people felt about it. The music teacher knows the songs both sides sang. The math teacher knows how to figure how much it cost, how to compare the cost to a modern war. The art teacher knows the painters who put their impression of the calamity on canvas or carved their memories in stone. The home economics teacher knows the old recipes and maybe the fashions. The science teacher knows how the muskets fired and how ballistic theory has advanced. The geography teacher knows where the battles were fought. The physical education teacher knows how soldiers trained their bodies for combat. The librarian knows the school's supplementary materials, records, videos, books, and artifacts, to augment it all. Newspapers, museums, court houses, and radio stations have community archives from the period. Parents know how a child's ancestors were affected. Put all of those resources together and, by comparison, the study of the Civil War could make a video game, MTV, or a trip to the mall a bore.

TEACHING TO LEARN

Bringing what you have to offer to the larger table might at first seem like a slapdash, potluck supper, but with planning, commitment, and the ability to give up a bit of power, it can transform your school into a

COMMUNITY OF LEARNERS. Librarians and teachers are acclimated to thinking of themselves as doers, but aren't as accustomed to considering themselves learners along with the children. When adults switch from doers to scholars who are also reading, writing, questioning, thinking, growing, what happens between them and their students loses the artificial aura canned lessons have been known to produce.

One of my fondest teaching memories happened when I was directing a demonstration center and the high-school-aged kids wanted to add a science fiction selection to the curriculum. The teachers and I said, "Sorry, none of us have read any." "We'll teach you," the students said, and they did. They chose the title; we read it and broke into small groups where the kids led the discussion, a very good one. Our standing as good sports went up with the kids. The students admitted they had never worked so hard on any book, but I thought they were standing a little taller.

Teaching to learn is an academic phrase I do plan to add to my working vocabulary and use often in this book.

INTEGRATING LANGUAGE ART SKILLS

Integrating the language art skills, as the phrase implies, is an approach that links the teaching of listening, speaking, writing, acting, and reading skills. Instead of a week where a fourth-grade class might be reading about dinosaurs, writing an essay on how to eat spaghetti, making speeches about their favorite TV show, listening to a *Peter and the Wolf* tape, and hearing about heroes of the Holocaust at the library story hour, they enrich their reading experience by practicing all the skills on the same theme or book.

Finding a place to stop is the problem when a class begins a book like Katherine Ann Paterson's *Bridge to Terabithia* (HarperCollins, 1987, reprint of 1977 edition). A teacher-and-librarian team splitting the tasks makes the most sense. Since, among other things, it's about boy and girl friendship, family problems, running, the magic of the imagination, the sixties, loss, and being a survivor, possibilities for writing and speaking explode like popcorn.

When appropriate, the whole language approach takes writing across the curriculum a step further. Kids still write to learn their math, music, science, and read their art, but after reading *Bridge to Terabithia*, where Jess's favorite teacher and Leslie's parents are hip-pies, they might want to do a history research paper on the political climate and events in the sixties that produced these flower children. Leaving the language arts classroom and going to history shouldn't be like entering unconnected planets. There should be a bridge from Terabithia to history class.

Nipping in and out to connect what is happening in the story to what a child has experienced makes all the difference. When Daisy can tell how she felt when she lost someone, she'll not only have more empathy for Jess's pain in losing Leslie, his pal in Terabithia, but also more respect for and interest in Paterson's language that expresses the loss so poignantly.

The class will want to hear recordings of the songs Jess's hippie teacher plays, like "This Land Is Your Land," "Blowing in the Wind," "My Beautiful Balloon," and especially, "Free to Be You and Me." The librarian will have not only the records ready, but other good boy/girl friendship books like Paul Zindel's *The Pigman* (Harper & Row, 1968), M.E. Kerr's *I'll Love You When You're More Like Me* (Harper & Row,1977), Lawrence Yep's *Sea Glass* (Harper & Row, 1979), Norma Klein's *Just Friends* (Knopf,1990), Myron Levoy's *Alan and Naomi* (Harper & Row, 1977), Patricia MacLachlan's *Arthur for the Very First Time* (Harper & Row, 1980), Marilyn Sachs' *Peter and Veronica* (Scholastic, 1987), and Jan Slepian's *The Alfred Summer* (Macmillan, 1980).

Poet Kenneth Koch told us literature is about wishes, lies, and dreams. Middle-school children, even the boys (although they're usu-ally less apt to admit it), dream about having a friend of the opposite sex. When I talk to students about my first book, *Megan's Beat* (Dial, 1983), they never fail to ask me if I really had a friend like Tom when I was Megan's age. I tell them no, not then, but that's what's fun about being a writer. I made him up and suggest they can write their wishes into their stories too. The young writers share the joke when I tell them about the day I was signing books in my hometown, and a woman came in and said, "I don't know if you remember me, but I'm Tom's mother."

INTEGRATING PARENTS

An exceptional child who makes it in spite of a parent as indifferent as Huck Finn's pa is as rare as that book itself. Educators have few truths to rely on. That children whose parents are involved in their learning have a better chance to achieve is one. Asking families to become involved in their children's learning not only helps to integrate school and life experiences, it builds everyone's self-esteem. Given a choice, even indifferent parents would prefer their children do well in school. Most would like to help. Not all know how.

Whole language programs ask parents to serve on committees, give nonthreatening student assignments to be done at home like interviewing family members, provide reading lists for mothers and fathers who want to read and discuss stories with their children. Although Jess and Leslie are fifth-grade characters, few adults can put down *Bridge to Terabithia*, or finish it with dry eyes. Paterson's *The Great Gilly Hopkins* (Crowell, 1979), Vera Williams' *"More, More, More" Said the Baby* (Greenwillow, 1990), Patricia MacLachlan's *Sarah, Plain and Tall* (Harper & Row, 1986), Virginia Hamilton's *M. C. Higgins, the Great* (Macmillan, 1974), Margaret Mahy's *The Tricksters* (Macmillan, 1987), Shirley Hughes' *The Snow Lady* (Lothrop, 1990), and Eve Bunting's *Fly Away Home* (Clarion, 1991) are a few of many stories that appeal to readers of all ages. Suggesting parents or older siblings read them too is a way to involve a child's family in her learning and to give her another opportunity to retell her version of the story at home. Also, it doesn't hurt a child's self-esteem to realize what she is studying interests adults, too.

When the science class studies the leaves of trees and plants, the parents are informed, so their backyard or street can become part of the exploration. They provide costumes for plays and skits, read and tell stories. If mothers, fathers, or siblings have an expertise such as marine biology, making steel, computer science, throwing hot rivets, playing chess or the tuba, they are invited in to talk to, or perform in, the class. The most important factor is giving parents tasks they are comfortable with.

Librarians plan parent-child events, encourage volunteers, suggest books, and provide relevant speakers. The majority understand human nature and realize parents are just kids grown up who want to be accepted—but everyone has bad days. When my nephew, Dannon, was a fifth grader in a Peoria school, his mother volunteered to be a library helper. Arriving the first day, eager to please, she noticed a stack of Norma Klein's books on the librarian's desk.

Unaware of the controversy Norma had created by breaking taboos in fiction for young readers, my sister hoped to find common ground when she said, "Dannon and I know her. She's my sister's best friend."

"Then I suppose your sister knows she writes dirty books." Shooting the books at a box on the floor, the librarian said, "I'm sending them back."

My sister switched her service to after-school sports.

INTEGRATING THE COMMUNITY

Tapping community resources is another part of the plan. Every thinking person in the country shares concerns about the education of our children. Too often business people and community leaders only have been asked to contribute money. The whole language approach seeks another resource—KNOWLEDGE. Field trips, speakers, films, print and software material, demonstrations, a holistic view of how the world works are all assets the community can contribute to tomorrow's leaders.

Publishing a classroom newspaper takes on another dimension, becoming a much more serious business, after visiting a publishing site or listening to a publisher explain the many different skills needed to put out a paper. Learning and practicing the different approaches to reporting news, writing a feature, and expressing an opinion should not only sharpen students' writing skills, but make them better readers, less apt to be swayed by bias or propaganda.

Civic organizations devoted to improving neighborhood conditions, such as cleaning up the streets, eliminating graffiti, recycling waste, caring for the elderly, welcome the opportunity to alert children to how they can help.

Not enough young Americans choose to be engineers or scientists to meet the national need. I remember a middle-aged woman in a continuing education class who said, "Maybe if I had known what a brand manager was, I would have been one." Maybe if children knew early enough what research scientists in corporations, medical facilities, and research labs do, they would be one. Maybe if they knew engineers come in as many different varieties as ice cream flavors, from those who build bridges to Barbie dolls, they would find an aspect that interested them.

Play Sherlock Holmes. Look around your town, your community for resources to enrich your child-centered curriculum and the children's lives. With a little luck, this holistic approach to learning could make Renaissance men and women of us all. The method generates so much energy it refuses to stay in the school house. Ideas and challenges chase children down the streets of the community and follow them home (see the example of the New York School that adopts a block of Broadway, p. 171). As alert educators, we catch the contagious spirit, broadening our own perspectives along with the students'.

INTEGRATING THE LIBRARY AND THE CLASSROOM

In whole language schools, more teaching is done in the library. Some librarians bristle at the thought. They want children to enjoy books, to become lifelong readers. They do not want to become pedants or preachers using good books in a didactic manner. Good for them. The idea is again the holistic approach. When teachers and librarians plan together, the theme in the library—on the bulletin boards, in the exhibit case, the books on display—can reinforce the classroom activity. Or a librarian can announce a math or science month. Teachers can follow through with counting books, puzzles, experiments and games. Integrating the efforts of faculty and staff makes all the difference.

Children from whole language classrooms come to the library with different expectations. They are taught reading and writing—everything from science to history—in tandem. They think like writers. After story hour, they will want to discuss ideas they picked up for their own stories and the responses they will put in their journals, if they are old enough to write. The story will not be enough. They want to know everything about the author. When librarians respond to their needs, it sounds like teaching to me.

Especially a public librarian can raise a cynical eyebrow in a whole language discussion. No one likes to be told what she already knows, be asked to do what she has been doing all her professional life. Granted, not all of the whole language ideas are new or revolutionary. Some are. There is a new vocabulary. Some of it is inventive. Some has a buzz. Whole language is curriculum-based. In the past, the curriculum was the teacher's territorial imperative. What is new is the librarian's role in curriculum planning. Whole language programs rely on a team.

Librarians can offer more support to whole language classrooms when:

1. Administrators allow time for brainstorming, etc.
2. They serve on the curriculum committee.
3. Teachers remain in the library while the librarian tells a story, so that they can follow up with related discussions, writing, drawing, math, science, geography, music, and other activities to reinforce the impetus of the story.
4. Teachers give feedback on their success or failure with choices the librarian has made for particular themes.
5. Classroom activities support books, ideas, themes, holidays, historical times the library's displays are featuring.
6. Curriculum does not ignore the necessity for providing quality literature for children we are all trying to hook on books. Programs are most successful when curriculum committees are ex-

panded to include the librarian and other experts in addition to language art professionals.

Adopting the Holistic Theory

I wish I could promise the whole language approach, using literature rather than textbooks or basal readers, would make your life easier, but although students respond more positively to reading complete works, publishing, dramatizing, the new approach requires more planning, imagination, and energy. Activities and questions are not provided at the end of each chapter. The answers aren't in the back of the book. The new way lacks order, takes more time, and demands more ingenuity from educators, but even though it's messy the results are better. After they've accepted the point of view, teachers and librarians say the challenge makes their work and their lives more enticing. They become more acute observers of the world. *Wise people work in teams.*

II. PRACTICES

Practices to Implement Whole Language Theory

Making the ball bounce the kids' way is the secret to implementing whole language.

The most promising aspect of the approach, when children have been reading and writing all day, every day at school, is the prospect of a generation of people not intimidated by reading or writing anything—job applications, their college-entry essays, letters to future mothers-in-law, reports for the boss, pages in their diaries. I also believe it is possible to accomplish nationwide literacy. Not every child will read at the same level with the same degree of competency, but everyone can learn to read and write just as they can learn to speak. The desire to communicate is a natural instinct. Watch how babies learn to tell mothers and fathers when they are hungry or uncomfortable. Wanting our attention, they talk before they can talk. The need for language is born in children. To help them acquire and learn to use words, what we have to do is to make learning real, sensible, interesting, and purposeful.

Whole language procedures like writing before you can write, inventive spelling, mini-lessons, modeled and process writing, drafting, rehearsing, revising, author cycling, peer evaluation, predicting, pretending, and retelling remind me of preventive medicine. You start early, monitor, encourage, educate, and reinforce before the intimidation begins to fester.

MODELED WRITING

The first day in a whole language kindergarten, children hear they will be writing and drawing pictures every day. The teacher goes first, demonstrating the steps as a dance instructor might. When you say,

"Follow my lead," the idea is to keep the steps simple, give ample time for practice, and convince the kids they have the potential of Fred Astair and Ginger Rogers.

Perhaps you will say you want to tell them what happened to you on your way to school. First, you write your name at the top of the easel paper you're using for demonstration so everyone can see. For the children who have not yet mastered writing their names, you could also suggest and show other ways of identifying their work, like drawing a self-portrait. You might add distinguishing glasses or earrings to the face on your paper while allowing the students to discuss ways to portray themselves. Explaining what made you late for school, you draw a car with one tire flat as an empty envelope.

Writing Before You Can Write

The next step is to convince children in kindergarten that the ideas they want to express, the stories they want to tell, are most important. As you tell the story of your perverse tire, you use scribbles, letter-like symbols, random letters, words, and sentences to show ways they might express their thoughts until they have the terms.

As dancers need a floor and proper shoes, writers need a place to practice their art. With a little encouragement, the children will begin to help each other find a way to communicate. A big table where they can spread out would be a good idea, especially in kindergarten where the kids don't sit at desks. Paper, pencils, crayons, and rulers should be easily accessible in the writing corner, and the students will need to be able to see the alphabet in upper and lower-case letters. Communicating with each other will be half the fun. Whole language rooms for all ages have a class mailbox. The idea is to create an atmosphere inundated with print and writing materials where children read and write all day. A special place for writing in the library also reinforces the idea that writing is important.

Mini-lessons, like miniskirts, are short. They have replaced drills and occur when the need arises. Model mini-lessons, too. You do it; the kids watch; then they try it. The kindergartners need to know to put spaces between words, to make their words walk left to right, to capitalize important words, to put in punctuation so the reader can take a breath.

Some teachers start each morning with a *daily edit*. On the board, they put two or three sentences containing errors they have covered in previous mini-lessons. The children make a game out of finding the errors, like finding Waldo. Mini-lessons work for learners of any age, if you keep in mind starting where they are and with what they need to know.

As younger children gain their sea legs, mini-lessons will deal with the different writing genres such as reports, letters, lists, journal entries. If you have been successful in turning your class into a community of scholars who share their work, they will give each other mini-lessons.

A mini-lesson on inventive spelling will empower your young writers, but without proper preparation can raise the hackles of parents and more traditional colleagues. Most people are reasonable. Explaining, if possible, in a meeting where you can respond to concerns and questions, or in writing, that creative or inventive spelling is a *temporary* means to generate writing should clear the track. When parents can visit the classroom and see displayed samples moving from scribbles to close approximations, they are apt to be more fascinated than anxious. They will see how children begin by discussing what they want to say, then finding words, finally saying the terms slowly to hear the sounds and finding letters to make the sounds.

At the start, they might spell creatively like Patricia MacLachlan's Arthur in *Arthur for the Very First Time* (Harper & Row, 1980). (Reading MacLachlan's books, it is obvious she once was an English teacher.) Visiting his aunt and uncle when he was seven, Arthur wrote in his journal, "Their house is big like a manshun. It smells like banas." Rereading the entry in preparation for his next visit, he corrected bananas and mansion, his "baby spelling."

In his *Spel Is a Four-Letter Word* (Heinemann, 1987) J. Richard Gentry says he believes inventive spelling is a natural foundation for building spelling abilities. Kids who invent spellings think about words and in so doing generate new knowledge. He thinks letting kids take risks in their own writing is the best way to teach them to spell, just as speaking and making mistakes helped them to learn to talk.

As I prepared this book, talking to teachers, librarians, administrators, students, and parents around the country was the best part. I only became discouraged when the adults told me, of course, they would like to try something new, but the parents or the principal or an unidentified "they" would never stand for it. Besides, they and the children were judged by test results. Several years ago, I had a similar experience when I was writing a censorship guide for Dell Press. After considerable research, discussions, and observations, I realized, too often, teachers, librarians, writers, and publishers were giving in to the bullies and the bigots. The last line of that guide was "the enemy is 'us.'"

There is no reason for such a conclusion here. In 1992, the U.S. Department of Education released the results of a survey showing U.S. children in traditional classrooms write seldom, with only 10–20 minutes per week devoted to writing in elementary schools, and they were not writing well. Assistant Secretary of Education, Diane Ravitch, called the survey results "one of the most important events in education for 1992." She said it could stimulate the revival of writing in American schools by breaking the iron grip of the standardized multiple-choice test in the nation's classrooms. (Karen De Witt, "Survey Shows U.S. Children Write Seldom and Not Well," *The New York Times*, 17 April 1992.)

"They" are coming around to the whole language approach. If we have the courage of our convictions, explain our goal for language competency and the steps for achieving literacy, this book can have an upbeat conclusion.

PROCESS WRITING

The theory of process writing compares to a coach who doesn't stress winning, but learning to play the game. The focus is on the procedures rather than the product. Literate children who enjoy reading and writing are the actual products. The idea works best and is more fun for everyone involved when you become a community of learners—teachers, librarians, parents—not only encouraging a child to write, but also writing and talking about the process (see Thinking Like A Writer, p. 45).

Start with a discussion about the students' choosing a subject or topic that has real interest for them. Melville's good friend Nathaniel

Hawthorne, the customs house clerk, could never have written *Moby Dick*. He didn't give a hoot about whaling. Melville's passion for the sea and the challenge of the fight with these incredibly clever, mammoth creatures made that book awesome. Kids will probably be quick to point out the closest they are apt to come to a ferocious fish is the piranha in the aquarium. This situation gives a whole language teacher or librarian an opportunity to encourage children to talk about their interests, their values, and the life experience they bring to school. "What do you care passionately about?" not only sparks the process-writing session, but builds a child's self-esteem when she realizes her ideas, hobbies, and pursuits are taken seriously. Many well-known children's-book writers admit their ideas come from goofy interests they had as children.

Finding a topic is only the first choice. Where to start, what details to include, what to leave out, and how to build the subject all continue the discussion about the process of writing. Mozart is supposed to have composed at four, but most of us, even when the desire is strong, are not born with a ready-made gift for creating or doing much of anything without raising a sweat.

REHEARSING, DRAFTING, AND REVISING

If I had three wishes, I would be tempted to use one to ask for the ability to write with the clarity and the deceptive ease of William Zinsser (*On Writing Well*, HarperCollins, 1990; *Writing to Learn*, HarperCollins, 1988). But I know he would say, "Stop wishing and start writing." There is nothing easy about it. Writing is a craft you learn by doing it . . . over and over and over. Good writers rewrite sentences again and again to remove the clutter and weasel words, to clarify, to improve the style, syntax, and sound. Zinsser reminds us that E.B. White and James Thurber rewrote their pieces eight or nine times. Mark Twain labored over *Huckleberry Finn* on and off for seven years. Young people would probably appreciate the analogy of how many times a football or basketball team practices to play one game, or the number of rehearsals actors must have before performing in a play. They polish their styles, perfect their techniques as a writer does.

The teacher or librarian, who starts the process by rehearsing—explaining something *real* she wants to write—talks about all the decisions she must make as a writer. Let's say her purpose is to write a newsletter for parents. With input from the students, she discusses the length—how much detailed information do mothers and fathers want to know about classroom activities? Would it be more effective to write a paragraph about the work each individual student is doing, or should she talk about the class projects as a whole? Should she use a personal-letter form, opening with Dear Mr. and Mrs . . . or would it work best as a report? Should she use the past tense, "after reading Mary Downing Hahn's *December Stillness* (Avon, 1990), the class worked on projects to help the homeless," or the present tense, "reading *December Stillness* raises our awareness of what we can do. . . ."

Another modeled rehearsing possibility is to choose a student's project and follow the same process described above. As soon as students have developed the knack for considering all options before they start to write, they can continue the practice with a partner.

When students work on their writing with peers, it frees the teacher or librarian to do other things, like concentrating on an individual who needs help. It's not an excuse to put her feet up, although hard working whole language teachers and librarians, who sometimes feel as if they're ring masters in a three-ring circus, deserve to rest their bones. Most important, it is an opportunity for the youngsters to practice all their language art skills—like presenting, listening and responding, reading for intent, developing constructive critical skills, as well as honing their own writing. Peer evaluation also increases students' sense of responsibility rather than leaving all evaluation decisions for the teacher to orchestrate.

The practice, sometimes called *author cycling*, pairs students who have meaningful writing tasks like a thank you note, letter, report, story, a new chapter for a favorite character, a different ending for a novel. The first step—rehearsing—is to talk through their projects, discussing aspects like intent, starting point, structure, viewpoint, audience, tone. Next they do drafts and then come together again to give and receive feedback before doing a revision, often revising many times.

Preparing for author cycling starts with building trust among the kids so they don't feel as if they are about to become a character in Shirley Jackson's "The Lottery" (*The Lottery and Other Stories*, Noonday Press, 1991). For the process to work, children have to be willing to write and discuss honest thoughts and ideas, as well as give and receive feedback in a constructive way. Trust builds when teachers and librarians have encouraged children to talk about their interests, values, themselves and to listen to and respect each other. The aim is to develop a community of scholars by emphasizing sharing rather than competing. Stress learning, not winning. Leave prizes for "the best," "the most," "the fastest," "the slickest" for the adult arena. The children will be there soon enough.

A child also has to have an opportunity to build faith in his responses to other people's writing. He sharpens his observation and listening skills in story hour or after reading a book when he is asked to explain what he noticed, what the writing tells him, what it makes him think about, what he liked or disliked about the language, characters, or what happened to them.

Children soon learn that repeating the same words causes their writing to be boring. They see how action verbs that create an image like "rumble," "roar," "rumple" make their stories more interesting. If a child's companion can't make heads nor tails of a paragraph, together they might discover he forgot to put a period at the end of a sentence or that where he put "green" made it sound as if his sister, not her sucker, were green, and she wasn't even supposed to be sick. As they improve their critical skills, the kids will probably decide " 'I hate you!' she said angrily," could do quite well without the "angrily."

Tempting as it is to want to write everyone's stories our way a good critic considers what the author wants to say (intent) instead of telling her how she, the commentator, would approach it. Whole language teachers and librarians praise the good critic as well as the good writer.

PREDICTING, PRETENDING, RETELLING

Predicting is one reading strategy to help your students focus on meaning. You can delete words from a text, asking the kids to predict the word or words you have deleted. For example, you are reading the following sentence from Elizabeth Spurr's *The Biggest Birthday Cake in the World* (Harcourt, 1991): "Led by the Richest-and-Fattest, boys, girls, and cooks dived into the cake, burrowing, smudging and sludging, licking and sticking making the Most Horrendous Mess in the World." You leave out "the Most Horrendous Mess in the World," show the grubby picture, let the children predict what these cooks and kids have made, and then give them the sentence to figure out if they have guessed right. They might have to sound out "Horrendous," but they will do it to make sense of the whole sentence, the whole story. Children's wanting to know, to find meaning, puts any isolated exercise in the shade. Taking the risk of guessing, skipping, and predicting to make sense of print has led learners from reading *Peter Rabbit* to tackling James Joyce's *Finnegan's Wake*.

Predicting plots from covers, titles, characters' names can whet a reader's appetite as well as arouse her imagination. Try it with titles like *Charlie and the Chocolate Factory* by Roald Dahl (Bantam, 1977); *Just Friends* by Norma Klein (Knopf, 1990); *Middle School Blues* by Lou Kassem (Avon, 1986); *Shadow of a Bull* by Maia Wojciechowska (Macmillan, 1965); *Park's Quest* by Katherine Paterson (Viking/ Penguin, 1988) or characters like Maniac Magee; M.C. Higgins, the Great; Weetzie Bat; Black Beauty, or Willy the Wimp.

If Shakespeare couldn't have pretended to be a prince, a Moor, and a madwoman no one ever would have read, *Hamlet, Othello*, or *Macbeth*. Find any writer who did not grow up playing pretend. Find an avid reader who does not sit in an armchair pretending to float down the Mississippi, catch the crook, or who doesn't crawl into the skin of Nick Adams, Scarlett O'Hara, or Peter Pan just for a little while. Pretending to be a character, the author, or an animal is like creative spelling; it generates new knowledge as well as making reading and writing enjoyable rather than a chore. Thinking from someone else's viewpoint also helps children to become better team players, less egocentric, which is what maturing is all about.

Retelling a story we love gives us double pleasure. We relive it, enjoying it again, but also we're giving a gift to our listeners. Children not only have fun when they tell about the stories they've read, but are learning to put together pieces to make a whole and finding words to fit their feelings and impressions. If the other kids listen, ask questions, it helps their self-esteem. When involvement isn't happening, the kid-watching teacher assists. He asks the teller questions to help her clarify, stay on track, find the interesting details.

To gain confidence in speaking in front of a group, summarizing and ordering material, sometimes the students retell the plot for the whole class. Other times they break into small groups to exchange suggestions about good books to read or those to avoid.

Retelling a story by writing about it locks in the knowledge. Finding the words to express why she likes *Harriet the Spy* by Louise Fitzhugh (HarperCollins, 1990) better than any books she has ever read forces a child to find the words to communicate an emotional response that would have floated away if not expressed. Recommending books in letters to cousins or friends who moved away is an opportunity to learn how to do a written précis.

THINKING LIKE A WRITER

Blondes don't have more fun. Writers do. The whole world is possible material. (For whole language teachers, librarians, and parents, as well as the kids.) Thinking like a writer sharpens your senses. You must be alert, observant for the unusual, the interesting, the obnoxious, the beautiful, the humorous, the scary, the touching. Nothing is lost. A writer notices if people slouch, sleep, sprawl, or shove on the subway or bus. Eating a slice of lemon meringue pie becomes a scientific experiment. How does one compare the slick yellow center to the fluff on top that might have a suntan? Eavesdropping is encouraged. When your mother told you not to, she didn't realize you were going to be a writer. A nursery-school child says, "Spring is coming in on a bus." A writer doesn't smile until she records it in her NOTEBOOK . A writer never leaves home without one. Neither do whole language teachers, librarians, and their students.

An editor friend is trying to find a waterproof notebook. She has her best ideas in the shower, but they evaporate faster than the soap bubbles. Writer-as-sponge is the cliché, but unless you have a photographic memory, it's best to let the notebook be the sponge.

Patricia MacLachlan's characters know how it's done. They all think like writers. Arthur records that his uncle has a small head "much like a graying tennis ball," and his aunt "was shaped like an uncertain circle, made up of large shifting spaces like an easy-to-color coloring book" (*Arthur for the Very First Time*, Harper & Row, 1980). In *Cassie Binegar* (Harper & Row, 1982), Cassie writes that her Gran has "sharp eyes, quick, darting, like the sandpipers" and her baby cousin "walked precariously on tiptoes, first one way, then the other, like a drunk dancer."

Children might not recognize "idiom" if they met it on a page, but thanks to Peggy Parish's character Amelia Bedelia they have sharpened their ear for language quirks—like "hit the road," "pitch the tent," "catch the fish"—and probably drive their families mad trying to catch them in the act.

Look at how rich and famous Erma Bombeck has become by watching with amusement what goes on in her own house. Bombeck has motivated me to write an Edgar Allen Poe-type story about my enemy, the vacuum cleaner. There is an opening line in my notebook, "I'd rather tangle with a sumo wrestler than my big-bellied Electrolux."

When novelist Nora Ephron visited her mother, a writer, on her deathbed, her mother said, "Nora, take notes." Some discretion is advised, however. Nora's ex-husband sued her when she wrote *Heartburn* (Knopf, 1983) chronicling his affair and their divorce. Relationships also have been damaged when buddies recognized themselves caricatured in published works, but usually friends and families are prepared. When my sister read *Katy Did* (Avon, 1992), she called immediately to point out three instances when Katy's dialogue had been taken straight out of my sibling's mouth. She was right, but I convinced her I carried my notebook when I visited her because she said such interesting things.

Maira Kalman says she spends hours wandering around New York, notebook in hand, writing in cafes or at the Museum of Modern Art. notebook in hand, writing in cafes or at the Museum of Modern Art. It works. In *Sayonara, Mrs. Kackleman* (Viking, 1989) her character Max, the dog, packs up, goes to Paris, where he sleeps in the Bleu Suite, a la Picasso, and dreams that a *bleu* horse is playing checkers with a *bleu* woman in a garden of *bleu* trees.

When Doug Florian decided to write *Auto Mechanic* (Greenwillow,

1991), the third book in his working series, he had never been a mechanic, so he found himself a job working in a garage. You can bet he sketched in his notebook.

Natalie Goldberg, author of *Writing Down the Bones* (Shambhala Publications, 1986), meets friends in cafes, not for lunch, but to do writing practice together. We should all get rid of our desks, if this habit inspired her to write lines like: "I am not happy. I am lonely. Loneliness is a dog that has followed me for years. It is a black dog and I have no peace."

Teaching in a New York High School, M. E. Kerr made a note when she met a fat, black girl with a do-gooder mother. The note became Dinky Hocker of *Dinky Hocker Shoots Smack* (Dell, 1973), who actually did not shoot smack.

Peter Sis was still a foreigner to our culture and lonely, when he thought someone was waving to him, but they were hailing a cab. He wrote it down and now kids see it happen in *Waving* (Greenwillow, 1988).

While reading the newspaper, Norma Klein saw an item that went into her notebook. The teenagers in the newspaper story, who traded their baby for a red Camaro, were the basis for Maddy and Jed in *The Swap* (St. Martins, 1983).

David Gates claims to have written his novel, *Jernigan* (McKay, 1991), in his notebook on the subway. Mary Cahill wrote *Carpool: A Novel of Suburban Frustration* (Random House, 1991) in the front seat of her Toyota where she overheard kids saying things like, "If you hold your breath when you're doing it, the girl won't get pregnant."

Encouraging children to think like writers is like building their self-esteem. You have to be there to get it. Whole language teachers and librarians share the nuggets in their notebooks with their students. If driving the same route every day to school has become as stale as yesterday's doughnut, then searching the streets, the shops, the signs like a spy looking for clues to a story could add zip to the trip.

Whole language educators and converted parents often write when the kids do. They point out funny, clever, or lovely phrases in the newspaper or poems; make up word games, like trying to find the words to describe Grandpa's nose or how jalapeño peppers taste; suggest things or people that might be interesting to write about, like a person with a black eye patch, a treehouse, sand in your sock, a prissy parrot, or characters in the stories they read, such as another adventure for Rotten Ralph, the bad, red dog, or Julie and her wolves, or Norma Mazer's Dump Queen. Who has ever read *Little Women* without wanting to rewrite it right with Jo married to Laurie?

Notebooks

My notebook looks as if it has been stepped on by a bucking horse, chewed on by a mouse, and dropped in the maple syrup. It probably has, but not to worry. What is inside is what matters. Fancy leather-bound books intimidate me. Only profound thoughts can be inscribed. Mine is one of those spirals with five divisions purchased at the supermarket, where I can scribble, even drivel, thoughts that might eventually go through a frog-to-prince metamorphose.

The first section contains long lists of possible names for characters, one of the more important decisions an author makes about his story. Imagine if Mark Twain had called Huck Finn Hubie Fink, Ishmael and Ahab were known as Bill and Joe, Maniac McGee were Clarence Cooper, or Kermit the Frog had been named Albert. Would we read "The Love Song of G. Benny Wilson," or *Weetzie Bat* (Francesca L. Block, HarperCollins, 1989) if her name were Wanda, or *Witch Baby* (HarperCollins, 1990) if Weetzie Bat had named her Baby Sue?

Sometimes names just sitting there in the notebook begin to develop a personality. Hoover has been hanging out in my notebook forever. At first I thought he might be a bulldog, but he seems to be a dwarf who rides in the sidecar of somebody's motorcycle. I suggest to young and not-so-young writers if women with two names—like Lucy Ann or Melba Sue—usually seem to be interesting, or you've always wanted to meet a guy named Chip, you've dreamed of having a dog named Socrates, or you would have paid your parents to have named you Ashley or Chauncey, write the names in your notebook, they could begin to speak to you as characters.

Once I met a woman called Mary who named her daughter Mary Junior. Then I read about Julia Dash, a producer making films about black American women's experiences, who called her daughter N'Zing after an Angolan warrior. You can bet neither of these women were anybody's patsy. Of course, there was also Eleanor Roosevelt's mother, a beautiful woman, who not only did not think her daughter was attractive, but so misunderstood her seemingly old fashioned child she shamed the girl by nicknaming her Granny, scarring Mrs. Roosevelt's self-confidence for years and years.

As Mary's choice showed her sense of self-worth, and Dash's showed her pride in her heritage, names the people in your stories choose for their pets, toys, and children can make a statement or be used as character development. For examples look at Laurence Yep's horse, Red Rider, in *Dragonwings* (Harper & Row, 1975); Anne Lindbergh's dog, Ronald Reagan, in *Nobody's Orphan* (Avon, 1983); M.E. Kerr's raccoon, Graham, in *Gentlehands* (Harper & Row, 1978).

In my notebook there is another page of titles I think about writing. *Small Pleasures* or *Black Sheep* have possibilities. After learning my West Point cousin's son was attending his fourth high school in three countries, I added *Army Brat*.

Titles, like characters, can inspire stories. They can also sell books. Who could resist *Busy Buzzing Bumblebees*; *Soap Soup*; *The Cat Ate My Gymsuit*; *Maudie and Me and the Dirty Book*; *Tales of a Fourth-Grade Nothing*; *The Chocolate War*; *My War with Grandpa*; *Middle School Blues*; *Philip Hall Likes Me, I Reckon, Maybe*; *Tuck Everlasting*; *The Hunky Dory Dairy*; *Blubber*; *The Pigman*; *I Love You, Stupid!?* Even though it didn't get very good reviews, I dashed out to buy Pam Houston's *Cowboys Are My Weakness* (Norton, 1992), because they're mine too.

Sculptors use stone, carpenters favor wood, computer engineers have their chips, Van Gogh relies on lots of paint. Writers' tools are words. They pirate, loot, plunder, and commandeer them in the street, at the movies, from everything they read including letters from Aunt Sadie, the back of the dill-pickle jar, and the telephone directory (all those names). They collect rare ones, new ones, and old favorites like stamps or baseball cards. Trading is advocated. What will you give me in exchange for flibbertigibbet or razzmatazz?

One section of my notebook is filled with lists of words like "sissy," "silly," "sassy" because I like the sound and writers are always trying to set their words to music. "Apple dumpling" is in there because it's fun to say, and "knickers" because the image makes me giggle. There is a serious column of impressive words I'll use some day like "pernicious," "complicity," and "duplicitous"; a special register of beautiful words like "gossamer" and "twilight" and pages of hard-working verbs like "swish," "sashay," "squeak," "squeal," "squiggle," "squirm," " splinter," "wham," "whack," "whoop." Patricia MacLachlan's Cassie Binegar, whose name rhymes with vinegar, likes "infinite" because it is a big word with a big meaning. "Colossus" is another big word with a big meaning. You're welcome to add it to your list.

I also make lists of synonyms. I have a verbal drawerfull of hose, tights, stockings, pantyhose, socks, leotards, nylons, hosiery, and I choose carefully when dressing my characters. A grandmother who wears tights wouldn't live on the same block with the one in the story who wears socks. A young Wall Street broker might wear pantyhose to the office, but I'd put her in leotards for the weekend. A prissy character wears hose; a sexy one always sports tights.

Kids could practice thinking like a writer by noticing what people wear to cover their heads. After they've filled their notebooks with bonnet, beret, fez, fedora, derby, stocking cap, bowler, straw hat, sombrero, hunting cap, cloche, panama, bandanna, baseball cap, helmet, chapeau, picture hat, boater, earmuffs, sailor cap, and scarf, they can make up characters to dress up in the proper headgear. Try to imagine Holden Caufield in a derby or Tom Sawyer in a bowler.

No matter how young, writers soon begin to realize the words they choose not only develop characters, but also reveal a great deal about the writer. For example when an American President contracted the stomach flu on a state visit to Japan, there was an embarrassing moment when he threw up . . . some say on the emperor. Writers had a field day. One wrote an article about all the synonyms for throwing up and their connotations, like "vomit," "was taken ill," "sick to his stomach," or euphemisms: "went whoops," "boot," "barf," "upchuck," "talk to Ralph on the big white phone," "hurl," "tossing your cookies," "blowing your doughnuts," "losing your lunch," "laughing at the carpet," "yawning in Technicolor;" or Shakespearian—"puke." A reader didn't have to check a columnist's voting record, just his verb, to know his politics and attitude toward the President. Children could practice writing a sentence describing a similar incident showing respect and a contrasting one that doesn't. They would be apt to gain more respect for their verbs and less for reporters.

Why make lists of words until something like the President's misfortune moves us to write? To say again that writers learn to write by writing is not a redundancy; it's an answer to many whole language questions. I know a busy editor who got up an hour earlier every morning to write one page of his novel. In 350 days he had a novel. Writers—young and not so young, old salts and rookies, whole language teachers and students—write every day, more often than they talk on the phone, if that's not wishful thinking pushed to the limit. The kids write for and with the teacher, librarian, and their parents. They write for each other and for themselves. Sometimes one word like "jealousy" can jump-start a writer who is stuck, be she five or fifty-five. Doing writing warm-ups to start the words flowing is like stretching before a run.

The writing warm-up exercise that got one of the best responses I've ever received was simply: "Better luck next time," your character says or someone says to him. I was amazed when adults wrote about death, reincarnation, blind dates, divorce, and stock market swindles in tones ranging from ironic to tragic. I tried it with kids and their pencils took off, too. Many of them wrote about losing a contest in the classroom or on the playing fields, but there were birthday cakes that fell; funny, money-making scheme failures; and touching attempts to impress or coerce that went awry.

Striving to remove the intimidation of the written word, the plan is for children to write so often and with such encouragement that writing becomes as easy and natural as talking. Speaking to kids, Madeleine L'Engle told them writing is like playing a musical instrument; you can't do it just when you feel like it. You have to do it regularly. In whole language classrooms they do all kinds of writing, formal and proper as an essay or a letter to an author, informal as notes to themselves in their journals, and always their own stories. Children given the opportunity to play with words like building blocks are less apt to clutch when asked to express themselves on paper. The goal is for children to feel like Willa in Patricia MacLachlan's *Unclaimed Treasures* (HarperCollins, 1984), who, looking at a box of alphabet letters, had an epiphany. With these letters, she realized she could make any word in the world, tell all the stories.

Identifying with Your Character

In *The Poetics*, Aristotle explained why literature, deserving the name, is character-driven. When people in stories we care about fail, experience misfortune, or die, we feel pity and fear, but the catharsis comes from realizing their fate was inevitable because of their nature. Their actions and decisions determine their fate. Oedipus' hubris, not an unfair universe, was responsible for his downfall.

Today, we say good writing tells it the way it is and commercial or sentimental writing tells it the way we wish it were. If Holden Caufield had ended up living happily ever after in New York with his little sister Phoebe rather than in a psychiatric ward in Hollywood, Salinger would have had to give him a lobotomy in the last chapter. Most readers prefer S.E. Hinton's *The Outsiders* (Dell, 1968), but my favorite book by this author is *Rumble Fish* (Delacorte, 1975), which I consider her most ambitious book. When she was not much older than her character, Motorcycle Boy, it seemed to me she was trying to write a classic tragedy for teenagers about a hero whose fate was determined by his tragic flaw. Readers root for Motorcycle Boy, but know his demise is inevitable. He couldn't have acted any other way.

What does Aristotle have to do with the whole language approach to language, literacy and learning? Actually, a great deal. The aim is to develop children with high self-esteem who will be lifelong readers and writers. I don't know one person who ever lived happily ever after and neither do these kids. Giving them stories—about families who never fight; Judy, who never lies, cheats, nor wears a hole in her sock, and is always asked to the slumber party; and John who is never late for his paper route and always hits a homer—doesn't do much for their self-esteem or their respect for literature. Fake or sentimental stories neither protect their innocence (that gets battered in the streets or on the bus coming to school) nor teach them anything useful about writing—or life.

What young writers want to know is how an author makes up a character as real as Big Bad Bruce, Gilly Hopkins, Harriet the Spy,

Tom Sawyer, Ponyboy, M.C. Higgins, Alice, Miss Blue, Hatter Fox, or Charlotte. After a writer finds her character, learning what motivates her creation is like method acting. Flaubert hadn't had a sex change when he said, "I am Madam Bovary." The writer becomes the character even if he's a dog. Maira Kalman says, "Max is me—a way to work out questions in my life."

Kids will understand the technique when you ask them to remember an imaginary friend or if, after seeing a movie, they have ever pretended to be the person in the film. I saw *Gone With The Wind*, when I was a child. For weeks, playing all the roles, I constantly said, "I'll think about that tomorrow," and when my mother wasn't listening, "Frankly, my dear, I don't give a damn."

Joyce Maynard says she sees herself in the third person, a character in a book, an actor in a movie. In *To Die For* (forthcoming), the novelized version of the story of Pam Smart, a high school adviser who seduced a fifteen-year-old student into killing her husband, Maynard wrote from the viewpoint of Smart and twenty-three other characters through spoken segments, addressed to an invisible interviewer. She said she enjoyed writing in those voices, like a fifteen-year-old boy driven by his loins, because she loves losing herself in other people's lives. According to Maynard (reputed to have lived with J.D. Salinger for several years), the period when she was writing *To Die For* was a time of heartache for her, so she wanted a subject that was completely separate from her.

In my adult writers' group, Virginia, who has a fear of flying, is writing a novel about Maggie, a character who can find humor in any situation. When Virginia had to fly to San Francisco, Maggie wrote me a letter on the plane telling a hilarious story about this passenger white-knuckling it across the country, bejeweled in rosary beads and a Saint Anthony medal. Maggie and Virginia landed safely.

The writer crawls into the skin of her character, views the world— even at thirty thousand feet—from her perspective. She reads, looks at movies, eats a pizza from the viewpoint of the person she is coming to understand. Let's say Daisy in your sixth-grade class has created a little girl named Lolly Bee. What does she need to know about Lolly Bee? Everything! What she likes for breakfast; what she would do if the school caught fire; what she is ashamed of; her favorite book, color, song, and holiday; if she would ask a boy to dance; if she is jealous of her cousin in Cleveland; if she likes fudge and pistachio ice cream; if she is afraid of the water; how her hair behaves in the rain. . . .

After Daisy knows her character well enough, Lolly Bee will begin to tell her what to write. "Skip school? Lolly Bee, why would you do that when there is a math test? . . . Oh, I get it. . . .You know you'll end up in a jam, but, feisty, that's just the way you are, isn't it? Okay, I'll write it, but, Lolly Bee, you're going to be in big trouble."

When the character is sullen and refuses to dictate, one of the best "jump starts" is *what if*. Robert Cormier tells about his son, an athlete who had to work hard to keep up his grades, asking his father's permission to talk to the priest about not selling candy to raise money for the school in the annual sale because he simply didn't have time. Cormier said he would support him, but that morning when he dropped the boy off at school, he didn't drive away when his son walked up the steps to the school. Robert Cormier is a writer. He said *what if* the priest were really a rotten guy. . . . Actually, the understanding priest excused the boy from the candy sale, but Robert Cormier's *The Chocolate War* (Dell, 1986), about a priest who's mean as a snake, is on its way to becoming a classic young-adult novel.

Teachers and librarians can make up lists of what-ifs like the following. The children will probably have some good ones, too.

What if your character got lost at the zoo. . . .

What if your character's mother forgot his birthday. . . .

What if your character lost her shoe at the movie. . . .

What if your character saw ants in the peanut butter his sister was eating. . . .

What if your character saw someone pilfering lockers. . . .

What if a new kid transferred to your character's school. . . .

What if your character saw her boyfriend with someone else. . . .

What if your character learned she were adopted. . . .

What if your character learned his best friend were adopted. . . .

What if the cat ran away. . . .

What if your character dreamed about a panther. . . .

What if licorice made your character sick. . . .

What if your character only got a Valentine from the teacher and Mary who sent one to everyone. . . .

What if your character's father sold her horse. . . .

What if your character were blind. . . .

What if your character won. . . .

What if it rained. . . .

Reading Like a Writer

What if you read other people's books with the eye of a writer? Would it make any difference? Probably. It's like being able to see through your skin to find out how you're put together.

Author Bruce Brooks says he writes like a reader. In whole language schools, readers write and writers read. Human beings have a natural urge to hear and tell stories, our own and other people's. Look at how much time we spend on the phone saying "wait till you hear this." Half the fun of seeing a movie or reading a book is telling someone about it.

The first question asked by readers who are writers is "who is telling me this story?" Then they must decide if the narrator can be trusted to tell them the truth or would she be biased, have an ax to grind, or not have enough experience to understand the situation? How would the story be different if one of the other characters told it? Imagine the stepmother's version of Cinderella's life or A *Separate Peace* (Bantam, 1985) as Finney would have told it while the story was unfolding rather than Gene returning fifteen years later, still feeling guilty about Finney's death.

Understanding point of view is not only what allows us to comprehend and appreciate literature in a profound way, and come to grips with our own writing voice, but it also affects the way we see every aspect of our universe, causes most of the tensions in the world, determines how our tax dollars are spent. When we help children to grasp the concept, we are preparing them to deal not only with literature, but to be better prepared to make important decisions in their everyday lives.

Animal-rights activists tell us to think about the red fox's agony when we put on our fur coats. Environmentalists remind us spray net might make our hair behave, but it plays havoc with the earth's ozone layer. Muslims' reaction to Salman Rushdie's novel, *The Satanic Verses* (Viking, 1989), shows us how different religions view good and evil as well as freedom of expression. Ralph Ellison's *Invisible Man* (Random House, 1989) turned an eternal spotlight on the black man's experience. Dee Brown's *Bury My Heart at Wounded Knee* (Holt, 1991) not only changed General Custer's heroic status, but caused us to rethink our view of the people whose country we invaded in the seventeenth century. Native Americans have also suggested we take another look at Columbus. As the country celebrated the five-hundreth anniversary of his arrival, they considered it a day of mourning. The New World he discovered had been their home from the beginning.

Another way to understand the power of viewpoint is to compare history text books written before and after the Cold War or Canadian history told from the perspective of the French and the English. It's enough to make you think cynical Oscar Wilde wasn't entirely wrong when he said history was only gossip.

Anne Frank's *The Diary of a Young Girl* (Doubleday, 1967) was the first of a long list of children's and young adult books looking at the Holocaust and World War II from the viewpoint of children on "our side." *I Was There* (Puffin, 1987) is a first-person account of the turmoil and terror of Nazi Germany from the perspective of a member of the Hitler Youth movement. Hans Peter Richter's story is so understated he manages to offer neither propaganda nor an apology. In addition to broadening students' perspective of war, the book offers an excellent opportunity for studying a writer's method where it is difficult to separate style from substance. Richter's words are as controlled as his character's life was. His style makes a strong statement.

Teaching in a Chicago high school, one of my most successful point-of-view activities was to ask students to describe Al Capone's character from the viewpoint of his mother, his moll, his lawyer, one of his henchmen, the widow of one of his victims, and the district attorney.

WRITING FROM A DIFFERENT PERSPECTIVE

Rewriting stories from a different point of view is another whole language practice not only popular with school kids. One of the best literary jokes is Tom Stoppard's play, *Rosencrantz and Guildenstern Are Dead* (Grove, 1988), Prince Hamlet's tale told from the viewpoint of two inconsequential characters. *West Side Story*, Jerome Robbins' version of *Romeo and Juliet*, not only helped to raise the self-esteem of Hispanic kids, but became a popular Broadway musical. Jane Smiley's *A Thousand Acres* (Knopf, 1991) tells the King Lear story as if he and his three daughters were Iowa farmers. Jean Rhys' *The Saragasso Sea* cleared up the mystery about Mr. Rochester's mad wife in the attic when she told the story of *Jane Eyre* from Mrs. Rochester's point of view.

New York playwright Paula Vogel's brother Carl had AIDS. He asked her to go to Europe with him, but she was too busy. He died. In her play, *The Baltimore Waltz*, a woman has ATD (a deadly disease Vogel invented). The plot is about a last trip to Europe the woman takes with her brother.

Perhaps Virginia Woolf, who has always left notes in the margin of my mind, started the trend of thinking about literature told from another point of view in *A Room of One's Own* (Harcourt, 1991) when she created Judith, Shakespeare's brilliant sister no one would take seriously because she was a woman. Norma Klein often said the book she wanted to read was Tolstoy's *Anna Karenina* told from Anna's point of view. And wouldn't it be fun to give Hemingway's women a chance to talk back to some of those macho men? Hester Prynne's interior monologues might not be so docile, and I've always wondered if Becky Thatcher wasn't mad as heck about Tom and Huck having all the fun.

Tom and Huck weren't the only guys who seemed to have all the fun. History used to be owned by white males, until blacks, Native Americans, and women began to say, "Wait a minute we were there, too." Retelling history from the less dominant point of view not only changes the way minorities feel about themselves, but fills in the blanks in our culture. In his introduction to *Now Is Your Time: The African American Struggle for Freedom* (HarperCollins, 1992), Walter

Dean Myers says, "What we understand of our history is what we understand of ourselves."

In the year of the five-hundreth anniversary of Columbus's discovering America, too many books were written about him, but Jane Yolen's *Encounter* (Harcourt, 1992), a quality story told from the viewpoint of a young native boy, puts the discovery in a perspective our children deserve to see.

Robert Miller knows Gene Autry and Roy Rogers do not represent all cowboys because two of his great uncles were cowpokes in Texas and Mexico and, following the Civil War, his great grandfather was recruited into an all-black unit with the U.S. Army to help open up the West. In his four-volume series, *Reflections of a Black Cowboy* (Silver Burdett Press, 1991), Miller says that of the 20,000–30,000 cowboys in the 1850's, over 8,000 were black.

While all of this revision was going on, The Big Bad Wolf, whose real name was Alexander T. Wolf, knocked on the door of Jon Scieszka's imagination. "I was framed," he said. "Let me tell you my side of that story." Scieszka wrote down what Al said. Illustrator Lane Smith drew some pictures, and lo and behold, we finally have *The True Story of the Three Little Pigs* (Viking, 1989). At PS 87 in New York City, the third graders read both versions. After they enjoy the stories, they have a lesson in "conflict resolution."

Then one day William J. Brooke, a singer and actor who had assumed the viewpoint of many characters, asked himself the writer's magic question, "what if . . . ?" What if Cinderella didn't want to try on the glass slipper? What if Paul Bunyan, the greatest tree chopper of them all, met up with Johnny Appleseed, the fastest tree grower? What if Sleeping Beauty didn't believe she'd been asleep at all? He wrote A *Telling of the Tales* (HarperCollins 1990).

Why let Scieszka and Brooke have all the fun? Think of all those princesses children have read about who were saved by the prince. What if the princess who felt the pea under her mattress thought the prince was a nerd? Or imagine Trenker's (*Gentlehands*, M.E. Kerr, Harper & Row, 1978) version of the summer he spent with his grandson Buddy. I would like Marcus, Dawn's little brother in Anne Lindbergh's *The Shadow on the Dial* (HarperCollins, 1987) to have his turn at telling what it was like to have a sister who picked on him.

Younger children love to make their own big books by rewriting and illustrating stories. In teacher Gail Lockart's Vandalia, Illinois, first-grade room, I saw a dandy revision of Eric Carle's *The Very Hungry Caterpillar*, where the kids had changed what he ate to the things they liked best, such as pizza and cheeseburgers.

Perhaps if, all along, we had been paying closer attention to children's play and their ideas, we wouldn't have had to wait until the eighties and go down under to find some of the whole language practices. When we were young, didn't most of us assume the roles of characters we read about in books or saw in movies, add our own twist, make up the next escapade?

The Woodward Park School in Brooklyn didn't call it whole language, but when I received a letter saying my young adult novel, *Gleanings* (Harper & Row, 1985) had won The Woodward Park School Book Award for 1985, I learned that each year a panel of kids read the new books and made their choice without faculty input. They also invited the author to the school to see a presentation of the award winning book to the other students and faculty. The children had turned *Gleanings* into a play, which they acted out for us in costume with props. The only problem had been casting. All the girls, and some of the boys, wanted to play Pepper Junior—no Becky Thatcher—but a good/bad girl who had more fun than her gentle friend the good/good boy Frankie.

The award and the ceremony, a Woodward Park tradition for many years, had been the kids' idea. They had always been the judges, had always prepared the program. Today we call what was going on there a child-centered curriculum, building students' self-esteem, encouraging independent and critical thinking. Sounds like whole language practices to me. Maybe the children knew all along.

WRITING THE NEXT CHAPTER OR THE SEQUEL

If the urge to do sequels to literary classics continues, books lovers are conscience-bound to encourage children to begin practicing early. Many of the adult writers, who have tried, needed an apprenticeship.

When Alexandra Ripley wrote *Scarlett* (Warner, 1991) for which she poached the characters from *Gone with the Wind* and took them to Ireland and back, Margaret Mitchell fans screamed outrage, and the critics cried foul, but it became a best seller. A columnist for *The New York Times* asked, perhaps a bit tongue in cheek, whether no literary legend was safe. Would these trespassers turn Oliver Twist into a banker and send Anna Karenina to a convent?

Lin Haire-Sargent defended *H.—The Story of Heathcliff's Journey Back to Wuthering Heights* (Pocket Books, 1992) as her homage to Bronte's classic, not a ripoff. Her goal was to explain what happened to Heathcliff during the three years' absence from Wuthering Heights that brought him back a changed man. She was at least successful in changing him. In the sequel, the potent character early critics called a force of nature returned transformed into a well-dressed sadist, a manipulative and obsessive bully.

High school teacher, Richard White, said he wrote *Mister Grey, or the Further Adventures of Huckleberry Finn* (Four Walls Eight Windows, 1992) because he couldn't stop thinking about what happened to Huck when he headed out to the territories.

As we go to press, the adult version of Huck has not yet made his journey to the bookstores, but we do know what happened to Dorothy from L. Frank Baum's book, *The Wonderful Wizard of Oz*, published in 1900. Known as Dynamite Dot, the strange old lady who claimed television had stolen her life, died in a Kansas nursing home in 1956 soon after the inmates had gathered around a brand-new TV to watch the network premiere of *The Wizard of Oz* starring Judy Garland.

Even though in his novel, *Was* (Knopf, 1992), Geoff Ryman goes farther in asking us to suspend belief by making author Baum and Judy Garland (Frances Gumm) characters, plus adding Jonathan, a present-day movie actor dying of AIDS, novelist and critic John Crowley said he got it right (*The New York Times Book Review*, July 5, 1992).

In children's and young adults' literature, the end is only the beginning. The young characters, like Huck and Dorothy, still have most of their lives to lead. Students have great fun writing the next chapter and might even show more imagination than some of the sad sequels being published.

PUBLISHING

Even the youngest kids know that writers publish. If you are going to convince them to go along with you and think like writers, you will have to go all the way encouraging them to go public with their work. Writers write for real readers. Children who start out in whole language kindergartens, where they write before they can write, will be veterans by the time they can spell Mississippi. These youngsters immediately became accustomed to writing every day, and will never again be satisfied with writing a weekly expository theme that only the teacher reads. In the beginning, they might have used pictures, a letter or two, even squiggles were accepted as long as the children tried to tell a story. The little girl with pigtails, who might have drawn a box, put a "k" underneath it and drawn a face with braids on the top, was telling her story about her cat who hid in the grocery box and almost got thrown out with the trash. Then she signed it with a self-portrait, but by the time she is in your third-grade story hour or fifth-grade class, she will be thinking of herself as an author and expecting her writing to be on display.

How does a child begin to think of himself as a writer, gain the confidence to want to be published?

Bobbi Fisher of Sudbury, Massachusetts, kindergarten teacher and author of *Joyful Learning: A Whole Language Kindegarten* (Heinemann, 1991) has created an *author's chair* in her room, an idea I like a lot. I can't imagine a student any age, who has built self-confidence about his writing not finding this the best seat in the house. Librarians will probably want to have an author's chair in the library writing corner. Beginning and seasoned writers are suckers for giving readings. Fisher structures her writing activities on Don Holdaway's Natural Learning Classroom Model: demonstration (by the teacher), practice and performance, participation (*Build a Literate Classroom* by Don Holdaway, Heinemann, 1991).

When it's the pigtailed little girl's turn in the author's chair, she holds up her picture demonstrating the symbols she has found to communicate her ideas. Beginning with invented, ear, or creative spelling, in a short time, the teacher helps the child find a word, then a string of words to put under her picture (see Mini-Lessons, p. 38). This is when the little girl learns what she needs to know to tell her story. With guidance from the teacher until they get the hang of it, the author's audience tell what they see in her story and ask questions to help her think through where she wants the story to go. After young authors are comfortable in the author's chair, inviting parents or the class next door to be part of the audience is a good idea.

The author's chair has several positive spin-offs, like developing critical thinking skills and giving the children an opportunity to take responsibility. Since everyone will have a turn, it's a "do unto others" situation. In advance, they discuss and decide upon the rules for audience and author, like not acting silly and not talking while the author is presenting her story.

For children who can write, the bulletin board in the classroom or the library is a place to start publishing. A class newspaper gives everyone a chance to see her byline. Collecting everyone's stories, putting them into a folder, selecting a title for the collection, illustrating the folder, preparing a title and author page, a table of contents, gives the writers a sense of accomplishment and pride.

For a student old enough to write longer stories, individual binders with the author's name and title on the front, her photograph and a biographical blurb on the back can't help but make her feel like an authentic author. She will probably also want a dedication page.

Until they gain confidence in their work, it's best to let the children decide the when, how, and to whom about going public. The audience will be extremely important to the writer. Surveys indicate that when given a choice, most students prefer receiving feedback from their peers, but in the beginning they might want to take their work home.

After being inundated by movies, books, and newscasters telling us about people meeting disaster because of their "files," the word has taken on a sinister connotation, but presented in a positive way, teachers can explain student-writing files without raising alarm. An individual folder to collect each child's work can give the teacher, the student, and parents an idea of his progress. The file also offers an option, rather than going public with something personal or a draft he hopes to improve or expand. When he chooses the file, the student knows he is writing for the teacher's eyes only. What he writes for himself goes into the notebook. Having choices makes his writing freer and raises his awareness of writing for a particular audience.

LEARNING ABOUT THE AUTHOR

Be prepared. Children who publish are no longer satisfied with only reading other people's stories. They want to know where the author found her idea, what other books she has written, how old she was when she started writing, what she eats for breakfast, when she had her first kiss, where she found her ideas for the books, if she were a cheerleader or an outsider, if she has any kids.

What second grader wouldn't want to read teacher/writer Jon Scieszka's, *The Good, the Bad, and the Goofy* (Viking, 1992) when they hear he wrote it because there weren't many books out there for his favorites, "the goofiest of the second graders." ("Jon Scieszka: Tell the *True* Story," by Allen Raymond, *Teaching K-8*, May, 1992)

And the kids will be delighted to know the secret is out: James Marshall really did have a teacher who looked and acted just like Miss Swamp.

If the teacher forgot, again, to tell you—the librarian—what authors and which books he will be using, don't fret. You might as well ask him because you'll have to collect the biographical and critical material anyway. It's better to do it on your schedule than have twenty-eight fifth graders swarming around asking for information about Katherine Paterson just when you have all of those computer entries to make.

They want to know about authors because children whose work is taken seriously begin to think like writers. When they know Rosemary Wells' West Highland white terrier, Angus, had the shape and expression to become Benjamin, Tulip, Timothy, and most of the animals she made up for her stories, they'll probably take another good look at their dog, Corky.

Every child has an embarrassing moment. After knowing Pam Conrad used hers in *Pedro's Journal: A Voyage with Christopher Columbus*,

August 3, 1492–February 14, 1493 (Caroline House, 1991), they might decide to write about it after all. Conrad, who is not a very good swimmer, tried to slip over the side of a boat without attracting everyone's attention. But wouldn't you know it, she caught her bathing suit on a cleat. There she was, hanging in the air, looking positively ridiculous.

What young person wouldn't be inspired to examine his own experience more carefully, when he learns S.E. Hinton wrote *The Outsiders* when she was sixteen years old and the story began when she saw a gang fight in the park on her way home from high school?

Younger children will understand why Jean Marzollo wrote *Red Ribbon Rosie* (Random House, 1988) when they learn she listens to a sports radio station all day and in her next life wants to be a major-league shortstop.

Early writers should be encouraged to learn that William Joyce—who at nine began making up and illustrating stories like "Billy's Booger," about a boy who sneezes up this highly intelligent little snotty man—says that in *Dinosaur Bob* (HarperCollins 1988) and *A Day with Wilbur Robinson* (1990), he is still simply meticulously rendering the goofiest musings of his childhood.

When Landmark Editions sponsored a nationwide "Written and Illustrated By. . . " contest, they received more than seven thousand submissions. Thirteen-year-old Anika Thomas from Pittsburgh wrote an autobiography, *Life in the Ghetto* (Landmark, 1991), about crack houses, crime, and boarded-up buildings, about racism and despair. She said she wished a tornado would grab her and her mom, like Dorothy in *The Wizard of Oz*, and take them away to another land, but if no tornado came, then she would do it herself. She just might. Anika's book won the contest. She received a $5000 scholarship and a 5 percent royalty for her book that is in its second printing. For many young writers, *Life in the Ghetto* could be the kind of inspiration Anne Frank's *The Diary of a Young Girl* was for an earlier generation.

Entering a contest in 1912, Edna St. Vincent Millay shattered the myth that poets live unsung lives, starving in a garret. Twenty years old, this young woman of limited means from Maine submitted her poem "Renascence" to an annual competition sponsored by a poetry anthology publisher. The poem did not even win a money prize, but

Millay was catapulted into the spotlight where she remained until she died.

Kids sometimes are scared that their stories aren't good enough. It helps to hear novelists Norma and Harry Mazer say they were so frightened when they decided to write for a living, they wrote sitting close enough to touch, to reach over to edit the other's work. They had four little kids, not much money, and a bushel each of insecurity. Young writers might find hope knowing, in spite of their fears, the Mazers fed their children, published many books, and today even write in separate studies and have grown children who write and illustrate books.

The Mazers have coauthored some books published under both their names, but kids might be surprised to learn Hadley Irwin is the pseudonym for two women, which makes writing about her/them a bit tricky when one has to use a pronoun. The Hadley Irwin story might motivate pairs of children to try a joint writing venture.

Shame gnaws away at children's self-esteem, especially if they think everybody else's life is hunky dory. Dad got fired, cousin Joey hot-wired a car, Mom drinks, Uncle Harry is in jail, she has to share her room with two sisters or sleep on the couch, she can't run fast, or she has big feet.

Not all writers were born perfect or grew up on Easy Street either. Bruce Brooks wrote *No Kidding* (HarperCollins, 1991) to come to grips with his growing up with an alcoholic mother. Anne Lindbergh's brother was kidnapped and killed. Mark Twain's family was so poor he had to quit school and go to work at twelve. Laurence Yep, raised in a black neighborhood, too American to fit into Chinatown, too Chinese to fit in elsewhere, grew up feeling like an outsider. Until he was fourteen, Robert Lipsyte weighed over two hundred pounds. Paula Danziger has had a weight problem all her life. Sue Ellen Bridges was so afraid of the water that getting her hair washed was an ordeal, and she sat on the beach with her back to the ocean. Hans Peter Richter's father was a Nazi, M.E. Kerr's brother a mercenary. Learning more about writers could help kids to realize they, their families, or their situations don't have to be perfect to make it.

With a little luck, children in whole language schools are going to appreciate, but no longer be intimidated by great writers and their work. After reading *Ulysses*, *Crime and Punishment*, and *The Sound and the Fury*, it took twenty years for me to have the audacity to think I might be able to write a novel. Of course, no one else can write *To a Lighthouse*—that was Virginia Woolf's voice, her experience and viewpoint woven into her imagination. The whole language approach encourages young writers to trust their voices, to dip into their lives. Rather than worshiping at the altar of writers they enjoy, kids look at the techniques successful writers use like flashbacks, interior monologues, overheard conversations, and then try the methods in their own work.

TALKING BACK TO AUTHORS

"What I like best is a book that's at least funny once in a while. I read a lot of classical books like *The Return of the Native* and all, and I like them, and I read a lot of war books and mysteries and all, but they don't knock me out too much. What really knocks me out is a book that, when you're all done reading it, you wish the author that wrote it was a terrific friend of yours and you could call him up on the phone whenever you felt like it." (from *The Catcher in the Rye*)

If Holden had been in a whole language classroom, he would have been encouraged to pick up his pen to respond to "old Thomas Hardy" in his journal.

In most of the professional literature you will see it called a literature response journal or log, but kids are more apt to keep one if you tell them it's a way to talk back to an author. Talking to the author could remind children of Judy Blume's Margaret who was even more gutsy in *Are You There, God? It's Me, Margaret* (Macmillan, 1982).

A child whose friends call him a tub of lard might read *One Fat Summer* (HarperCollins, 1991) and want to thank Bob Lipsyte something like this:

"Remember when that guy called Bobby, Crisco Kid because he was fat in the can and Bobby pretended he didn't hear, so the guy would think he wasn't getting to him? I wanted to thank you because I tried it and it worked, sort of."

Or while reading *The Search for Grissi* (Avon, 1985) a child might tell Mary Francis Shura he hoped she didn't mind, but he was going to name his stout cat Guinness, too. He was also planning to write a story about Guinness running away, but his cat was going to be found because he thought it was terrible that she never let DeeDee find Grissi.

The response journal is also a way for children to make their literature discussion groups more interesting or lively. They make a note to bring it up in the group when they especially liked or disliked an incident, a character, the language. When they don't understand, they put that in too, because one of the other kids might be able to explain it.

Rookie readers can also come to understand character development, pacing, structure, and tension when they go back to read their journal entries. If, for instance, in the beginning of *Taking Terri Mueller* (Avon, 1981), they had told Mazer they couldn't understand why she had Terri and her dad moving around all the time without explaining the reason, at the end they would see that the mystery was one of the techniques Mazer used to create tension and tension or suspense is what makes the reader keep turning pages to find out what happens.

READING SELF-SELECTED BOOKS
NOT DISCUSSED IN CLASS

The whole language approach looked like a winner to me as soon as I learned there was to be a free-read time. When fat bookmobiles, perhaps purposely designed to look like bread trucks, still delivered books to nourish the souls of students in rural schools, and desks had tops that pulled up, I kept mine stuffed with stories about girls and their horses. You wouldn't believe the machinations I went through reading those stories with the desk top up, so I wouldn't get caught doing "something bad." Recently, I winced when a young, Indiana cousin's parents received a note from his well-intentioned teacher saying Mitch was doing sloppy work because he hurried so he could "sluff off" to read story books. This is a child who read *Lord of the Flies* in the fourth grade.

We've always known that children, who come from homes where there are books and parents set aside time to read, are more apt to enjoy reading and become high achievers. Doesn't it seem only logical that legitimate school time should also be allotted for free reading? Some teachers call it Choice Time, where kids can write, draw, or read. Most rooms have a shelf where children may put books they think friends would like, but they don't have to do anything with their selections other than enjoy them.

The question always comes up, what if all students read are series like thirteen accounts of Sweet Valley High or every available edition of *Wildfire*? The sales figures make a strong case for concern. In a 1988 *Wall Street Journal* article, M.W. Apple reported Bantam's Sweet Valley High series averaged more than 350,000 books for each first-print run and had printed over twenty-six million books. Then there is the publisher's marketing strategy of jointly marketing teen and adult romances, based on the theory they have hooked lifelong readers, especially female readers, eager to follow the recurring themes of romance, sexuality, and making themselves beautiful. This does not give male readers a leg up on taste however. Boys and men can be equally as obsessed with sports, horror, wild West, and cops-and-robber stories. There was a time when my nephew Dannon could have told you Mafia kingpin John Gotti's preference for breakfast cereal.

In "'Transitional Novels for Readers of Teen Romances" (*The Alan Review*, Fall 1991), Patricia Kelly suggests teachers and librarians tap into this interest by a respectful discussion, helping the readers to critically reflect on their identification with the characters, compare books and their versions of femininity, analyze their appeal, and evaluate the realistic and unrealistic elements of the story.

Kelly offers a list of bridge books dealing with romance, which also include more realistic and complex issues relevant to the plot. She suggests *Acts of Love*, Maureen Daly (Scholastic, 1986); *In SummerLight*, Zibby Oneal (Bantam, 1985); *The Last April Dancers*, Jean Thesman (Avon, 1987); *All for the Love of That Boy*, Linda Lewis (Archway, 1989).

For love stories with believable characters, Kenneth Donelson and Alleen Nilsen (*Literature for Today's Young Adults*, 3rd ed., Scott Foresman, 1989) recommend *Bright Shadow*, Joyce Carol Thomas

(Avon, 1983); *Very Far Away From Anywhere Else*, Ursula K. Le Guin (Athenaeum, 1976); *If Beal Street Could Talk*, James Baldwin (Doubleday, 1974); *Fair Day and Another Step Begun*, Katie Letcher Lyle (Lippincott, 1974); *Rebels of the Heavenly Kingdom*, Katherine Paterson (Lodestar, 1983).

I would add *Forever*, Judy Blume (Bradbury, 1975); *Beginner's Love*, Norma Klein (Dutton, 1983); *Unclaimed Treasures*, Patricia MacLachlan (Harper & Row, 1984). Perhaps these bridge lists, combined with yours, eventually land the reader in Brönte, Austen, and Hardy country. Wouldn't that be a journey worth the trip?

Another possible means of luring readers addicted to fantasies might be to introduce a unit on "Role Models, Real and Fictional." I once heard a forty-something Duke University professor say that at a meeting of her feminist history group, Queen Elizabeth I and the Virgin Mary were the only childhood female role models they could remember. As a tomboy growing up on the plains, my heroines were less erudite and had more warts. For years, I proudly put on the personae of Belle Starr, Bonnie Parker, and Scarlett O'Hara. The bookmobile must not have carried Willa Cather.

Parents and educators can deliver well-intentioned pedantic lectures about limited dreams until their vocal cords shrivel, but self-discovery makes a more convincing sound. In an age when Sally Ride goes to the moon; Marguerite Yourcenar is admitted into the Académie Française; Madonna makes more money than the president and sets more fashion trends than Ralph Lauren; Ann Richards governs Texas; Hanna Gray heads The University of Chicago; and Judy Blume is a household name, young women will surely come to realize they can have goals beyond the bedroom and the beauty parlor. Suggesting that students not only read biographies, but form groups to discuss and defend their choice of role models might help them turn a reading corner.

FOLLOWING INTERESTS AROUSED BY STORIES

I strongly believe that people would rather know than not know. Know what? EVERYTHING. When a child says, "that's boring," or "I don't care," I think it has more to do with his self-esteem or the image she has been sold as the "desirable one" than the subject at hand. The boy who believes poetry is for sissies, the girl who thinks her sex has a deficient math gene, the kid who was laughed at when he tried, the child who feels so far behind he thinks the race is over, or one made to feel like a dummy early on, wear armor, but it's man-made. They wear it on the outside and it's penetrable. Until further notice, I shall assume that in the right climate, with enough resources, a child can enjoy learning and will follow the string as far as it's rolled out.

Take dinosaurs. I've yet to meet a K-4 teacher who doesn't have a "How the Dinosaur Lesson Got Out of Hand" story. Introduce a bunch of little kids to those creatures by reading one story and then say, "that's all, folks." If a teacher plans to try to get away with one tale, she should warn the librarian to dig out several dozen stories, dinosaur encyclopedias, and to be prepared for a swarm of not very tall, independent researchers with a need to know what dinosaurs ate, where they lived, how big they really were, whether kids could ride them, and most important, why those marvelous, magic creatures disappeared before these kids had a chance to see them. They probably will also get a kick out of seeing how artist Bruce Degen makes them dance in his illustrations for Jane Yolen's *Dinosaur Dances* (Putnam, 1990).

The most ardent whole language supporter can't promise reading Mary Francis Shura's *The Jessie Gambit* (Avon, 1986) will insure our country's winning the next international chess match, that Scott O'Dell's *The Island of the Blue Dolphins* (Dell, 1961) will inspire a dozen children to become oceanographers, or exposure to Bruce Brooks' *Midnight Hour Encores* (Harper & Row, 1986) and Patricia MacLachlan's *The Facts and Fictions of Minna Pratt* (Harper & Row, 1988) will fill the string sections of the nation's symphony orchestras, but then we shouldn't totally dismiss the idea. As a boy, rumor has it, John Kennedy read the biographies of every president, even the Republicans.

Some students will finish *The Contender* (Harper & Row, 1967) and want to read every other book Robert Lipsyte has written (see Sports for All Ages, pages 119–125). Others will want to know more about boxing and might switch to biographies of great fighters like John L. Lewis, Jack Dempsey, Joe Lewis, Rocky Marciano, Muhammad Ali.

Those who enjoy a broader range of sports stories might move on to Richard Blessing's A *Passing Season* (Little, Brown, 1982); Walter Dean Myers' *Hoops* (Delacorte, 1981); and *The Outside Shot* (Delacorte, 1984); Bruce Brooks' *Moves Make the Man* (Harper & Row, 1984); Chris Crutcher's *Running Loose* (Greenwillow, 1983); Roger Angell's *The Summer Game* (Simon & Schuster, 1977).

Entering a new source of knowledge and pleasure through the back door is ethical. For example, in our culture a majority of boys are more apt to be exposed to sporting events than art galleries. If Maurice Sendak's *Where the Wild Things Are* (Harper & Row, 1985) didn't arouse a child's interest in art when he was two, maybe he can enter through the gym. In 1992, IBM put together an exhibition of fifty-six works, "Sport in Art From American Museums." The selections included: Thomas Eakins on boxing; Elaine de Kooning on basketball; Winslow Homer on croquet; Childe Hassam on golf; Henri Rousseau on rugby; Marjorie Phillips on baseball; Andrew Wyeth on fishing; and Andy Warhol, who once said that everyone would be famous for fifteen minutes, on a group of sports celebrities who have lasted considerably longer. Finding a piece of art a child would relate to because of its subject could be the first stage in learning to *read art.*

Integrating the arts and the disciplines can take children down circuitous routes to new interests. In a room where the kids' art work is intermingled with the display of Jasper Johns, de Kooning, Rembrandt, and Picasso posters—where a Haydn violin concerto might be the background music and they can communicate their ideas about rain by drawing, sculpting, dancing, acting, photographing, or writing a story or a poem—everyone is an artist of some sort. Artists become interested in forms, natural and created—the shape of a leaf, the structure of a story or a building, movements in music, dance and transitions in writing. They explore materials, words, paint, notes, numbers, wood, facts, stone.

III. IMPLEMENTATION

Whole Language
Activities That Could
Work for You

Writing this section, I collided with conflicting concerns, both legitimate. Librarians fear the whole language approach will "basalize" (that's creative spelling) all literature. They shudder at the thought of over-structuring, overworking a book, teaching beyond a child's interest, bending good literature they love to fit a curriculum need. Everyone has a "ninety-page teacher's guide for a nine-page picture book" story. On the other side, teachers and librarians in systems where whole language is being mandated without in-service training are eager for as much curriculum help as possible. They say they are being asked to go out on a limb with no safety net, no guidance on ways to talk to parents. These people want ideas they can adopt immediately until they can come to grips with the philosophy and practices. My suggestion to both contingents is to be aware of the situation and to use common sense.

Following are suggestions and ideas in a variety of sizes and shapes. The sports theme is lengthy and detailed. The one on family relationships short with most decisions for integrating the books left to the teacher or librarian. If people already using the whole language philosophy were to use everything I suggest, I would be amazed. I envision them dipping into something like the homeless theme discussed in this chapter, perhaps using *Fly Away Home* to supplement their list, or picking up on how myths are made in the section on *Maniac Magee*, maybe using the "what if" writing game. For those trying whole language for the first time, I hope the recommendations give you a good start.

SOCIAL-ISSUE BOOKS

The Homeless

When I was a child, the Illinois Central Railroad had long before cut the Willett land straight down the middle. The hobos used to camp under a trestle, down the track from my grandfather's farm. The myth was these drifters made the best Mulligan stew you ever tasted in an iron kettle my friends and I could always find hidden in the weeds. Tramps also used to knock on our back door, offering to split kindling or pump water for the horses in exchange for a meal Mother always provided. My father was certain the bums secretly marked our gate to let their fellow travelers know about Mother's soft heart and good cinnamon rolls. I used to sit on the well curb, while our visitor tried to eat his meal between my volley of questions about where he had been, where he was going, what he had seen.

These men, jumping freights to ride the rails, were romantic, mythical figures to those of us forced to stay put. Vagabonds with itchy feet, we said. Always moving on by choice, we thought. Considering how long the Great Depression had lingered on, perhaps that was a mythical idea too, but these wanderers, who seemed as free as the wind, touched children's imagination and wanderlust; they didn't break our hearts.

Today's children do not and should not romanticize the many people, sometimes entire families, forced to live in the streets, because they have no other place to go. Homelessness has become a strong rallying cry for the nation. For class books, I've chosen three—all with different views of the problem. In *December Stillness* (Avon, 1990), homelessness, the effect of the Vietnam War, prejudice, all touch Kelly's conscience, but she has a safe and secure life. *Maniac Magee*, a myth, and realistic *Fly Away Home* look at the problem from the perspective of the victims.

Maniac Magee by Jerry Spinelli (Harper, 1992)

ABOUT THE AUTHOR

According to Jerry Spinelli, while he was growing up in the West End of Norristown, Pennsylvania, he did the usual kid stuff with bikes, balls, popsicles. He got poison ivy, wondered about girls, and thought stuff he would never say out loud. He was sixteen when he made a decision to say many of his thoughts out loud. His high school won an important football game. He wrote a poem about the game that was published in the local paper. " . . . right about then I stopped wanting to become a Major League shortstop and started wanting to become a writer," he says (*Sixth Book of Junior Authors and Illustrators*, Sally Holmes Holtze, ed., H. W. Wilson, 1989).

In the beginning, he wrote grown-up novels nobody wanted. Then in his thirties he married a writer, now known to readers as Eileen Spinelli, who brought to the marriage a "wagonload" of published works and a half-dozen kids. (Later, they had one more.) One night, one of the half-dozen swiped the fried chicken Spinelli was saving for his lunch. The kid was lucky. So was Spinelli. The way he dealt with the problem was to write about it. What he wrote eventually became *Space Station Seventh Grade* (Little, Brown, 1982), his first children's book. Everybody has wanted his stories for kids, which include *Dump Days* (Little, Brown, 1988), *Jason and Marceline* (Little, Brown, 1986), *Who Put That Hair in My Toothbrush?* (Little, Brown, 1984) *Night of the Whale* (Dell, 1988), *There's a Girl in My Hammerlock* (Simon & Schuster, 1991), *Fourth Grade Rats* (Scholastic, 1991).

Spinelli received an A.B. degree from Gettysburg College and an M.A. from Johns Hopkins University, but he received the material for most of his books from his seven kids and his memories of the West End days. Like that period when his daughter Molly, a feisty boy-hater, and son Jeffrey, who liked to lift weights, were always fighting. Spinelli doesn't say whether *Who Put That Hair in My Toothbrush?*, a story about sibling rivalry, stopped the spats.

Although *Maniac Magee* (winner of the 1991 Newberry Medal and the 1990 Boston Globe-Horn Book Award for Outstanding Fiction) grew out of Spinelli's memories of his childhood in Norristown, he deliberately made Maniac legendary to try to capture the sense that our childhoods are bigger than life, mythic and heroic. He says you go back to your hometown to look for a big old scary alleyway and can't believe that innocent looking pathway is what you remembered.

Racial harmony, one of the themes in the book, also came from the author's childhood memories. He frequently played basketball with black kids and remembers once being the only white kid at a birthday party. In the book, Spinelli has Mars Bar be the only black kid at a white birthday party, but being free to rewrite history is part of the fun of being a writer.

BEFORE READING THE NOVEL

Whole language teachers have intriguing ways for presenting class books. Following is another suggestion:

Who was Daniel Boone? Betsy Ross? Paul Revere? Geronimo? George Washington Carver? What made them heroes? When the stories we know, and those we make up about people like these, have been handed down through the generations and are "loosely" based on historical fact, they are called *legends*. What other American heroes can you name, whose fame is based on legend? Legendary heroes have grown out of World War II, like Generals MacArthur and Patton. Who are the immortals from the Holocaust? The Civil Rights Movement? The Sixties? Why do you think all countries have these legends about people whom we like to think were braver, stronger than the rest of us?

Myths differ from legends in that they have less historical background, and are based more on supernatural qualities—incredible strengths, feats, etc.—more the way we wish things were than they really are. A country's myths are stories that explain why the world is what it is and why things happen as they do. Myths and legends give us something to believe in, to make us proud. For example, cowboys are uniquely American. The mythology surrounding these fearless, independent loners who braved incredible odds to settle the wilderness and bring law and order to an untamed land is a way we explain who we are as a nation, and why we behave as we do. Outstanding sports figures like Red Grange, Joe DiMaggio, Joe Lewis make good mythical heroes, too.

In your family, is there a legendary hero people talk about at family gatherings? What myths have grown, or are growing out of your family history? Are there any myths about you? Do we have any mythical heroes in our school, community, city, state?

If you are short on heroes, don't despair, you may adopt Jefferey Magee, better known as Maniac Magee. But wait a minute, what does maniac mean? Isn't that someone who is crazy, loony, a madman?

Now, when I chose this book for the class to read, I was told it was about a young, heroic character. And just look at that cover. Does a hero wear sneakers with the soles flapping like snapping turtles? Please, open your books. Let's clear up this mystery.

The narrator warns us: "The history of a kid is one part fact, two parts legend, three parts snowball." Who might be telling this story? Do you think he is going to be a character in the story? Where did he get his information? Who are the "they" who say Maniac was born in a dump? And why do you think this Maniac Magee is carrying a book in his hand even on the football field?

As you read the story think about a bigger-than-life character you might like to write about.

AFTER READING THE NOVEL

Discussion Questions

1. Retell Jeffrey Magee's story, explaining how he got to Two Mills in the first place.

2. When did this story take place? There are no dates, no Model-T Fords, or a president's name to help us place it in time, but in "Before the Story" how does the narrator makes it sound as if it happened a long time ago? If it is a legend, why would it make sense for it to have been far in the past? But turn to page 91, to find a detail that makes it seem to be a current story. Do you think Spinelli made a mistake with the Egg McMuffin? Is he is playing a joke or do you think the time is now? If you had been his editor, would you have asked him to remove or leave the egg?

3. When you think of the word "home," what is the first thing to come to mind? All Maniac wanted was a home. He had one with his uncle and aunt, so why didn't he stay there? Then in Two Mills, almost immediately, he found another one with Amanda Beale's family. Why couldn't he stay? Living in a band shelter might not be everyone's idea of a perfect home, but why did it suit Jeffrey's, after he'd painted a house number on it, of course? At the end, when he went back to the Beales' to stay, what had changed? How much of the difference had been Maniac's doing? If you had to pick only one of the things the story is about, would you say it is mostly about—homelessness or prejudice or love? Defend your answer.

4. A symbol is an object that has meaning itself, but also represents something abstract, like a cross. What does the knot at Cobble's store represent? When Jeffrey arrives, what else in the town is so twisted you couldn't find the beginning or end of it? How does he untangle it?

Amanda has a whole suitcase full of books; why do you think the author picked *The Children's Crusade* for her to give to Jefferey? What does the title symbolize in relation to the rest of the story?

What is the significance of Grayson's glove?

5. Point to episodes in the story where Jeffrey played the role of teacher. How does this minor theme, learning, relate to the major issue of the book?

6. Even heroes get the blues. When did it happen to Maniac? Why? Point to the one time in the story when he did not show courage. Explain. Do these episodes make the story more believable or take away from Maniac's role as hero?

THINKING LIKE A WRITER

1. The cover says "legends are made, not born." What do you think it means? If this is not only a story about Maniac Magee, but about how stories are told over and over until they become legends someone writes down, isn't it also about the process of writing? Look at the way Spinelli organizes his story. On the first page he gives some facts about what an unknown kid does on a football field. What do you find in "Before the Story"? After the legend section, he begins his tale, weaving the facts and the myths with his imagination. Notice how Spinelli has Maniac do things that *might* be possible. He doesn't give him the ability to fly or create lightning, but to run on a railroad track, hit difficult pitches, bring black and white people together, teach an old man to read—outstanding things, but within the realm of possibility.

Try his method: Think about a character who "people say" did all of the things you would like to do. Make a list. Next think of an incident where your character accomplishes one of your dreams, like breaking a horse that was so wild no one could ride him.

Now think about who your character is, how did she have the opportunity to do something outstanding? Notice how Spinelli got rid of authority figures who would have made Maniac go to school, had a fit if he had eaten the buffalo's carrots. What is your character's situation? Also, mythical characters have to do things that not only benefit them, but make the world better—more like we want it to be, like Maniac's breaking down the line that divided the East and the West sides. What will your character do that will help other people?

When the story opens, what did Maniac want? Wanting an address was his motivation—the justification for his actions. What does your character hope to accomplish? What motivates her?

How did Spinelli make Maniac seem real, but more interesting than the people we know? Carrying the book around was a good touch. His fetish for butterscotch Krimpets and the beat up sneakers helped to identify him. What *props* will you give your character?

Finally, think of what will happen to your character in the end. Myths and legends are only made when the character wins. How can you find a credible way for your character to accomplish her purpose?

Work with a partner to plan your story. Tell him what you want to accomplish, the incidents you plan to include, what the conclusion will be. Rehearse. Ask for feedback. Write a draft, ask for feedback, and revise until you have done what you set out to do. When you have finished your stories, we will collect them and *publish* our own collection of myths (see Publishing, pp. 61, 158).

ACTIVITIES

1. Pretend that one day Maniac Magee ran into your town. Where did they see him first? Who saw him? What did he do? Tell what happened.

2. Hold a panel discussion on the homeless. One student will present the facts—statistics about how many exist, what percent of the population they represent, where they are, major causes for people not having homes. Another child will present plans different states and cities have devised to ease the problem. A third will explain what she thinks the federal government could or should be doing. A fourth will explain why he feels *Maniac Magee* will raise kids' awareness of the problem. A fifth child will take the opposite opinion, stating why she thinks fiction romanticizes something very serious, making us feel it will all turn out all right in the end. The panel will take questions and opinions from the other members of the class.

3. Set *Maniac Magee* to music. Pick five scenes from the novel.

Choose songs or instrumental music that you feel set the tone of the episodes. Explain your choices. Play the music if possible.

4. Describe a place in your neighborhood that has a reputation like Finsterwald's.

5. Write Maniac a letter. You may invite him to come to visit, telling him why you would like to meet him, or tell him why the two of you are alike in some ways, or explain to him some problems you would like for him to untangle in your family or your town or. . . .

6. Find five well-known historical legends, such as George Washington's cutting down the cherry tree, that are probably myths.

Brother Eagle, Sister Sky: A Message from Chief Seattle, adapted and illustrated by Susan Jeffers (Dial, 1991): A Controversial Myth

If the children are interested in myth, they might be interested in discussing the controversy over Chief Seattle (1786–1866), the Native American for whom the city in Washington was named. When an adult book, *Brother Eagle, Sister Sky: A Message from Chief Seattle* by Richard Duffy (Erie Street Press, 1991), hit the best-seller list and the chief's words began to be quoted by environmentalists, historian David Berge, who is writing a book about Seattle, said the chief is probably our greatest manufactured prophet. Other debunkers claim much of the chief's famous oratory was written in 1971 by a Hollywood script writer for an Earth Day movie.

Part of the dispute grew out of a letter attributed to Seattle in 1854 in which he reportedly wrote, "The earth is our mother. . . .I have seen a thousand rotting buffaloes on the prairies left by the white man who shot them from a passing train." But it seems there were no bison within six hundred miles of the chief's home on Puget Sound, the letter is dated about fifteen years before the first railroad crossed the Plains, and the great buffalo slaughter took place at least a decade after Seattle's death.

Those same words appear, however, in a best selling children's book, *Brother Eagle, Sister Sky*, but in an afterword we find, "The origins of Chief Seattle's words are partly obscured by the mists of time." Author and illustrator Susan Jeffers said in an interview in *The New York Times*, "Basically, I don't know what he said, but I do know the Native American people lived the philosophy and that's what is important." Dial president and publisher Phyllis Fogelman said, "For want of a tape recorder, maybe we have a book that will change children's view about the environment."

To add a dash of irony to the discussion, you might want to include the fact that Chief Seattle died in 1866, one year after the city named for him passed a law making it illegal for Indians to live in Seattle. (Timothy Egan, "Chief's Speech of 1854 Given New Meaning [and Words]," *The New York Times*, April 21, 1992)

December Stillness by Mary Downing Hahn (Avon, 1991)

ABOUT THE AUTHOR

When Mary Downing Hahn was growing up, she thought all writers were dead or living in England. Even though her teachers said she had "too much imagination," she read books when she should have been studying her spelling words, doodled all over her homework, and even added illustrations in the margins of her picture books, no one— including Mary—thought about her becoming a writer. Ordinary people growing up in College Park, Maryland, didn't write books. Much to her regret, she didn't begin to put scenes from her own childhood into stories until she was almost forty.

In *December Stillness*, Kelly's father's expectations for his daughter do not match her desires. Hahn knows something about that conflict. When she and her best friend Ann were young, both of their mothers taught in the local elementary school. Daughters who got into trouble with teachers, colored and drew pictures in their storybooks, climbed trees, messed up their clothes wading in the creek, followed mysterious strangers, did not fit the definite ideas the teacher/mothers had about proper behavior for children. Mary and Ann dealt with the problem imaginatively, as writers would. They simply eliminated the prickly parents. The girls played "Orphans," making up stories about poor, mistreated children who, running away from the orphanage, dashed straight into exciting adventures.

Born in Washington, D.C., Hahn graduated with a B.A. degree in Fine Arts in 1960 from the University of Maryland, where she had been encouraged to make new illustrations for old stories and had a sketch pad where she could color any pictures she wanted to, all over the pages. After marrying and having two daughters, she wrote *The Sarah Summer* (1979), *The Time of the Witch* (1982), award-winning *Daphne's Book* (1983), *Wait Till Helen Comes* (1986), *The Jellyfish Season* (1985), and *December Stillness* (1988), a story about a girl who follows a homeless man. Now where do you think she got that idea?

BEFORE READING THE NOVEL

Following is only one of many possible whole language approaches to this book that might go like this:

The next time you are asked to write a research paper for a class assignment, it might be a good idea to take notes in your journal about the process. *December Stillness* is a story about what happens to fourteen-year-old Kelly when a teacher rejects her original topic for a current-issues paper. Judging only from the cover, what do you think she finally wrote about?

William Zinsser has written a book called *Writing to Learn*. What do you think he means by that title? Zinsser contends that the only way we really learn anything is by having to find the words to express our ideas, facts, and feelings on paper. Take geometry. Rather than memorizing a theorem, Zinsser would say you won't be able to apply the theorem to anything practical until you can explain in words what it means and how it works. How do you feel about his view?

Assuming Zinsser is right, if you were given Kelly's assignment, what issue in our society would you choose? To make it meaningful— worth the effort—it would have to be something you sincerely want to learn more about. Plant your issue in your notebook. As you read this novel, perhaps it will begin to germinate ideas.

AFTER READING THE NOVEL

Discussion Questions

1. Who would like to retell the plot? Now, who can tell what the story is really about? Is it about Mr. Weem, the homeless, the Vietnam War, Kelly's relationship with her friends, her mother, her father? Adding all these elements together, what does Kelly finally learn through the process of researching her paper?

2. Who is responsible for Mr. Weem's death?

3. How did you feel about Kelly's father? Explain why you think he behaved as he did. If Hahn had written one more chapter after he and Kelly returned from Washington, do you feel he would have acted the same as he had before? What implication does the author leave for you to consider about their future relationship? Do you find her insinuation credible? What other believable endings might she have written? If you had been her editor, would you have suggested another conclusion or accepted it as is?

4. Has anyone ever been to the Vietnam Memorial? If so, how would you describe the experience? Do you know about anyone whose name is on the wall?

5. The Vietnam War was a conflict in Southeast Asia, primarily fought in South Vietnam between government forces aided by United States troops and guerilla insurgents aided by North Vietnam. The war began soon after the Geneva Conference in 1954 and escalated from a civil war into a limited international conflict in which the U.S. was deeply involved. The combat was virtually halted by peace agreements in 1973. Why was it such a controversial conflict?

6. Although it was an unpopular, often protested war that many young people refused to serve in, America lost 58,156 known dead. In 1981, Maya Ying Lin, a twenty-one-year-old Yale architecture student was commissioned to create a memorial, made from black granite which reflects the sky, trees, and faces of the people searching for names. The faces on the cover of this book are superimposed on an artistic rendition of the monument. Like the war, in the beginning the memorial was controversial. Now it is one of the most frequently visited sites in Washington, D.C. Why do you think this piece of stone with names has become so popular?

7. What other books have you read that focused in some way on the Vietnam War? If you liked *December Stillness*, you might want to read Bobby Ann Mason's *In Country* (Harper & Row, 1985), a young girl's concern about her father who was killed and her uncle who couldn't recover from his experience in Vietnam.

8. Hahn deals with the issue of homelessness at a distance, told not from the homeless person's perspective, but from one observing his plight. How would the story have been different if Mr. Weem had told it? Eve Bunting's picture book, *Fly Away Home* (Houghton Mif-

flin, 1991), about a boy and his father who live at the airport or Jerry Spinelli's Newberry Award winner, *Maniac Magee* (Harper Trophy, 1992) look at the problem from the victims' viewpoint (see p. 87 and p. 76). If you are interested in reading more about homeless people Carol Hurst, Children's Book Editor for *Teaching K-8*, suggests Marilyn Sach's *At the Sound of the Beep* (Dutton, 1990); Lois Lowry's *Taking Care of Terrific* (Dell, 1984) and Paula Fox's *Monkey Island* (Orchard, 1991).

I especially like Fox's story about eleven-year-old Clay Garrity who ends up living in Monkey Island, a small park, when his parents lose their jobs. Although it's a heartbreaking story, there is hope and a cast of wonderful characters like Calvin, a mainly mad philosopher.

In conjunction with the current homeless issue, Hurst also suggests you look at books about pioneer children taken captive by Indians in the eighteenth century. She lists Sally M. Keehn's *I Am Regina* (Philomel, 1991); Conrad Richter's *A Light in the Forest* (Knopf, 1966); Mary Smith's *Boy Captive of Old Deefield* (River City Press, originally published in 1904 & still in print); Elizabeth Speare's *Calico Captive* (Houghton Mifflin, 1957); James E. Seaver's nonfiction book, *A Narrative of the Life of Mrs. Henry Jeminson* (Syracuse University Press, 1990). ("Dealing With the Homeless," *Teaching K-8*, April, 1992)

As Far as Mill Springs by Patricia Pendergraft (Philomel, 1992) tells the Great Depression story about Robert and Abiah, boarded out to the Hicksons, who treated them badly. The boys run away to ride the rails in search of the town Mill Springs where Robert hopes to find his mother.

THINKING LIKE A WRITER

1. Building on the impression you received from Kelly's mother, write a scene that might have happened between Mr. and Mrs. McAllister before they were married.

2. Form small groups. Think of happy endings Hahn could have written. In good writing, character drives the plot of a story (the way life is, not the way we wish it were). Discuss which would make you feel better and which would be the best literature.

3. Write a character sketch of an imaginary homeless person or

family. Include his/her age, physical appearance, reason for being on the street, and attitude toward life.

4. The idea for this story came from Hahn's habit of following mysterious strangers when she was young. Look through your journal. Can you find any entries describing things you do when you're having fun that you might use as the basis for a story?

ACTIVITIES

1. Interview someone in your family, school, or community who served in the Vietnam War. Prepare five major questions and three follow-up questions for each one. From your interview notes, prepare an oral presentation to the class. Begin by explaining whom you interviewed, his/her answers to the questions and conclude by explaining your feelings about the interview.

2. Divide into groups. The task is for each group to decide on two things you think the federal government could do to help the homeless, two things the community could do, and two things kids in your school could do.

3. Design a T-shirt with a message that you think would be appropriate for Kelly to wear.

4. Write a character sketch (if you have enough information) or a descriptive passage about someone in your community who fascinates you. It could be the butcher, who makes you laugh; the shy person who delivers your paper; the woman with the weird hats whom you sit behind at church; or _____.

Fly Away Home by Eve Bunting (Houghton Mifflin, 1991)

ABOUT THE AUTHOR

Several of the young-adult novelists mentioned here are friends, most are at least acquaintances. More often with the younger children's books, I relied upon research, but being so personally touched by *Fly Away Home*, I felt I actually had to talk to Eve Bunting. Clarion publicist Margery Naugton agreed, bent the rules, and gave me her phone number. Irish-born Bunting, who has written 150 books for publication, was the delight I had anticipated. After her children had grown up, she says she handled her mid-life crisis by taking a writing course. Hundreds of children and her four grandchildren who love her books are thankful. *Fly Away Home* happened this way:

Having read a newspaper article about the number of homeless who live at Chicago's O'Hare Airport—not perfect accommodations, but better than the street or shelters—Bunting, who travels a lot, began to look around at major airports. "But I didn't see them," she said. Knowing they were there, but that they were looking anonymous, like "nobody" gave her the idea.

Bunting wrote the text, gave it to Clarion and they decided Ronald Himler was the right illustrator. When she saw the drawings, she agreed. When they discovered, while talking on the phone, that they were to attend the same meeting in Phoenix, she asked how they would recognize each other. "Oh, I don't think it will be a problem," Himler said wryly. Of course Bunting recognized him immediately, because he looks exactly like the father in *Fly Away Home*.

When I asked Bunting which of all her many books were her favorites, at first she seemed reluctant, but then she began to discuss *The Wall* (Clarion, 1990) another book illustrated by Ronald Himler, and she couldn't stop. Perhaps to appreciate her passion, you must remember that, born in war-torn, Northern Ireland, Bunting emigrated to the U.S. in 1960 to find a safer place to raise her three children. When she first visited the wall, seeing the wives, children, parents, suffering the same pain she had left in Ireland touched her deeply.

Not wanting to write a political book, it took her a long time to find her way into the wall—which she finally saw as the repository of sadness, but, as in *Fly Away Home* where there is hope, she concentrates on the living. "I try to leave out the parts people skip," Bunting says.

BEFORE READING THE STORY

Following the children's interest is the best way into a good book. Here are some additional ideas:

Look at the cover. Where are these people in the picture? See the airplane flying away through the clouds. Have you ever been to an airport? Did you go to meet someone, or to take a plane to another city? What do you think the lady in the yellow dress and the man in the tan sweater are doing? Yes, they could be looking for the plane they will take to fly away or watching for a plane bringing a grand-parent. If Granny is coming for a visit, what will these people do after they collect her luggage? You're right, she might be tired, so they will take her home where she can have a snack and lay down to rest.

Now, look at the little boy and his father. What are they wearing? What do you think they have in the two bags? How would you describe the expressions on their faces? Do you think the little boy likes his dad? What was your clue? Predict: Why do you think they are at the airport? Where do you think they might be going? Why do you think they aren't looking out the window like the other people?

I know a secret. There's a bird in this book. Don't miss him. After you've finished the story, tell me why you think Eve Bunting put him in there.

AFTER READING THE STORY

Discussion Questions

1. Why do the little boy and his father live at the airport?

2. What is their biggest problem? How do they keep from being noticed? How did Mr. Slocum and Mr. Vail get caught?

3. What mistakes did the woman with the metal cart make?

4. Look at the picture on page 12. What is different about the little boy's face? Why is he smiling? Why doesn't he sit down with his friends? Why do you think his dad never smiles? The artist, Ronald Himler, knows how to draw smiling grown-ups. Remember Mr. Slo-cum and Mr. Vail?

5. That bird is on page 16, but he is in trouble. What is his difficulty? How do he and the little boy have similar problems? Why does the bird make the little boy so happy? What did the bird give him? Have you ever seen a bird that kept flying into a window when he wanted to get out? Was it stupidity or circumstances beyond his control? Have you ever felt like a bird who ran into an obstacle you couldn't see until you hit it?

6. How did the little boy and his father keep clean? Where did they eat? Have you ever gone camping and had to "rough it" for a few days? How was Arthur's situation different?

7. How old is Denny? Arthur? How do their families feel about their going to school? Do you think it makes any difference?

8. Is Arthur's dad a lazy, irresponsible bum or just down on his luck? Give examples from the story to support your answer.

9. Based on how they are coping with their situation, do you think they will ever fly away home, singing like the bird? What are your reasons?

10. Why do you think Eve Bunting wrote this book? What do you think she hoped you would feel after reading it?

THINKING LIKE A WRITER

1. Look at the picture on page 6, where Mr. Slocum and Mr. Vail are singing "as loud as two moose bellowing." "Bellowing" is a word that makes a sound like the one it's describing. So do "swish" and "rustle." Think of some others.

2. Say the word "nobody." How does it make you feel? Take the words apart, and what do you have? No body. The poet, Emily Dickinson wrote a line people can't forget, "I'm nobody, who are you?" Have you ever felt like nobody? On page 8, the little boy says "Not to be noticed is to look like nobody at all."

3. Modeled writing: Let's write a story about Nobody. You tell me what to say. First I'll write the title in the center like this. Now, who is Nobody? Is she an alley cat, or a baby elephant who got left behind by the circus, or a little girl no one will play with, or. . . .

4. On pages 14 and 15 everything is on the move, even the language. Pick out the words that make things move, like "bounces." Let's make a list of other words like "flaps," "streaks," "hurdles," "soars." . . .

5. In a good story, the end is only the beginning. There is always "And what happened next was . . ." for someone to write. What would you write about Arthur and his father? Tell me what the first sentence would be.

ACTIVITIES

1. The bird who flew away home gave the little boy hope he could too, someday. Draw a picture or symbol of something that has given you hope.

2. Put on a skit that could have taken place at the airport. It could be when the little boy and his father almost get caught by security, or a scene between Denny and Arthur on a weekend, when the father was working or one that you make up.

3. Make a class collage showing Arthur's life at the airport. Everyone contributes something like an airline advertisement, a cut out bird, an airplane, a scrap of denim.

REALISTIC FICTION

For our children's hearts and imaginations to be touched only by dancing dinosaurs, baseball games, family reunions, and young love, they would have to live in bubbles. People they love die, drink too much, do bad things. They do bad things too. In our complex society, the young constantly have to make hard choices, find ways to live with loss. When I began to plan my novel, *Katy Did* (Avon, 1991), a girl's maturation story, I had no idea it would lead to the issue of mercy killing. Too many young people are victims of random violence and people with evil intent. On the journey to maturity, everyone has to try to balance self-interest with the greater good. As we see in Avi's *Nothing But the Truth* (Orchard, 1991), for some it's a short trip. True to the whole language principle of encouraging the young to bring their life experience into their reading and writing, the following selections reflect the world as it is, not the way we wish it were. The real problems of real kids are presented candidly and with respect, which should encourage readers to tell and write their own realistic stories.

A good book never deals with only one issue, one problem. For example, Jean Thesman's *The Last April Dancers*, appropriate for middle school and young adults, balances a touching story of young love with the death of Cat's father. In Robert Cormier's *We All Fall Down*, a complex novel for older readers, his major theme is random violence and its victims, but he also deals with alcoholism, fathers who abandon their children, revenge, and for the first time—a love story. Avi's *Nothing But the Truth* raises a baker's dozen of ethical problems, not only for young people, but the entire society they cope with—parents, schools, politicians, the media. Beverly and David Fiday's *Time to Go*, a picture book for all ages, presents a farm boy's loss of his home, but also his dreams and his memories.

Random Violence

We All Fall Down by Robert Cormier (Delacorte, 1991)

After *The Chocolate War* knocked the socks off the young-adult literary world, including mine, I went to Leominster, Massachusetts, to interview this young-adult author who pulled no punches, expecting to find a dour pessimist, a scoffing cynic with a sneer or a smirk. Instead I found a gentle, serious man, a loving father of four, a husband who still thought his wife was terrific, the kind of person who made friends for life.

However, Cormier, who has an abhorrence for bullies and no faith in elevators, is what we used to call a worrywart, and rightly so. Troubled by corruption in government, greed, loss of faith, the breakdown of the family, prejudice and bigotry, haphazard violence, and the lethargic television generation, he thinks it is important not only to recognize the seriousness of real life problems that cannot be solved in an hour like in a sitcom, but even more important for honorable people, young and old, to do their utmost to bring change. Following *The Chocolate War* with *I Am the Cheese* (Pantheon, 1977) and *After the First Death* (Pantheon, 1979) it were as if he were saying, sorry, but this is the way it is, now what is to be done.

Although, in my opinion, the bizarre ending causes *We All Fall Down* not to carry the wallop of the novels mentioned above, it is like saying I prefer *King Lear* to *Richard III*. In 1979, *Newsweek* magazine said Cormier was the author who could challenge J.D. Salinger and William Golding, and he has continued to do so. I call him the Faulkner of young adult literature because, as with Faulkner, you have to read Cormier's books at least twice—the first time racing through to find out what happens, then again, and maybe again, to find out what it means and how he did it. For example, I didn't stop to ponder the significance of Buddy's smashing the Jeromes' mirrors with a Statue of Liberty; the symbolism of his divorced mother's unmade bed; the irony of Amos's books—two Stephen Kings and *The Adventures of Tom Sawyer*; the subtlety of Harry's talking black; or Cormier's reason for choosing several points of view, until the second read.

We All Fall Down would work well in a heterogeneous class where a record of students' interests and abilities resembles a longitudinal measure of the prime meridian. The most reluctant reader could hardly resist the shock of Cormier's opening line for that book that could scratch a diamond:

"They entered the house at 9:02 p.m. on the evening of April Fools' Day. In the next forty-nine minutes, they shit on the floors and pissed on the walls and trashed their way through the seven-room Cape Cod Cottage."

(*The Chocolate War*'s first line was, "They murdered him.")

The serious literary student won't miss the symbolism of the event happening on April Fool's Day, the wannabe writer will want to dig deeper into the flat—just-the-facts—tone of the narrator. Who is he? Where is he? How did he know what happened? Dedicated thriller readers can use their expertise to compare the story to the formula for the genre. For those with a heightened awareness of social issues and an interest in current affairs, this beginning will promise a realistic view of the problems and the challenges for their generation.

To appreciate what sets Cormier apart from lesser writers, all students should be encouraged to explore how the plot grows out of the characters' actions. The trashers picking the Jeromes' house might have been "dumb luck" as Harry Flowers says (note the irony of his language and name), but he is the corrupting evil force much as Archie was in *The Chocolate War*. Not only what Harry does, but how Buddy and the Avenger react to him set off a drastic chain of tragic events. The kids will want to talk about the Harrys who have or have tried to influence them.

Following are a list of questions for discussion, small group work, or writing assignments. This book would be an excellent choice for a team teaching, integrating the disciplines venture with a social studies teacher exploring crime, the changing suburbs, breakdown of the family.

- What did Cormier gain or lose when he chose to use multiple points of view? What could not have been included if the entire story had been told from Jane's viewpoint? Buddy's? The Avenger's?
- Did the alternating viewpoints heighten the suspense or make the story difficult to follow?
- Explain the effects of misdirected anger. Have you ever spent your fury on the wrong person or had it done to you?
- How did people treat the Jerome family, the victims? If this is realistic, how do you explain society's reaction? Has it ever happened to you or to others you've known or read about?
- Are the fathers the real villains in the story? Defend your answer.
- Explain the relevance of the metaphor when Buddy says his father "always left a trail of disarray and debris behind him." Point to other places where a metaphor strengthened Cormier's point.
- If Harry's father had not bought him out of trouble, how might things have turned out differently?
- Early in the story, Jane's mother says, "People are not always what they seem to be." Trace that as a prophetic statement for the rest of the novel. Write or tell about someone you know or have met who is not what he/she seems to be.
- The story begins with the trashing of a house. Explain how it ends with the trashing of love. Did the author's use of irony make Buddy and Jane's story more compelling or detract from the impact?
- Dramatic irony is when the reader knows something the character does not. If you had been writing this story, would you have kept Buddy's identity as a trasher a secret from the reader, too? How would the change have affected the plot?
- To test the impact of dramatic irony, if you have read Judy Blume's *Forever* (Bradbury, 1975), compare your reaction to Blume's couple vowing to love each other forever to Jane and Buddy making the same vow.
- *The Chocolate War* did not have a love story to counterbalance

the emotional aridity of evil as does *We All Fall Down.* If you have read both books, explain which structure has the more powerful impact.

- Does hope survive the trashing? What character is saved and who is doomed? If Jane is the moral center of the story, how does she add an optimistic glimmer to the story? Predict what you think will have happened to her in five years. To Buddy?

- On one level, the psychotic Avenger, with his voyeuristic fascination for Jane—attracted by her wholesomeness, troubled by her sexuality—is Mickey Stallings (Loony), a strange neighbor, a real character in the story. On a deeper level, what element of society does Cormier mean for him to symbolize?

- The critics disagreed about the Avenger. Defend or attack the following or give your own opinion about his effectiveness:

More familiar territory is a suspenseful subplot involving a character called "The Avenger," whose goal is to exact revenge for the trashing. Although it certainly will keep readers turning the pages, this may be the weaker part of the novel, particularly its resolution which seems some what glib. *School Library Journal* (September, 1991)

The characterizations of Jane, Buddy, and the Avenger are particularly well developed and convincing. *Booklist* (September 15, 1991)

Although Cormier clearly understands that he is writing for an audience reared on the novels of Stephen King, this sensational episode with the killer clouds over some important issues raised in the novel— questions of the dissolution of family and societal violence, of personal responsibility and guilt. *The Horn Book* (November/December, 1991)

- Was there any way Cormier could have written a happy ending? If the ending is a challenge for change, who is responsible? What is to be done? What can you do?

(Good readers who wish to go further with the theme might want to read adult writer Joyce Carol Oates, who throughout her prolific career has been obsessed with the theme of violence and randomness of modern life—"the unspeakable turn of destiny," as she once called it, that can instantly shatter an individual's hopes and dreams.)

Nothing But the Truth by Avi (Orchard Books, 1991)

No one who is breathing will need suggestions on how to approach this story, a whole language teacher's dream. Finding a place to stop could be a problem. If you and your kids think like writers, you will say, "Whoa, this isn't a novel. It's a series of letters, diary entries, phone conversations, faculty memos, newspaper stories, snatches of conversations." Looking at how the author put together this crazy quilt so that it has a beginning, a middle, and an end; develops characters; and tells a story is a fascinating must-do exercise for apprentice and accomplished writers.

Self-interest, one of many themes to follow, is probably the sharpest cut to the center of this complex story with no heroes.

Philip Malloy wants to be on the track team, but his English teacher, Miss Narwin, whom he thinks doesn't like him, gives him a disqualifying "D." He concocts a nutty plan—humming to the "Star Spangled Banner," which is supposed to be observed in respectful silence, to get out of her homeroom and English class. Instead, he is expelled. Miss Narwin, a dedicated teacher, asks for a stipend to improve her teaching, which becomes "proof" she can't do her job. There is enough irony here to build a battleship when the media and local politicians pick up on a slick "suspended for patriotism" story, the school district retreats to save their budget, Philip's parents who don't own a flag, but love their country, all get into the fray. No one wins, and the conclusion, like Paula Fox's *Moonlight Man*, is a punch to take your breath away.

Preachy approaches—teaching the children a moral lesson—is my nightmare about what can happen to good books. Not a chance with this one. After the students read the story, stand back and let them have a go at discussing what happened, why did it happened, whose fault was it, what about ethics, how can "truth" shift, how is this incident like a recent, actual event, how do you feel about it and how did Avi make it happen in this story? (For more about the author, see the discussion of *The True Confessions of Charlotte Doyle*, p. 104)

Death of a Father

The Last April Dancers by Jean Thesman (Avon, 1987)

ABOUT THE AUTHOR

There isn't anything, or much of anything, about the author. Although one can't help but wonder if she could be a distant relative of the isolate J.D. Salinger or the late Greta Garbo. A very private person, Thesman has politely refused to fill out the proverbial publisher's profile sheet or to be interviewed. Perhaps the mystery will intrigue the students as much as knowing her story. It certainly should help them to understand the private women in the novel.

This is what we know: Thesman lives outside of Seattle, Washington, with her husband and three children. She says she wrote *The Last April Dancers* because she wanted to show that courage is not an attribute of a particular age. She has also written the following other titles published by Houghton Mifflin: *When the Road Ends* (1992), *The Rain Catchers* (1991), *Rachel Chance* (1990), *Appointment with a Stranger* (1989).

BEFORE READING THE NOVEL

1. Discuss the title. Who do you think the "April Dancers" might be? The key word in the title is "last." Does it make you think this will be an ominous or a melancholy story? Does any other feeling come to mind? When choosing a book to read for pleasure, are you influenced by titles? What are some of your favorites? Critics have praised Scott Fitzgerald's decision to call his book about Jay Gatsby, a Roaring Twenties bootlegger, *The Great Gatsby*. What's the key word? Would you be intrigued about why he called a crook "great"?

2. Let's read the first page aloud. How does Thesman capture your attention? What do you want to know? Cat says she knows who Shelia is. Do you believe her? By the time you finish the story, you should know who she is, too. If not, why has the author played a dirty trick? Although you don't meet the author of most books you read, it is as if you've signed an unwritten contract. What is your role in the agreement? What is her part of the bargain?

3. *Tone* (the implied attitude toward the subject and the reader) is

as important in literature as it is in music. Picture people you know who usually have a sarcastic or a menacing sound in their voice. Now think of someone whose optimistic attitude toward life is expressed by her inflection as much as her words. Writers use tone to develop their characters. How would you express the tone of Cat's letter to this mysterious Shelia?

4. As you read the story, keep a literature-response journal. It's a way to talk back to Thesman. Tell her when you think you have figured out who Shelia is. After you know how the story turns out, tell her if you think she made a wise or unwise choice by opening the book with this puzzle. Compare entries with your classmates'.

AFTER READING THE NOVEL

Discussion Questions

1. If you were asked to review *The Last April Dancers*, would you describe it as a love story, a young person's struggle to deal with death and loss, the lack of communication in a family, or _____?

2. One of the major challenges a writer faces is braiding all the plot lines together. Explain how Thesman related the three listed above.

3. How did the author *show, not tell,* you that Cat's father had more than a physical problem? Point to places where Cameron's and Cat's behavior toward him revealed their characters. Was the mother a sympathetic/unsympathetic character? Was she realistic? Did she try to keep up appearances because she was a snob or because she couldn't face what was happening to her husband? Have you ever known someone who tried to cover up a problem? Did it work? Have you ever tried to hide something that was hurting you? What happened?

4. In her last unmailed letter to Sheila, Cat suggests the St. John women should try to forgive each other. What had Cat, her mother, her grandmother, and Leah done to Mr. St. John that needed to be forgiven? What had they done to each other? To themselves?

5. How do you think *The Last April Dancers* "shows that courage is not an attribute of a particular age"?

THINKING LIKE A WRITER

1. Do you have any ideas for a title of a story you might write? Think of five, list them in your notebooks.

2. Authors sometimes choose to give their books the name of their protagonists like *Tom Sawyer*, *Huck Finn*, *Maniac McGee*, *Cassie Binnegar*. When do you think using the hero's name is a good idea for a title? Think of a character's name you feel might appeal to readers. How important is the sound? George Eliot wrote a book about a character named Daniel Deronda which are fun words to say because of the *alliteration* (repetition of an initial sound in two or more words of a phrase like Maniac McGee.) Make up some characters' names that are examples of alliteration. Thesman could have called her book *Cat and Cameron*. Which title would you have preferred?

3. A *symbol* is something that has meaning on its own, but can be used also to represent something abstract. For example, a dove is a bird, but it is also the symbol of peace. In the last chapter, Cat flies a red kite, but then she cuts it loose. Why does she cry? What else is she letting go? Therefore, what did the kite symbolize? Think of ways you could make the following symbols in stories you might write: a marble, a yoyo, a foghorn, a long white scarf, a cross-eyed cat, a lacy antique Valentine.

4. When a writer finds characters he wants to write about, it is not possible to include their entire lives and everyone's perspective in one book. He must select what to tell, what to leave out, which person's point of view he wants to explore in depth. When Thesman decided to limit her story to Cat's viewpoint, she left a lot of material on the cutting-room floor. What else would you like to know about this family? If you were going to write more about the St. John saga, would you go back to Leah's youth, the early days of Cat's parents' marriage, her father's life as a young man, the relationship between Mr. St. John and Leah, or would you tell the same story, but narrate it as Cameron saw it?

ACTIVITIES

1. Choose one of the titles, a character name, a problem from your notebook, and a classmate for a partner. Discuss the story you would like to tell. Rehearse: Who would tell your story? Who are the minor characters? What is their significance to your protagonist? How would the problem affect your hero's life? How much time would the plot cover? Would you need to flashback to an earlier time? How would

your character finally deal with the problem? (He could fix it, come to understand and live with it, overcome it through strength of character, give up.)

2. After talking through the story, write a draft. Meet with your partner to read each other's stories. Give feedback on: what you liked and disliked, how well you thought he accomplished his purpose. Point out spelling and grammatical corrections that need to be made.

3. Using the constructive criticism you received, revise your story. Continue the process until you feel your story is ready to publish.

4. Surrealistic art, popular in the twenties, expressed imaginative images and ideas revealed in dreams, free of the conscious control of reason and convention, like Salvador Dali's melted clocks. Make a surrealistic painting or drawing to symbolize some aspect of the novel. You might choose the world as Cat's father saw it, the scene where Cat and Cameron were the April dancers, or one of your choice.

Loss

Time to Go by Beverly and David Fiday, illustrated by Thomas B. Allen (Harcourt, 1990)

ABOUT THE AUTHORS & ILLUSTRATOR

Until Beverly Fiday's death in 1992, she and her husband David both wrote books on their own, but what they enjoyed most was working together. Good chemistry, they said, common interests, too. They met and were married in college at Northern Illinois University, but as teenagers both of them had loved to read and tell stories. Both had poetry published in local and school papers when they were kids.

Beverly became a reading teacher, David a school media specialist. After their daughters Jennifer and Jessica were in school, the Fidays began to write seriously. They have published several nonfiction books, but *Time to Go* was their biggest challenge. Where did that story come from?

The Fiday clan originally settled on a farm, but the cows were gone, no smiling pigs, no treehouse with a view of the stars any longer existed. Years ago the homestead had become a subdivision with houses that looked like Monopoly pieces. Then one day Joliet, Illinois, city-dwellers Beverly and David took a drive to an Amish settlement in Indiana. Beverly saw a farmer standing on a plow as a horse worked to unfurl the earth. She had a strong feeling that he loved his land. As a writer, she began to think as writers are apt to do, *what if.* . . . What if he had to leave his farm? What would he do? What would his youngest son feel about leaving his homestead, the only place he had ever called home?

Thomas B. Allen, born in Nashville, Tennessee, during the Great Depression, is now the Hallmark Distinguished Professor of Design at the University of Kansas, father of a teenage daughter, two older children, even a grandfather, but there was a time he traveled the globe looking for an answer to the proverbial question, "who am I?" At forty-three he spent three Spartan years, what he calls his Thoreau period, in a cabin on a pond in Cold Spring, New York, finding a new direction, a new quest for his life.

Allen says the journey that began in Cold Spring continues. He learned that questions are more important than answers. The pictures in *Time to Go* are finished, but Allen hopes, in the reader's mind, they still raise some questions about the experience of life.

BEFORE READING THE STORY

What is your favorite title of a book, not necessarily the story you liked best, but just a nifty title, like *Mom, the Wolf Man and Me*, or *The Five Little Peppers and How They Grew* or *Little Women*, or *A Wrinkle in Time*? How do you like *Time to Go*? What do you think the story will be about? Time to go where?

Close your eyes and picture a farm. What colors do you see? Yellow corn, red apples, green fields, black-and-white-spotted cows, pinkish pigs—those are bright colors. Look at the colors Thomas Allen used for his picture on the cover. Describe them. Why do you suppose he used muted shades? Do you ever use colors to express your moods, like wearing a red shirt when you're feeling full of pep or a black sweater when you're sad or a grey sweatshirt when you have the blahs?

WHILE READING THE STORY ALOUD

Did you ever see a two-seated tandem bike which both riders peddle while they move on the same path? That is the way the authors and the artist have worked to make this book. The writers say endless acres stretch before the little boy, and the artist stretches acres clear across the page. The boy says today all that will change. When we turn the page, it has.

Compare and contrast what you see on the left page with the right page on which the boy is talking. The left side is now-parched corn stalks; the right is the way it used to be—lush and green. Is there any significance in having the way it used to be on the *right* side?

How has the artist used color to make the empty henhouse look as lonely as the writers describe it? How are the colors different on the right side showing the hens and their chicks?

Those pigs are smiling. Turn the page and Biscuit is smiling, too. Why? On what side of the page are the smiling animals?

Why do you think the artist drew the silent tractor, whose job is over, so big?

What does water symbolize? How does the lack of water relate to earlier pictures we've seen in this book? Old Nell is gone, so there's no milk, the silo is empty and the squirrels are eating the apples before they are ripe. What does this tell us about the farm?

Sleeping in the treehouse, sleeping under a quilt Mama stitched by hand are the boy's memories. What will he do with those when he leaves?

When the family drives away, where is the sun? Why? But, look at the last page. What has happened to the boy? He has faith he'll grow up like this and come back. Do you?

THINKING LIKE A WRITER

1. The writers also draw pictures of what has happened to the farm. They use words like "shimmering heat," "dry kernels," "cracked and baked mud." Find other word pictures. Write some word pictures to describe your house or yard.

2. We not only see the decay of the farm, but we hear how it sounds, like a weathered door that squeaks on rusty hinges. Find sound words to let me hear the noises on your bus this morning or the playground yesterday.

3. How do pigs behave? What does their squealing, nudging, pushing tell you about their natures? Find action words to describe the personality of a cat, goldfish, dog, or pony you have known.

4. The writers said the scarecrow is wounded like a soldier, comparing what has happened on the farm to a war. Compare something in your life to a flat bike tire, a broken mirror, a melted stick of butter, a runaway kite, a cracked cup.

5. When the authors write about the pump and the windmill, how do they appeal to your senses? Find words to describe how it feels to take a shower. Don't forget to include how the soap smells.

ACTIVITIES

1. What color is winter? Saturday? Friendship? Loneliness? Church music? The shopping mall? Easter? Your best friend? Is Saturday brown because it is as good as chocolate, or orange because it makes you want to dance like a flame? Pick something and write a sentence explaining what color it is and why.

2. Build a model of some aspect of the farm—the windmill, a cornfield, as it is, as it was or will be when the boy returns.

3. Take a field trip to a farm. Carry a sketch pad or your notebook. Write or sketch your impressions. Don't forget the colors, the sounds, the smells, and the expressions on the animals' faces.

4. Research. Find articles in newspapers and magazines or interview farmers or people at the Farm Bureau to find out why many small farmers are having to give up their farms.

5. Math (for older kids). Interview a farm-implement dealer. Ask him for the prices of farm equipment today compared to twenty years ago. Ask a realtor to give you figures comparing the price of farm land now and twenty years ago. Do the same at a store which sells fertilizer and pesticides to farmers. Analyze your figures to see if they tell you why the small farmer is having trouble.

6. Put yourself in the story. Pretend you are the boy's brother or sister. Tell how you feel about going, how you feel about your brother.

ADVENTURE AND ROMANCE

When children grow up in a world where the nightly news chronicles violent teenage gangs, drug abuse, divorce, custody feuds, homelessness, AIDS, crack babies—and many of the books written for them deal with the frightening realism of such problems—they often need an escape.

The big wide world is never more alluring than when a kid is still too young to drive and probably not even left at home without supervision. Vicarious love and adventure through literature can help to ease the ache.

The original *romance*, written in a Romance language, was a form of chivalric and romantic literature widely diffused throughout Europe in the eleventh century through song, but later recited in the courts. The troubadours lengthened them into *chansons de geste* and the *roman d'adventures*, which told stories of love and adventure that have lured readers down through the ages.

In my early teens, an excellent English teacher gave me Tennyson's "Lancelot and Elaine" from *Idylls of the King* to feed my fantasies. On my own, of course, I searched for accounts of Belle Starr leading the Younger gang, real stories so romanticized who could tell the difference. When I became the English teacher, Herman Hesse's *Siddhartha* (Bantam, 1971) and *Steppenwolf* (Bantam, 1971), Tolkien's *Lord of the Rings* (Houghton Mifflin, 1974), William Golding's *Lord of the Flies* (Coward, McCann & Geoghegan, 1955), all dealing with quests that ended in finding wisdom, were popular with my students.

Today many young-adult novels fall into the category Donelson and Nilsen (*Literature for Today's Young Adults*, 3rd ed. Scott Foresman, 1989) astutely label "Wishing and Winning." In whole language classrooms and libraries, these books are most frequently offered as independent reading, but can also be useful in studying literary genres and helping students to develop critical skills. Literature, often defined as a mirror of reality, reflects social, political, and economic values and reforms similar to the way history and sociology record them. Analyzing how a formulaic genre adapts to the changes in society is one way to approach these books.

The True Confessions of Charlotte Doyle by Avi (Avon, 1992)

ABOUT THE AUTHOR

The Manhattan author's twin sister, the poet and literary critic Emily Leider, nicknamed him Avi. He rarely tells his real name, only teases by saying he doesn't use a last name because it saves ink. He is very open, however, about other aspects of his life such as how he became a writer. His story is not what you expect.

He flunked out of high school, not because of the stiff competition, even though Walter Dean Myers and Norma Klein were classmates, but because of his poor writing. Avi had and still has dysgraphia, a learning disability that is never cured (the inability to write properly, similar to dyslexia). On the brink of failing in the second school, he had a teacher who not only taught him the fundamentals, but convinced him he had writing talent.

When asked how he has been able to produce an incredible body of work that includes comedy, mystery, adventure, fantasy, and young-adult novels, he says by reading a lot, writing a lot, being stubborn, never giving up, and having a spell check on his computer.

Avi claims not to create characters, but to discover them within himself and his world. He often creates several drafts before even naming or physically describing the character. "It takes a while to get to know them," he tells Barbara Ann Marinak ("Author Profile, Avi", *The Book Report*, March/April 1992).

Not all of his books have required research, but for *The True Confessions of Charlotte Doyle*, he haunted libraries and museums, read thirty to forty books, and lived with maritime maps all over the house. But he is comfortable in libraries, since working as a librarian was his profession while raising three sons, until he became successful enough to write full time.

BEFORE READING THE NOVEL

1. Discuss the appeal of adventure and romance novels. Students are bound to realize that people like these far-fetched stories because they have happy endings, as readers' lives seldom do, and the writers are willing to embellish characters and events enough to make their plots more interesting than reality. Who but James Bond finds constant adventure dangling from airplanes, romancing extravagantly beautiful women, diving into the deep, and winning the chase in cars you could die for?

2. Ask students to retell outrageous storylines they have enjoyed.

Generate a list of appealing characteristics like:

- The plot will be driven by the hero's pursuit of justice, honor, revenge, love, truth.
- The setting will be as exotic as the kids' dreams when they're feeling confined in the same old room, on the same old street.
- Tension will be created by the protagonist's qualms, tests of strength and courage, lack of understanding.
- In the end, the hero will win, of course, and success will be sweeter because of the terrible trials that have to be overcome.

3. Talk about the cover. Ask for opinions about its appeal or lack of allure. What do the students think was the artist's intent? What do they predict the story will entail? Are kids influenced by a cover when they choose a book, or do they take recommendations, read cover copy or a few lines of the story?

AFTER READING THE NOVEL

Discussion Questions

1. On the board write the three stages Donelson and Nilsen (*Literature for Today's Young Adults*, page 127) suggest adventure stories contain that resemble rites of passage many cultures have set up for adolescents to accomplish before entering the adult world:

A. A young, naive person is removed physically and spiritually from the sustaining love of friends and family.
B. While being separated from loved ones, the protagonist, who has noble qualities, faces an intellectual, emotional or physical test of courage and stamina.
C. The hero is reunited with friends and family in a new role, having gained a more exalted status.

How true to the formula is *The True Confessions of Charlotte Doyle?*

2. If Avi had been writing such a tale in the forties or fifties rather than in 1990, how do you think it would have been different? Did his choice of a female heroine add to, or take away from, the story's appeal? Is your answer influenced by your sex? How could this story

have a positive impact upon society? Are there any disadvantages to having young women identify with such an adventure-seeking hero?

3. Novels are structured so that the action builds to a dramatic point—*the climax*—where something happens that causes a change. The hero comes to realize something she didn't know before, she makes an important decision, she has a reverse in fortune. The climax is the emotional center of the book—the point when the reader is most involved in the story. After the climax, the story winds down to the conclusion. What was the climax in *The True Confessions of Charlotte Doyle*? How would the story have been different if Charlotte had not decided to join the crew? Do you think it would have been a stronger or weaker story?

4. An anachronism is anything out of its proper historical period. For example, why couldn't Charlotte drink Cokes, wear blue jeans or listen to Bruce Springsteen? Did you find any anachronisms in the story?

5. Have you ever had to make a climactic decision that has had a strong effect on what has happened since in your life?

THINKING LIKE A WRITER

1. As we go to press, "Political Correctness" is a term often bantered around in literary criticism. How do you interpret it? When you, or any writer, sit down to create a story, do you think the idea that you must neither alienate nor discriminate against any group interferes with the creative process or that the challenge sharpens the author's thinking process? For example, Avi chose to have a girl be the hero in a story usually told from a male point-of-view, he made Zachariah—a black man—the good guy, and the bad guy was a white Anglo Saxon male. Would this be considered a politically correct novel? Did these decisions weaken or strengthen his plot and the book's appeal?

2. Avi chose to tell his tale as if Charlotte had written in her journal what happened. What other options did he have? What would have been gained or lost, if, for example, he had written it from her viewpoint, but had a third-person narrator tell the story? How would the story have changed if Zachariah, her father, or Captain Jaggery had told it in first person? Do you have journal entries you might be able to generate into an adventure story?

3. Adventure stories are more plot driven (action) than determined by character, but even so, a writer still has to make a character engaging enough for the reader to care about her fate. How did Avi make Charlotte interesting? Were you more intrigued by her looks, her personality, her thoughts, or the way she treated other people and their reactions to her?

4. Analyze chapter 14 (Charlotte's climbing the riggings in the storm) to determine how Avi created the tension. Find images that make the setting scary, point to language that helped you to experience the danger. *Structure* is the way the story is built, how incidents and information are arranged. Could you rearrange the order to make it even more sensational, add more stages of danger or do you think the author's design cannot be improved upon?

ACTIVITIES

1. Design a radio play dramatizing one chapter of the novel. Choose an announcer to introduce the program, people to do commercials selling a product, a cast, a director, and a producer. The cast sits on stools, reading to make the listeners see the action through their words and intonation, rather than acting out what is happening. The emphasis is on the actors' VOICES. The director instructs them and the announcer how to say their lines. He decides on what sound effects to use. The producer chooses the background music and is responsible for playing it and making the sound effects at the appropriate time. She also decides when to break for a commercial and when the announcer speaks.

2. Pretend you are Charlotte. Write a letter she might have written to her parents after she returned to the *Seahawk*.

3. Act out a scene that might have happened in the Doyle family when they discover Charlotte has skipped. You will need a playwright, a director, a cast, and a person in charge of props.

4. Write a journal entry Charlotte might have made when she was eighteen years old.

5. Lay tissue paper over a map of the world. Trace the map, plotting the route of the *Seahawk*.

6. Draw, paint, sculpt a scene, or make a collage representing the storm at sea. Your work can be realistic or impressionistic.

Across-the-Disciplines Adventures in Other Countries

Chitty-Chitty-Bang-Bang by Ian Fleming (Knopf, 1989)

ABOUT THE AUTHOR

Anyone who does not know that Ian Fleming created a string of best-selling, adventure-packed thrillers about superspy James Bond has to have been in a trance or does not own a television on which the macho Bond movies appear as often as the mailman. But a children's book, that's a different kettle of giddy adventures.

Fleming, born in England in 1908, was educated at prestigious Eton, Sandhurst, the University of Geneva, and the University of Munich. Joining Reuters News Service in 1929, he was based in London, Berlin, and then Moscow. In World War II he spent a number of years in the British Intelligence Service, a job that amply qualified him for writing the James Bond thrillers.

As an adult writer, Fleming has been severely criticized for Bond's chauvinistic attitude toward women, but in *Chitty-Chitty-Bang-Bang*, although Mrs. Pott is portrayed as a "whatever you say, dear" type, Jemima shows as much courage as her twin brother Jeremy.

More sensitive to language than women's issues, in 1964 Fleming already had a feeling for how whole language readers approach a story, so he helped them out. For example, in the first line, "Most motorcars are conglomerations . . . ," realizing kids might have to skip or guess at conglomerations, he defined it "(this is a long word for bundles)." On page 28, he explained "transmogrifications (which is just a long word for changes)"; and again on page 47, "schuyt (a kind of small barge you see a lot of in the Channel, though when it's at home, it pronounces itself skoot)."

BEFORE READING THE NOVEL

Make the story an adventure, a trip abroad the class takes through the magic of a book. Your discussion might go something like this:

When people plan a trip to another country, in addition to packing their clothes, what must they do? They need a passport. (Show one, if possible, explaining how they are obtained, how often they must be renewed, etc. You can explain the photo is not a still from a horror movie. *Everyone's* passport picture is ghastly.) Learning the value of the country's money, and as much as possible about the language, is also essential.

Since Fleming is inviting this class to have an English adventure, he has been kind enough to explain the money (the British are noted for having awfully nice manners). Look at "The Note for the Observant Reader." At these rates of exchange, how much American money would you need to buy ten British pounds? If a soft drink costs three shillings, how much U.S. money would you need?

Look on the world map. We'll put a pin where we are. Who can find London, the city where the Pott family lives? The body of water John Burningham has drawn on the cover is the English Channel. Find it on the map. If you cross the Channel from England, in what country do you land? The Potts' adventure takes them to France, so we will go with them—leaving this map up so we don't lose our bearings.

To whom has Fleming dedicated this book? Some people are fascinated with their cats, but others have as much affection for their cars. Has your family ever been especially attached to an automobile? In this story, the Pott family is rather eccentric, another British trait— they treasure people who are a bit daft—but the Potts have especially strange ideas about picking their car.

You are almost ready to take off, but even though the British speak English, be alert for the differences in usage. Do you know any British expressions? For example, they call elevators "lifts" and when they're angry, they are more apt to say they are "cross." Note other differences in your notebooks.

AFTER READING THE BOOK

After the kids have had a chance to retell the story and explain what they liked best about the madcap adventure, they will probably enjoy continuing the trip with discussion questions, some math and money challenges, a few insights into the history and the geography of the story and a look at the story through the eye of a writer.

Discussion Questions:

1. What was unconventional about the Pott family? How did their being a bit eccentric affect the choice they made when buying a car?

Do you know anyone whose habits, interests, behavior seem peculiar to others? How about your family? Has this unorthodox conduct created incidents you could use in a story?

2. On page 10, Mr. Pott received 1000 pounds for his crackpots (note the pun). At $2.80 equaling 1 pound, how many dollars was he paid? How much in dollars will he receive when they sell five million? In dollars, how much did he pay for Chitty? (page 17)

3. What was unconventional about Chitty-Chitty-Bang-Bang? Her license plates? To make the story interesting and funny, Fleming *personified* the car. What human traits did he give to this hunk of machinery? Have you ever had a bike, a family car, a boat, a school bus that seemed to have a unique personality, or a mind of her own, just like a person?

4. What uniquely British words did you find, like "jam puffs" on page 26? (Other examples: page 32—golliwog; page 63—Guy Fawkes' day; page 83—duckies; page 86—"Dash My Wig And Whiskers"; page 93—jolly; page 97—by jove.)

Write:

- A time when you did something "off the wall" that was funny or turned out all right in the end.
- A character sketch of a car, bike, bus, skateboard you have known.
- A tale about the most unconventional person you know.
- Pretend Chitty-Chitty-Bang-Bang is yours. Write about a trip you take.
- The Normandy Invasion. In World War II, the Allies could have used Chitty-Chitty-Bang-Bang on D-Day (June 6, 1944) when they crossed the English Channel. Write a report about what really happened or what might have happened if Chitty had been involved.

Draw:

- A car you would like to own.
- A car, bike, bus, skateboard you have known.

ACTIVITIES

1. Look in the newspaper or ask at the bank what the current exchange rate is for pounds and francs. (Both currencies have been re-evaluated since this book was written.) Compare the rate to the one in the Potts' day.

2. On the Continent, the Potts had to figure distance in kilometers, rather than miles. A kilometer is approximately .62 miles. Figure the distance from your town to the state capitol in kilometers.

3. On p. 43, Mr. Pott says a naval knot is 1.15 miles per hour. If you have a boat that can do 25 knots per hour, how many miles per hour will you travel?

Themes to Explore

SPORTS FOR ALL AGES:
A WHOLE LANGUAGE PROJECT
FOR THE WHOLE SCHOOL

Most teachers have a story about a freckled face kid, who, when asked to identify a famous scientist, author, artist, says, "Did he pitch for the Yankees?" Some children might not be able to identify Frida Kahlo, James Monroe, or Wolfgang Amadeus Mozart, but find me a child who has never heard of Babe Ruth.

Human beings, from the ancient Greeks playing Olympic Games to American cowboys holding rodeos at the end of a roundup, have demonstrated an instinctive need to compete and to win. Today when physical fitness has become a national craze, sports play an even more integral part in the lives of both genders. There is no longer a "Men Only" sign on the locker room door. Those who aren't bouncing around in the gym, jogging down the streets, smashing a ball across the net, rafting white water rivers, or jumping curbs on their skate-boards, are apt to be watching a sports event on TV. I could have lived without "couch potato" becoming such a popular idiom, but the image improves if you think about kids curled up with a good book like *The Contender* (Robert Lipsyte, Harper & Row, 1967); *The Moves Make the Man* (Bruce Brooks, Harper & Row, 1984); *There's a Girl in My Hammerlock* (Jerry Spinelli, Simon & Schuster, 1991); *Slugger Mike* (Gibbs Davis, Bantam, 1991); *The Official Baseball Hall of Fame Story of Jackie Robinson* (Mark Alvarez, Simon & Schuster, 1990); or *Baseball Ballerina* (Kathryn Cristaldi, Random House, 1992). The following unit has an ulterior motive. It's an offensive move to win a few sports fans over from the screen to the page.

If you are looking for an all-school whole language project to integrate the people and the disciplines with its universal appeal sports could be a good choice. There are a staggering number of books;

possibilities for math, history, geography, art, music projects; and a myriad of writing opportunities for all ages. Such an all-encompassing unit is a good way to encourage teamwork among the faculty, staff, students, families, and community members. This venture with its magnetic kid-attraction also extends an excellent opportunity for students' taking responsibility for their own learning. They will want to be involved in the planning as well as the doing. Use some of the following approaches plus your own ideas.

Language Scouts

The simplest way to judge America's obsession with sports is to observe how our passion is reflected in the language. The gym and the playing fields are not the only places you will hear phrases like "southpaw," "keeping your eye on the ball," "go the distance." Everyone talks that way. Dub the students in your school "language scouts." Their job is to listen for the jargon in the kitchen at home, on the bus, at the green grocers. Ask them to:

- write what they hear in their notebooks.
- look in newspapers, magazines, books, on signs—anything that has print.
- copy those discoveries in their notebooks.

Start a daily list on the board with newspaper headlines like, "The Longest of Long Shots Is Suddenly a Contender" (a politician), "New Big-Spending Team At The Museum. . . ." Every morning, ask the children to add to the list from their collection. Suggest they:

- enlist help by putting their families and friends on the sports-language-alert-scouting-team.
- trade words with kids from other classes.
- read the sports page to find examples of jargon, cliches that have become boring from being overused.
- look for funny, new and interesting ways writers find to describe sports.

- make a list of snappy verbs that grab readers' attention by having an interesting sound like "swish," or by presenting a picture of the action like "swoop."
- add vivid images or analogies.

At the end of the unit, vote to award a gold, a silver, and a bronze "medal" to the three best examples found.

Teaming Up

Ask the children to think of a sport they love or one they want to know more about. Since the definition of the word encompasses any recreational activity requiring bodily exertion, include dancing, fishing, wrestling, horse racing, skiing, skating, rafting, running as well as baseball, basketball, football, soccer.

Form teams. For example, those interested in ballet or boxing will work as a team to research and present that sport to the whole class. Divide the responsibilities:

- present the history/rules, necessary skills, how and where the sport began, countries that have produced outstanding players, performers. If a team is doing baseball, they will show their classmates how to calculate batting averages; or if it's football they will explain "downs." Give the measurement of the field if the size is regulated. Show and interpret significant statistics.
- make a list of memorable people associated with the activity, biographical sketches of a current and a past star.
- show photographs, videos, play music, or draw pictures that exemplify the sport.
- prepare a skit, acting out the activity, or present an imagined interview with someone connected to the game.
- show collections members of the team might have acquired, like baseball cards, pennants, posters, programs, articles of clothing, playing paraphernalia.
- suggest a list of stories, nonfiction books, or biographies pertaining to the activity.

Teamwork

Discussion Questions for After the Research Project

- What does it take to be a part of a team?
- Tell the class about experiences you've had playing or watching team competition.
- Analyze the process your team used to prepare its presentation (above). Discuss the advantages of teamwork. Look at what hindered the team's progress. What can you do about it? What can we as a class do about it?

Coaching

How boring life would be if everyone had the same talents and interests, but thankfully some of us are good at writing, running, or reading while others can draw, sing, act, or throw. Give everyone in school the chance to have a coach to help him in an area where he needs to build strength. The teachers will compile a list. Students can volunteer to coach as well as to be coached. Explain that, as coaches, they will have to plan a method to assist their player, starting with ways to build the confidence of the person they're helping and to win his trust. Suggest they think of times when learning something new was fun or easy because of the way the person teaching them presented the challenge.

Work out a coaching schedule with the other teachers.

Put Your Team on the Map

Construct a huge map of the United States to put on the wall. Students make pennants, helmets, ballet slippers, etc. to represent the sport they like, pinning them on the map in the appropriate areas. They will want to use the team logos, symbols or colors—like New York Yankee pinstripes—for their symbols.

Integrate math and geography exercises by asking the students to figure how far teams in the different leagues have to travel to play their games, how far the kids would have to travel to see a live game, etc. Study the map as they plan the trip. If they went by car, what rivers would they cross, what big cities would they pass through? Would they cross any mountains? What state is farthest from a professional team? What state has the most?

Making a Jackdaw

This idea for younger children came from library media specialist Susan Rogers who suggests younger children make a jackdaw—a container, like a basket, filled with items that symbolize the person or sport they researched. The items can be collected from home, made or drawn in class. They share the things in their jackdaw when they make their presentations.

Rogers also recommends kids make a sports card game. They draw or color a portrait or symbol of their athlete on the front of the card with events, dates, and statistics summarized on the back. The teacher gives clues and the kids guess the identity. ("The Sporting Life," Susan Rogers, *Instructor*, March, 1992)

Sportswriting

Red Smith, the Shakespeare of sportswriting, took readers by surprise with his humor and originality, such as his description of a quarterback who was "scraped off the turf like apple butter." Too often, sportswriters use tired, worn-out phrases, like "a hurler firing the old horsehide," or they rhapsodize about the "old pigskin." Talk to your students about how they can write fascinating sports stories using good English.

In *On Writing Well* (Harper Perennial, 1990), William Zinzzer points to John Updike's account of Ted Williams' final game in 1960, when the forty-two year old "Kid" coming up for the last time at bat in Fenway Park, hits one over the wall. ("Hub Fans Bid Kid Adieu," *Assorted Prose*, by John Updike [Knopf, 1965]) Compare Updike's style and language to run-of-the-mill accounts in the local newspaper.

Invite a local sportswriter to speak to the class about the sportswriting genre and how it differs from regular news reporting or writing a feature article.

Ask the students to write either a report of a school or local sporting event they cover in person, or a feature story on a sports-related issue, such as drug abuse, spectator violence, women's rights, paying college athletes, minorities in team management, or to write a profile of someone who plays sports in their community. If possible, ask those doing a portrait of a player to interview the subject—a member of the girls' high school basketball team, a local bowling champ.

Sportscasting

Have students pretend they are reporting live on the radio or television. In preparation for writing a three-minute script to present to the class, suggest they listen at home to the language, cadence, tone, and pacing of an actual broadcaster, or bring a radio or TV to class.

Assuming the Role of an Athlete or a Character from a Book About Sports

Kids prepare a three-minute presentations to the class that begins something like the following:

- "My name is Kristi Yamaguchi. I won a 1992 Olympic gold medal for skating."
- "My name is Pete Rose. I made a mistake."
- "My name is Maisie. I joined the boys' wrestling team." (*There's a Girl in My Hammerlock*)
- "My name is Nolan Ryan. They said I was too old."
- "My name is Muhammad Ali. I am the greatest."

The presenters could wear costumes or use props if appropriate.

Each student makes a time line to demonstrate either his character's progress, or when she ran off the track to success.

Families Pick Sports Heroes

Have the children interview each member of their family to determine their favorite sport and player. Ask parents and grandparents who were their heroes when they were young and whom they admire today. The students share their families' choices with the class.

The Critics Go to the Movies

Hollywood loves sports, too. Plan to show a film kids of all ages can enjoy such as *Field of Dreams* (movie version of W. P. Kinsella's *Shoeless Joe* [Ballantine, 1982]). Recruit the art class to make posters advertising the event. Call it a special showing for the critics. In preparation, look at movie reviews in newspapers and magazines to determine what critics include, how they structure their pieces. Teachers provide a list of important names like the cast, director, special-effects handler. Armed with notebooks, the critics go to the movies. The little kids can write a sentence or two telling what they liked best. The older viewers can pan or praise the production.

Sports in Literature

With the plethora of good sports stories available, if you put a selection in the classroom library, kids will probably read independently throughout the unit. Following are suggestions for treating books the entire class might choose to read. The approach can be adapted or modified for any selection. For example, everyone in your class might not wish to read Lipsyte's *The Brave*, but some would prefer *The Contender*, or *One Fat Summer*. You could introduce all the books with the biographical information provided, discuss his style as presented in BEFORE READING THE NOVEL, and then let the students divide into groups based on the book of their choice.

My intention is not to suggest that you work the story to death until the kids are turned off, but rather to offer many possibilities, assuming you pick and choose ideas and activities, add your own, and call it a day when students begin to lose interest.

For Older Readers:

The Brave by Robert Lipsyte (HarperCollins, 1991)

ABOUT THE AUTHOR

When Robert Lipsyte writes about sports, he knows what he's talking about. As a sports columnist for *The New York Times*, he has covered them all. He got his idea for *The Contender*, his award- winning first novel, on the job. As a *Times* boxing reporter, he was in Las Vegas covering the Muhammad Ali fight when a boxing manager told him about the narrow, dark, twisting flights of stairs that led to his gym on the Lower East Side of Manhattan. Lipsyte was not yet a novelist, but he knew the magic question, *"what if?"* What if a kid would come up those stairs some night, alone, afraid, but hoping to use boxing as his ticket out of the streets and out of the slums?

Twenty-five years later, Lipsyte met a seventeen-year-old Native American, desperate to escape his reservation, but afraid of what waited for him in the white world. The writer began to ponder, what if this kid, who wanted to box, stepped off a bus in New York? He decided, "Sonny stepped off the bus and the city smacked him in the face. . . ." In true whole language fashion, Lipsyte also lifted Alfred Brooks from the pages of *The Contender*, thinking what if twenty-five years later Brooks was a cop who collided with this kid from the reservation? *The Brave* became the sequel to Alfred Brooks', the contender's story.

Sonny is naive about New York, but Lipsyte, a native, knows it well. He graduated from Columbia College and the Columbia Graduate School of Journalism. In 1957 he started at *The New York Times* as a copyboy. Fourteen years later he left the paper to write books, (all published with HarperCollins): *The Contender* (1967), *One Fat Summer* (1977), *Free to Be Mohammed Ali* (1978), *Summer Rules* (1981), *The Summerboy* (1982), *Jock and Jill* (1982), *The Chemo Kid* (1992).

The books are not his only accomplishments, however. Lipsyte has been a correspondent for the CBS "Sunday Morning Show," where Charles Kuralt called him "one of the most knowledgeable and skillful of the country's tellers of sports tales." In 1990 he won an Emmy as host of "The Eleventh Hour," a nightly public affairs show on New York's PBS station. In 1991, after a twenty-year absence, he returned to the staff of *The New York Times* where they call him "The Comeback Kid," as if he were a hero in one of his own novels.

He just might be. Like Bobby Marks, the hero of *One Fat Summer*, *Summer Rules*, and *The Summer Boy*, Lipsyte was a fat boy. He weighed more than two hundred pounds, but he never found out how much more. Like Bobby Marks, he too always jumped off the scale when that mocking red arrow reached 199. Again like Bobby Marks, he lost a lot of weight the summer he was fourteen. Some of the material might also have come from his son or his daughter, who were teenagers in the eighties.

BEFORE READING THE NOVEL

Robert Lipsyte once said books for young adults provide "a bridge of words" that can carry a child into a lifetime of reading. Close your eyes. Think of a bridge made out of words. What does it look like? His figure of speech is a metaphor, an implied analogy which imaginatively identifies one object with another. "Bone head" is a metaphor heard too often to suggest someone is stupid. Think of an original one you might use in a story. Figures of speech are writer's tools, as important in making their work interesting as a carpenter's saw. Create a metaphor for a hockey stick, a football helmet, figure skates, a referee, an injured player in pain.

While I read the first page aloud, hold on to the images you see:

• Describe the picture you saw of Sonny Bear.
• Did you get a glimpse of what he is like on the inside?
• Could you visualize the setting?
• Can you characterize the atmosphere?

Examine the words to see how the writer was able to accomplish so much in two paragraphs. Look for images, powerful terms. Sonny "swaggered," "banged his gloves," "whipped his ponytail," "vaulted into the ring." How do his actions relate to his thoughts? Does the crowd's hatred actually "slap his body like a fine cold spray"? As you read the story, pay close attention to Lipsyte's choice of verbs that not only tell you what's happening, but paint a picture. Take any you like to put in your notebooks for use in your writing. He won't mind. In addition, be on the lookout for other strong, vibrant, visual verbs you see in print or find in your head like "squeal" or "squash." Put them in your notebook too.

• How does the author create suspense, making you want to turn the page to find out what is going to happen next? What do you think the monster stirring in Sonny's chest might be?

- Respond to the author in your journals. Tell him what you like or dislike about his writing technique. If you don't like the way the story unfolds, tell him where you think he went off the track and how you would have told it.

AFTER READING THE NOVEL

Discussion Questions

1. Retell the plot. Was Sonny someone you would want for a friend? He was both naive and wise. Give examples. Describe how his Native American heritage impacted his character. How did it make him an outsider? Was Sonny's temper, or his kind heart, his weakness? What is the significance of the title?

2. Lipsyte has said young-adult writers should be trying to write more truthfully about sports, writing books that acknowledge kids' fears about the contests and say that other people, even heroes, share the fears. (from HarperCollins author-profile sheet).

Reviewing *The Brave* in *The New York Times* (March 1, 1992) W.P. Kinsella (author of *Shoeless Joe*, the novel on which the movie *Field of Dreams* is based) said, " . . . though Sonny appears to have alternatives to a life in the ring—he is intelligent, a sketchbook artist of considerable talent—the dangers of boxing, the brain damage and mental devastation suffered by both winners and losers are never mentioned. The brutishness of boxing, the exploitation of the fighters are glossed over."

Do you think Lipsyte failed to write truthfully about boxing, or do you feel Kinsella's criticism is off the mark? Support your answer with examples from the novel.

3. In the same review, Kinsella also objected to the author's handling of the Times Square sordidness. "Those scenes do not capture enough pure evil to keep an immature adventurer—say, a reader—from wanting to sample the thrills. Doll, who lives with Stick somewhere underneath 42nd Street, has a baby who, incredibly, appears to be both happy and healthy." Support or attack the critic's position by explaining your reaction to such scenes.

4. As it turned out, who had the strongest influence over Sonny—Doll, Jake, the mythical Running Braves, or Brooks?

5. In the last chapter Martin said, tongue in cheek, "From the

Outhouse to the Penthouse, The Sonny Bear Story." Basing your answer on Sonny's character, predict if Martin's prophecy will or will not come true.

THINKING LIKE A WRITER

1. *Point of view* is the way a reader is presented with the material or the vantage point from which the story is told. Viewpoint and characterization are the most important elements of literature for a reader and a writer to understand. Whose point of view does Lipsyte choose for this story? What options did he have? How would the story have been different if Uncle Jake had been the narrator? Doll?

2. If you have read *The Contender*, you will remember a black kid named Alfred Brooks told that story. It was such a popular story, Lipsyte's fans and his publisher urged him to write a sequel. He did and he didn't. *The Brave* is a bit of a literary joke like Tom Stoppard's *Rosencrantz and Guildenstern Are Dead*, in which Hamlet becomes a minor character. Brooks reappears in this novel, but he too is a minor character. This is Sonny's story because it is told from his point of view. When a writer makes the all important viewpoint decision, he has begun to structure and select his material. He can only include information, scenes, action that develop Sonny's story.

- Rewrite the first page of this story from Brooks' perspective.
- Rewrite the first page as if it were twenty-five years earlier and Brooks were continuing to tell his story. In your versions try to assume Lipsyte's sports-columnist style—strong action verbs, colorful figures of speech, realistic dialogue, and a fast pace.
- If you have read Robert Cormier's *The Chocolate War*, you might want to look at the sequel, *Beyond the Chocolate War* (Dell, 1986), which picks up where the first book left off but switches to the villain's point of view. Which approach do you prefer, Cormier's continuation or Lipsyte's time-jump?

3. Would you consider the conclusion of *The Brave* a happy ending? A realistic ending? Writers of highly acclaimed literature tell it the way it is. Writers of popular culture or escape reading tell it the way we wish it were. In which category would you place *The Brave*?

1. Hold panel discussions on one of the following topics or one of the students' choice:
   A. The Pay Scale for Professional Athletes—Deserved Or Unfair?
   B. The Good and Bad Effect of TV Coverage on Professional Sports.
   C. Boxing as a Healthy Activity for Tough Kids or an Encouragement for Violent Behavior?
   D. In Our School, There Is Too Much or Too Little Emphasis on Sports?

2. Make a time line showing the heavyweight boxing champions in the past seventy-five years. Also fill in for each one who was president when each was champ, as well as the most important historical events at that time, such as the stock market crash in 1929, the bombing of Pearl Harbor in 1941, etc.

3. Pretend your dream has come true. You have become a world-famous performer or athlete—like a well-known jockey, a member of a modern dance team, an Olympic swimming champ, a starting goalie for a major hockey team. In the library, find as much information as possible about the athlete you have chosen. Work in pairs. One person will introduce the famous person to the class. Assuming the role, you will make a speech telling the group how you, the player or performer, reached your goal, including the obstacles you had to overcome. Then reverse roles.

4. Create a sports art gallery. Find a piece of art depicting an athlete—a photograph, a reproduction of a painting or piece of sculpture, an artistic poster—or best of all, create one. Explain what you find appealing about your contribution. Describe what you think the artist was attempting to do like show strength or speed.

5. Write a letter to one of the characters in *The Brave*. Explain who you are and how you felt about him/her in the story.

6. Boxing movies have been a Hollywood staple since the twenties. The formula goes something like this: A wise, veteran trainer finds a desperate young fighter looking for a break on the way up. Treacherous promoters, mobsters, and women (saints or hookers) interfere, but there is a climactic big fight that pits the underdog against

a favorite, and the contender wins. (Wallace Berry/Jackie Coogan in *The Champ*, 1931; John Garfield in *Body and Soul*, 1947, etc., on down to the Rocky movies of the eighties.) After viewing the original *Rocky*, Eddie Futch, a trainer who had worked with champs like Joe Frazier, Larry Holmes, and Ken Norton, was asked if he would now support a move to ban boxing. "No, but I certainly would support a movement to ban boxing movies," he replied. (Allen Barra, "For the Sweet Science on Screen, A Split Decision," *The New York Times*, March 29, 1992)

Critics say a boxing movie usually has more blood and torn flesh than one is likely to see in a year of viewing real boxing matches. Defenders of these films say the good movies use boxing as a metaphor for the larger battle of life outside the ring, and the violence inherent in the sport as a kind of cleansing agent, as well as a passage to some higher good. Analyze boxing movies you've seen. Do you think the theory that violence has a purifying element, as if the fighter has to drag himself through purgatory before redemption, is wisdom or baloney?

Think of a plot for a boxing film that does not fit the formula.

ADDITIONAL SPORTS FICTION:

Baczewski, Paul. *Just for Kicks*. Lippincott, 1990.

Blessing, Richard. *A Passing Season*. Little, Brown, 1982.

Crutcher, Chris. *Running Loose*, Greenwillow, 1983.

———. *Stotan!* Greenwillow, 1986.

———. *The Crazy Horse Electric Game*. Greenwillow, 1987.

Deuker, Carl. *On the Devil's Court*. Avon, 1988.

Myers, Walter Dean. *Hoops*. Delacorte, 1981.

———. *The Outside Shot*. Delacorte, 1984.

Dedicated readers are sure to enjoy some of the adult sports stories, like Mark Harris's *Bang the Drum Slowly* (Knopf, 1956). Many of them deal with major-league hopes of life's minor leaguers, a subject that could inspire some good response writing. *The Natural*, by Bernard Malamud (Farrar, Straus, 1952), is a story about the bush league in which Malamud devised a mythic bat for his star who came up from the sticks. With perfect pitch Ring Lardner's 1914 classic *You Know Me, Al: A Busher's Letters* (Macmillan, 1987) reduced his brash busher, the bullpen's Jack Keefe, to human dimensions.

Herbert Mitgang, a reviewer for *The New York Times*, in his March 25, 1992 review, called W.P. Kinsella's early novels, *Shoeless Joe*, and *The Iowa Baseball Conspiracy* (Houghton Mifflin, 1986) "fast balls." But Mitgang especially liked *Box Socials* (Ballantine, 1992) that begins, "This is the story of how Truckbox Al McClintock almost got a tryout with the genuine St. Louis Cardinals, but instead ended up batting against Bob Feller, of Cleveland Indians fame in Renfrew Park, down on the river flats in Edmonton, Alberta, summer of 1945 or '46. . . ." The story is narrated by Jamie O'Day, a teenager, which should be added appeal for kids.

ADULT NONFICTION:

Action, Jay. *The Forgettables*. Crowell, 1973.

Angell, Roger. *The Summer Game*. Simon & Schuster, 1972.

Ashley, Merrill. *Dancing for Balanchine*. Dutton, 1985.

Bradley, Bill. *Life on the Run*. Quadrangle/The New York Times Book Co., 1976.

Creamer, Robert. *Babe*. Penguin, 1983.

———. *Stengel*. Simon & Schuster, 1990.

Halbertstam, David. *The Amateurs*. Morrow, 1985 (about rowing).

Hynd, Noel. *Giants of the Polo Grounds: The Glorious Time of Baseball's New York Giants*. Doubleday, 1988.

McPhee, John. *Levels of the Game*. Farrar, Straus, 1969.

Maiorano, Robert. *Worlds Apart: The Autobiography of a Dancer from Brooklyn*. Coward-McCann, 1980.

Morris, Jeannie. *Brian Piccolo: A Short Season*. Dell, 1972.

Peterson, Robert. *Only the Ball Was White: A History of Legendary Black Players*. Prentice-Hall, 1970.

Plimpton, George. *Paper Lion*. Holtzman, 1981.

———. *The Curious Case of Sidd Finch*. Macmillan, 1987.

Ralbovsky, Martin. *Destiny's Darlings: A World Championship Little League Team Twenty Years Later*. Hawthorne, 1974.

Ryan, Bob, and Terry Pluto. *Forty-Eight Minutes: A Night in the Life of the NBA*. Macmillan, 1988.

Sayers, Gale. *I Am Third*. Viking, 1970.

Strodel, Ernsteine. *Deep Song: The Dance Story of Martha Graham*. Macmillan, 1984.

Will, George. *Men at Work*. Macmillan, 1990.

For Middle School Readers:

Summer's Chance by Patricia Harrison Easton (Harcourt, 1988)

ABOUT THE AUTHOR

Patricia Harrison Easton used to show quarter horses with her local 4-H, but when she graduated from Washington and Jefferson College in Pennsylvania, she had planned a career in psychology. Lucky for kids who like her stories, she shifted to writing when she married Richard Easton, a college writing teacher and began raising three children. The author of two young adult novels, *Rebel's Choice* (Harcourt, 1989) was the second, and *Stable Girl* (Harcourt, 1988), a nonfiction book, Easton often speaks to young writers, advising them that writing is a learned craft, not a miraculous act only for the gifted.

Easton's story about Elizabeth Harter's summer on her grandmother's horse farm should encourage children to learn their craft and then look closely at their own lives for story material. When she was growing up on a farm in western Pennsylvania, the author's father raised standardbreds for harness racing. Their farm, which is still in the family, became the setting for her novel.

If you have apartment-dwelling students, who point out the nearest they have ever come to a pasture is the crowded city park and whose experience with horses has been limited to a wild ride on the carousel, show them a line from the review of *Summer's Chance* in *Booklist*, "The story's harness-racing backdrop is convincingly drawn, but relationships are the core of the story." Every writer can fish in the family-relations pool. Urge young writers to use what they have.

BEFORE READING THE NOVEL

A discussion might go something like this:

What is your definition of chance? Think of synonyms for the word: likelihood, opportunity, gamble, prospect, luck, destiny, probability, possibility. Look at Easton's title. What do you predict this story is going to be about? She could have called it *Summer's Gamble*, or *Summer's Opportunity*. Do you feel she made the best choice?

Look closely at Ellen Thompson's illustration on the cover. Most covers have realistic pictures of characters or settings, as close to a photograph as possible, but this image isn't an absolute likeness. Look at the fence, the trees, the girl's shirt. What medium has Thompson used? Do you think her choice of a watercolor has any significance? How has she made the horse and the girl's hair appear to be in motion? Be alert for clues to the artist's choice of a painting as you read the story.

When you write a book, to whom will you dedicate it? Read this dedication. What does Easton's calling her husband and children her best friends imply about her? Since a writer's work reflects her values, you will want to pay special attention to how she presents the way families interact.

Let's read the first page. Easton and her immediate family might be best friends, but all does not seem to be well with Elizabeth Harter and her relatives. Think of possible reasons for her not having seen her grandmother in eleven years.

Among other things, this book is about the sport of horseracing. As writers you must always be on the lookout for new language you might use in your stories. Make a list in your notebook of new words or terms that Easton uses to describe the sport, the gear, the people involved or the trotters.

AFTER READING THE NOVEL

Discussion Questions

1. When Elizabeth is having difficulty understanding her grandmother's coldness, Carrie says Ruth Bates is hiding behind a mask. What is she hiding? Why? Follow that thread through the story explaining how Elizabeth finally sees behind the mask.

If you had been Elizabeth, would you have gone home or "toughed it out"?

Although Elizabeth resents her grandmother's concealment, for a while she, too, puts on a mask. Explain her reasons and how she is finally able to put it aside and be herself again. Linda Major only seems to wear her mask for Elizabeth. Why?

2. What did Elizabeth and Linda have in common? Did you think Linda was a sympathetic character? Has anyone at home or at school ever held someone up to you as a model you couldn't quite match? How did it make you feel?

3. Historically, the wicked stepmother has been a recurring stereotype in stories. Do you think the literary image has affected real family relations? Easton chose not to write the cliched version of Sarah, but to play against type. Describe Elizabeth and Sarah's relationship. Do you think this added to or distracted from this story about a young girl's attempt to understand herself?

In many sports stories, the main characters are heroes, but Elizabeth is afraid of horses. Describe her experience of driving Chance around the track. Do you prefer to read stories about people who are more like you or those who seem to be superhuman?

Easton also chose to have Lizzie and Ruth Bates' best friends be black. Did this seem believable? How did the author avoid treating any of these issues like propaganda written to bring about social change?

4. When a writer has done a good job developing a character, the reader should be able to imagine how she would behave in situations not included in the story. Imagine what will have happened to and among all of these people by the time Elizabeth is twenty-one years old. Will Linda and Elizabeth become friends? Will Nicky be romantically interested in either girl? Will Elizabeth inherit the farm? Will Mrs. Bates ask Sarah to visit the farm?

THINKING LIKE A WRITER

1. What has happened before the story opens? How did the author give you the information about Lizzie Bates' death, Elizabeth's father and grandmother's reaction, the relationship between Carrie and Lizzie?

2. Are Lizzie Bates and Sarah characters in this story? Do they appear in any of the scenes? How did Easton create characters who don't appear? Try to write a character sketch of someone by only having other people talk about the character you are portraying.

3. What other possible endings might Easton have written? How would you have ended it? Would it have been a more interesting book

if Elizabeth had turned out to be a natural horsewoman? Would you have had Grandmother Bates go to the cemetery and come to gripes with her daughter's death? Would you have enjoyed the story more if Chance had won the race? Which conclusion was the more realistic? How would Easton have had to "tinker" with Elizabeth's character if she had ended the story with her driving Chance in her mother's Memorial Race?

4. Reread chapter 9, where Elizabeth and Nicky go to the art gallery. Pay special attention to the language Elizabeth uses to read Degas' painting. If possible, go to a gallery where you can observe a painting or piece of sculpture showing the motion of a horse or an athlete doing another sport like fishing, dancing, running, jumping, skating. Interpret in words the action you see and feel in the art. If a gallery is not a possibility, look at a good reproduction.

5. Analyze Easton's language when she is describing a horserace. How does she appeal to all our senses like describing "the tattoo of the horses hooves"? Point to other examples.

ACTIVITIES

1. Design the mask, or a symbolic interpretation of the masks, the following characters wear in the beginning of the story: Elizabeth, Grandmother Bates, Linda Majors, Linda's father.

2. Work with a partner to write additional dialogue to create a scene that didn't happen, but could have, among or between the following:

Elizabeth, Linda, and Linda's father
Lizzie Bates and Carrie when they were young
Elizabeth and Sarah (Mom) at the end of the summer
Elizabeth and her father at the end of the summer
Elizabeth and Nicky the summer following the end of this story
Elizabeth and Linda the summer following the end of this story

Cast and act out your episodes.

3. Write an essay entitled "A Mask I Have Worn" or "I Know (or Have Known) Someone Who Wears A Mask." Explain the when,

where and why. Rehearse your intent with a partner before you begin to write. Write a draft. Ask your colleague to give you feedback. Revise until you are satisfied you have accomplished your purpose.

(Carol Fenner's *A Summer of Horses* [Knopf, 1989] also tells the story of a girl dealing with her love and fear of horses. Younger girls who, like Elizabeth, are not Belle Starrs, might enjoy Jo Ann Simon's *Star* [Random House, 1989] about chubby Toni Wallace whose first riding lesson filled her with terror.)

ADDITIONAL SPORTS STORIES FOR MIDDLE SCHOOL READERS:
FICTION

Adoff, Arnold. *Sports Pages.* HarperCollins, 1986 (poetry).

Avi. *S.O.R. Losers.* Bradbury, 1984.

Farley, Walter. *The Black Stallion.* Knopf, 1941.

Golenbock, Peter. *Teammates.* Harcourt, 1990.

Hughes, Dean. *Angel Park Soccer Stars, Kickoff Time.* Knopf, 1991.

Miles, Betty. *All It Takes Is Practice.* Knopf, 1976.

———. *The Secret Life of the Underwear Champ.* Knopf, 1981.

Park, Barbara. *Skinnybones.* Knopf, 1982.

Sinykin, Sheri Cooper. *Shrimpboat and Gym Bags.* Athenaeum, 1990.

Slote, Alfred. *Make-Believe Ball Players.* HarperCollins, 1992.

———. *The Trading Game.* HarperCollins, 1992.

NONFICTION

Brooks, Robert and Nancy. *For the Record: Women in Sports.* World Almanac Publications, 1985.

Carlson, Lewis, and John J. Fogarty. *Tales of Gold.* Contemporary Books, 1987.

Isberg, Emily. *Peak Performance: Sports, Science and the Body in Action.* Simon & Schuster, 1989.

Morris, Ann. *On Their Toes: A Russian Ballet School.* Athenaeum, 1992.

Schmidt, Diane. *I Am a Jesse White Tumbler.* Albert Whitman, 1990.

Sobol, Donald J. *Encyclopedia Brown's Book of Wacky Sports.* Bantam Skylark, 1984.

Wallechinsky, David. *The Complete Book of the Olympics.* Little, Brown, 1991.

Whitlock, Steve. *Make the Team: Gymnastics for Girls.* Sports Illustrated for Kids, 1991.

For Younger Readers:

Willy the Wimp by Anthony Browne (Knopf, 1984)

ABOUT THE AUTHOR

When British born Anthony Browne was a young boy, he wished to be a boxer, but he was a small child wanting so much to be like his big, powerfully built father who died when Anthony was seventeen. You can understand why Anthony admired his dad, who had a strong, outwardly confident manner and was a boxer, but who also taught art and had a shy, sensitive nature. He spent hours drawing or writing poetry for Anthony and his brother, as well as making delicate models of castles, boats, and houses.

Fortunately, Mr. Browne also encouraged his boys to play rugby, soccer, and cricket, to box and wrestle, to lift weights and to run because Anthony went to a tough school in the industrial north of England. Being good at sports kept him from being bullied.

When he wasn't playing sports, Anthony was drawing. In the beginning, inspired by his comic books, he did very detailed pictures of battles with macabre jokes and speech bubbles in the background. After he grew up, got married and had two children, urged on by a fascination with the insides of people's bodies, he became a medical artist painting finely detailed watercolors of muscle, blood vessels, fat, and bone to demonstrate operation techniques.

Strange as it might seem, Browne swears he learned to tell stories in pictures on that job. Because an operation is a mess—"all blood, instruments and hands"—a medical artist has to clean all this up, and make it clear what is muscle and what is fat, which is the artery or vein in order to tell the story of the operation. He has to decide what can be explained in pictures and what to explain in words, just like in a picture book such as *Willy the Wimp.*

Additional books written and illustrated by Browne include: *Through the Magic Mirror* (Greenwillow, 1977); *Bear Hunt* (Doubleday, 1979); *Look What I've Got* (Knopf, 1980); *Gorilla* (Borzoi Books, 1985); *Piggybook* (Knopf, 1986); *Willy the Champ* (Knopf, 1986); *The Tunnel* (Knopf, 1990).

(Based on information in *Sixth Book of Junior Authors and Illustrators*, edited by Sally Holmes Holtze, H.W. Wilson Co., 1989)

BEFORE READING THE BOOK

When the children have seen the cover and had a good giggle, a discussion might go like this:

Usually, when we read a book, we look for what the author has put into his story, but maybe in Anthony Browne's story we should try to find what he left out or what he lets his pictures tell us. But first, let's see what he put on the cover. I see a joke. Why a spray paint can? Who has been using it? What did Browne write?

Describe Willy's clothes. How would you characterize his posture? Do you think he looks wimpy or cool and preppy? What do you think is going to happen to him as he saunters down this street where there is spray paint on the walls?

AFTER READING THE STORY

Discussion Questions

1. Bullies had always been picking on Willy. Why did he finally decide to make himself strong? Have you ever had a nickname you hated? How did Willy change after his workout program? Who saw him differently? Where were they looking? Willy had changed on the outside, but how about on the inside? How do you know? If you cut your hair, learn to play the guitar, or win a skateboard contest will it change your nature?

2. How might Browne's father have given him the idea to write this story? How might his own childhood memories have added to the story?

3. Now, let's look for what the author left out. He doesn't tell you anything about the gorillas except that they were bullies. How did he let you know how tough they were? He doesn't tell you Milly is Willy's girlfriend either. How do you find out? Find other places where he lets the pictures tell the story, like the picture of Willy's diet.

1. Close your eyes and think about your dad, a big brother, or an uncle. Now, if you were going to make up an animal story that would really be about this person, decide what animal you would choose, but don't tell us. Do the same for your mother, sister, or aunt. Think of names for your animals. We are going to form a storytelling circle. I'll start by telling you why I would make my sister a lap kitten named Priscilla. I'm holding the storyteller's ball. When you are ready, hold up your hand and I'll pass the ball to you. No one else can talk while you hold the ball.

2. Close your eyes again until you can see what your animals look like, what kind of clothes they wear. We'll go around the circle again, giving you an opportunity to share your picture. Tomorrow I'd like for you to bring either a picture you draw of your animal or one found in a magazine or a book that looks like him or her.

3. Bully is an ugly word, and bullies are ugly people. Let's make a list of other words to describe a bully (persecutor, ruffian, terror, tease, tormentor). Now, let's think of words you would use to describe what bullies do to bother people (pester, browbeat, tease, domineer, harass, frighten, trample, punch, tyrannize).

4. Willy and Millie are fun to say because they rhyme. Think of other rhymes like Tillie and Gillie. Find a name to rhyme with your character's.

Kathryn Cristaldi's *Baseball Ballerina* (Random House, 1992), about a baseball player whose Mom not only makes her take ballet lessons, but through a fluke her friend, Mary Ann (a catcher) catches "staritis," is another good story to help younger children see their own experience as story material, as well as have a good laugh.

FOR YOUNG READERS:

Carlson, Nancy. *Making the Team*. Carolrhoda, 1985.

Davis, Gibbs. Never Sink Nine Series. Bantam, 1991.

Day, Alexandra. *Frank and Ernest Play Ball*. Scholastic, 1990.

George, William T. *Fishing at Long Pond*. Greenwillow, 1991.

Giff, Patricia Reilly. *Ronald Morgan Goes to Bat*. Viking Kestrel, 1988.

Kessler, Leonard. *Here Comes the Strikeout*. HarperCollins, 1992 (an I Can Read Book).

Marzollo, Jean. *The Pizza Pie Slugger*. Random House, 1989.

Sachs, Marilyn. *Matt's Mitt and Fleet-Footed Florence*. Avon, 1991.

Simon, Jo Ann. *Star*. Random House, 1989.

THE FOLLOWING ARE ALL RANDOM HOUSE STEP INTO READING BOOKS:

Buller, Jon, and Susan Shade. *Twenty Thousand Baseball Cards under the Sea*. 1991.

Cole, Joanne. *Norma Jean, Jumping Bean*. 1987.

Kramer, S.A. *Baseball's Greatest P-I-T-C-H-E-R-S*. 1992.

Marzollo, Jean. *Cannonball Chris*. 1987.

Standiford, Natalie. *The Bravest Dog Ever*. 1989.

FAMILY RELATIONSHIPS

Tolstoy's famous opening line in *Anna Karenina*, "Happy families are all alike; every unhappy family is unhappy in its own way," tapped into THE universal theme for young and old. Perhaps the best way to blend a child's life experience with his learning is to explore family relationships through his reading and writing. Another plus is the opportunity to involve families in the process. Decorate the classroom with family photographs and children's portraits of themselves and their kin. Invite the relatives to school. Find out what they liked to read when they were young. Give them an opportunity to read or tell a story to the class.

As with sports, you could spend the entire year exploring the theme, still leaving mountains of good books unopened, a multitude of activities to try next time. Following is a less structured theme approach than was suggested for sports, giving the students more independence. The trick is to offer many selections—from Virginia Hamilton's *Cousins* (Philomel, 1990), in which Cammy wishes her cousin bad luck and it comes true, to Will Hobbs' *Bearstone* (Avon,

1989) an upbeat story about Cloyd, a Native American boy, who was always in trouble until he found a surrogate father and the healing power of love. Nine-year-old klutzy Lily and her ballet-star sibling discover sister power in James David Landis' *The Sisters Impossible* (Knopf, 1979). John D. Fitzgerald's *The Great Brain* (Delacorte, 1985), the scheming adventure of a boy genius, told by his younger brother, is another good one, as is Tomi Ungerer's *No Kiss for Mother* (Delacorte, 1991), an early-childhood story about a little boy who is too big to be kissed . . . in public. Then there is Isabelle Holland's historical (set in the 1800s) novel, *The Journey Home* (Scholastic, 1990), about two sisters who travel across the country on a train filled with orphans like themselves, until a family in Kansas picks the sisters to raise, and Patricia Windsor's black-bound thriller, *The Christmas Killer* (Scholastic, 1991). And don't forget my all-time favorite, Barbara Robinson's *The Best Christmas Pageant Ever* (Harper & Row, 1972), in which the worst pack of siblings in town takes part in the Christmas pageant.

Daniel is black, his friend Oriental, his dog imaginary, but the baby sister who takes most of mother's time is real in *Daniel's Dog* by Jo Ellen Bogart (Scholastic, 1990). Joey and Marvin are mice, but mice have families, too, as we learn in a story within the story of *Dear Brother* by Frank Asch (Scholastic, 1992). Pork and Beans are pigs, but their play date is with a crybaby Billy goat (*Pork and Beans: Play Date* by Jovial Bob Steiner, Scholastic, 1989) . . . and so it goes in this theme that could go on forever.

One way to give the children a broader overview is to let them choose to read from one of the categories such as little brothers, but listen in on booktalks the other kids give. Perhaps the stories they didn't read, but that sounded good, could become part of their summer reading list.

After they have made their choices, but before they begin to read, give the kids the responsibility of finding out something about the author. (*Be sure to work with the librarian when planning the project.*) When the information is available, discovering things like the fact that Hadley Irwin is/are two people, or where the writer found the idea, makes reading the story more interesting. Take M.E. Kerr's young-adult story, *The Son of Someone Famous*, inspired by the author's embarrassing experience in college when she wouldn't believe a friend was Lizabeth Scott's sister until Scott's letter mentioning *trust* arrived, an incident Kerr describes in *Me Me Me Me: Not a Novel* (Harper & Row, 1983). Colleen O'Shaughnessy McKenna found her inspiration for *Too Many Murphys* (Scholastic, 1988) from her own four kids and claims to have written most of the novel at the playground.

Grandparent Stories

Johanna Spyri's classic, *Heidi*, might have started it all, but grandparent stories continue to flourish, from the traditional wise old sages to the avant-garde. Look at Norma Fox Mazer's approach. There is the offbeat *Mrs. Fish, Ape, and Me, the Dump Queen*, in which Grandpa runs the dump and falls in love with eccentric Mrs. Fish. *A Figure of Speech* is the touching story of Jenny's dealing with her beloved granddad's death, but Rachel's grandpa in *After the Rain* is a grouch. In M.E. Kerr's *The Son of Someone Famous*, Adam Blessing's grandfather Charlie drinks, but in her *Gentlehands* (HarperCollins, 1978) Buddy's grandpa was once a Nazi. And then there is Mildred Pitts Walter's *Justin and the Best Biscuits in the World* for younger children. Justin's grandfather is a cowboy.

ACTIVITIES

Students might enjoy writing a play and acting out a situation where all the grandparents from their stories have a chance to meet at a picnic, on a bus, during Grandparents' Day at your school. Or they might want to imagine how their own grandparents would get along with the fictional characters. Younger children making a big book featuring real grandparents could make everyone proud.

Creating a photography gallery featuring pictures of the kids' grandparents is another idea. Inviting them to be honored guests at the gallery opening could be a pleasure for everyone. Looking carefully at the pictures for background details, period clothes, etc., could encourage children to learn to *read photographs*. If you have a Polaroid camera, holding a Grandparents' Day when everyone has their photo snapped could also be fun, and could provide an opportunity to talk about how a photographer, another kind of artist, works.

Most of all, children like to imagine how they would have handled the situation the storybook grandchildren faced in tales like Hadley Irwin's *What About Grandma?* where Rhys Ann learns how important maintaining their independence is to older people. Little children especially like to retell stories in which kids have brought joy to a grandparent, as the child in Helen Griffith's *Georgia Music* soothes her grandfather's homesickness by playing music of the sweet sounds of summer in Georgia.

When I identify age groups, I hope you will ignore them. My ideal classroom library has books at all levels for everybody. After all, whole language is about meeting a child where she is.

FOR YOUNG READERS:

Cameron, Ann. *The Most Beautiful Place in the World*. Knopf, 1988.

Griffith, Helen. *Georgia Music*. Greenwillow, 1986.

MacLachlan, Patricia. *Through Grandpa's Eyes*. Harper & Row, 1980.

Walter, Mildred Pitts. *Justin and the Best Biscuits in the World*. Knopf, 1986.

Watson, Joy. *Grandpa's Slippers*. Scholastic, 1992.

FOR MIDDLE SCHOOL READERS:

Davis, Jenny. *Checking on the Moon*. Orchard, 1991.

Easton, Patricia Harrison. *Summer's Chance*. Harcourt, 1988

Kassem, Lou. *Listen for Rachel*. Avon, 1986.

MacLachlan, Patricia. *Journey*. Delacorte, 1991.

Polacco, Patricia. *Chicken Sunday*. Philomel, 1992.

———. *Mrs. Katz and Tush*. Bantam, 1992.

Smith, Robert Kimmel. *My War with Grandpa*. Delacorte, 1984.

Spyri, Johanna. *Heidi*. Dell, 1990.

Voigt, Cynthia. *Homecoming*. Athenaeum, 1981.

FOR YOUNG ADULTS:

Brancato, Robin. *Sweet Bells Jangled Out of Tune*. Knopf, 1982.

Irwin, Hadley. *What About Grandma?* Avon, 1991.

Kerr, M.E. *Gentlehands*. HarperCollins, 1978.

———. *The Son of Someone Famous*. HarperCollins, 1991.

Mazer, Norma Fox. *A Figure of Speech*. Dell, 1975.

————. *After the Rain.* Avon, 1980.
————. *Mrs. Fish, Ape and Me, the Dump Queen.* Avon, 1981.
Paterson, Katherine. *Jacob Have I Loved.* Crowell, 1980.

Fathers and Daughters

In our real lives, giving up the role of Daddy's little girl can prove one of the toughest family challenges. Shakespeare takes a look at the problem from the father's point of view in *King Lear*. Jane Smiley bagged a 1992 Pulitzer Prize for trying his theme from the daughter's perspective in *A Thousand Acres* (Knopf, 1991). Mary Rodgers bowed to Freud in *Freaky Friday* (Harper & Row, 1972) when a thirteen-year-old girl woke up one morning to find she had turned into her mother.

In her adult nonfiction book, *Women and Their Fathers: The Sexual and Romantic Impact of the First Man in Your Life* (Delacorte, 1992), Victoria Secunda interviewed many people who testified to what Secunda called "the great father hunger."

Earlier, Colette Dowling blamed Cinderella (*The Cinderella Complex*, Pocket Books, 1990). Dowling claimed modern women only substituted Daddy for the prince who would rescue Cinderella, so she could live happily ever after without growing up. Trying to set things right, William J. Brooke gave us a version of the story in *A Telling of the Tales* (HarperCollins, 1990) in which strong-willed Ella and the prince smash the glass slipper. But just in case Daddy was also that frog in another fairy tale who turned into a handsome prince and was supposed to take care of the princess for the rest of her life, Jon Scieszka felt compelled to tell the truth:

> Well, let's just say they lived sort of happily
> for a long time.
> Okay, so they weren't so happy.
> In fact, they were miserable.
> (*The Frog Prince Continued*, Viking, 1991)

Of course, the absent father can cause more problems than the overly protective father/prince. Having worked with Vietnamese immigrants, Sherry Garland tells the saddest father-daughter tale in *Song of the Buffalo Boy* (Harcourt, 1992), the story of Loi who has grown up not knowing her U.S. soldier father. The plot involves the decision she must make about leaving the boy she loves, and her country, in the hopes of finding her father in America.

Unfortunately, there are more grandparent stories for children than books dealing with the more complex relationship between fathers and daughters, even though many women say the relationship they had with their fathers affected the roles they have with all significant men in their lives. Take novelist and short story writer Jean Stafford (married briefly and tragically to poet Robert Lowell) about whom someone I once read said that she passed over the literary landscape of her day like some bright but wounded butterfly. Reportedly, she wrote to a friend that Lowell was so much like her father that, at first, she worshiped him and later she felt betrayed by him. Having begun her writing career brilliantly with a highly acclaimed novel, *Boston Adventure* (1944) and *New Yorker* stories admired by reviewers, she ended her career in the "red room," her metaphor for alcoholism.

Since the holding-on/letting-go conflict hits adolescent girls like a mack truck, here I've spotlighted two outstanding novels for young adults which I explored in more detail in "Stunting Readers' Growth" (*School Library Journal*, November, 1986).

Moonlight Man by Paula Fox (Bradbury, 1986)

Melville might still hold the "best-opening-line blue ribbon" for "Call me Ishmael," but Paula Fox deserves one for her closing line in this realistic novel. It's a shocker! The story is stunning, but tells it like it is.

Catherine Ames' parents divorced when she was three, but she has created a romantic figure out of her allusive father, who is, or at least was, a writer, as Catherine knows from reading his early novels and memories of their few, but usually dramatic, meetings. This story opens when she is fifteen, her charming father picks her up (three weeks late) from boarding school and they spend a summer of discovery in a remote cottage in Nova Scotia.

Henry Ames struggles to win his battle with alcoholism and to win Catherine back after she realizes the problem, but she sees through his charm. When she returns from "the moonlight man" to her "daylight mother," she plans to tell her how she finally understands why her mother cared for him, but couldn't live with him. She doesn't plan to tell her that when she left her father at the airport, Catherine said, "See you," and he said, "Not if I see you first."

In Summer Light by Zibby Oneal (Viking, 1985)

Oneal tells seventeen-year-old Kate's struggle with her selfish, competitive father, an artist, with pertinent allusions to Shakespeare's *The Tempest*.

This is a book for artists, as well as frustrated daughters. Oneal gives Kate the language of a painter. Morning light lays on the table like marmalade, her cat is the color of peaches and she sees, Ian, the boy she likes, as she would paint him. She also comes to realize her father is getting old, his best work behind him, but he still must have the foreground for himself, even if it means pushing his daughter into the background.

Kate finds a way to forgive her father and to free herself through a research paper she writes about Prospero. With a little luck, your students could find deeper insights into their relationships with their fathers when they read Fox's and Oneal's novels and explore the feelings they provoke through their own writing.

ADDITIONAL FATHER/DAUGHTER STORIES:

Brooks, Bruce. *Midnight Hour Encores*. Harper & Row, 1986.
Cleary, Beverly. *Ramona and Her Father*. Morrow, 1977.
Levitin, Sonia. *A Season for Unicorns*. Macmillan, 1986.
Mazer, Norma Fox. *Taking Terri Mueller*. Avon, 1981.
Yep, Laurence. *Child of the Owl*. Harper & Row, 1977.

Siblings

What Louisa Mae Alcott did for sisters in *Little Women*, S. E. Hinton has done for brothers. When Hinton cornered the market on teenage brothers, she also captured the attention of an often hardsell group of readers—adolescent boys. Her books for this group include the following, all published by Dell: *The Outsiders* (1967); *That Was Then, This Is Now* (1971); *Rumble Fish* (1974); *Tex* (1979).

Anne Lindbergh's stories began to make me feel little brothers with bossy, big sisters should have their say. Martha's little brother Kermit, who piles on lots of sheets and goes trick-or-treating as mashed potatoes, is a delightful character to everyone but Martha in *Nobody's Orphan*, and there should be a law against the way Dawn treats Marcus in *The Shadow on the Dial*. Another charmer who comes off better with his sister, is McGrew in Patricia MacLachlan's *The Facts and Fictions of Minna Pratt*.

Then there is Max who finds his sister Lisa's ballet class is a great warm-up for his baseball game. (*Max* by Rachel Isadora, Macmillan, 1976). Judy Blume's cute, show-stealing Fudge (*Tales of a Fourth-Grade Nothing*) has a brother, Peter, not a sister, but the kids could always create a sister just to see how she could handle him.

In *Three Sisters* (Scholastic, 1986), Karen is the youngest and even though Norma Fox Mazer, one of three sisters who has three daughters, intended to write from the middle, her place, kids might be able to figure out why Karen's story is the one finally to capture the author's imagination.

FOR YOUNGER CHILDREN:

Alexander, Martha. *Nobody Asked Me If I Wanted a Baby Sister*. Pied Piper Books, 1977.

———. *When the New Baby Comes I'm Moving Out*. Pied Piper Books, 1979.

Asch, Frank. *Dear Brother*. Scholastic, 1992.

Bogart, Jo Ellen. *Daniel's Dog*. Scholastic, 1990.

Browne, Anthony. *The Tunnel*. Knopf, 1990.

Byars, Betsy. *The Golly Sisters Go West*. HarperCollins, 1989.

Hoban, Russell. *A Baby Sister for Frances*. Harper, 1976.

Wilhelm, Hans. *Tyrone, the Double-Dirty, Rotten Cheater*. Scholastic, 1992.

FOR MIDDLE SCHOOL READERS:

Blume, Judy. *Tales of a Fourth-Grade Nothing*. Dell, 1976.

Lindbergh, Anne. *Nobody's Orphan*. Avon, 1983.

————. *The Shadow on the Dial.* Avon, 1987.

McKenna, Colleen O'Shaughnessy. *Too Many Murphys.* Scholastic, 1988.

MacLachlan, Patricia. *The Facts and Fictions of Minna Pratt.* Harper, 1988.

Manes, Stephen. *Chocolate Covered Ants.* Scholastic, 1990.

Metzger, Lois. *Barry's Sister.* Atheneum, 1992 (handicapped).

Ransom, Candice F. *My Sister the Meanie.* Scholastic, 1988.

Shura, Mary Francis. *The Search for Grissi.* Avon, 1985.

Spinelli, Jerry. *Who Put That Hair in My Toothbrush?* Little, Brown, 1984.

Wilson, Johnniece Marshall. *Oh, Brother.* Scholastic, 1988.

FOR OLDER READERS:

Hinton, S.E. *The Outsiders.* Dell, 1967.

————. *That Was Then, This Is Now.* Dell, 1971.

————. *Rumble Fish.* Dell, 1974.

————. *Tex.* Dell, 1979.

Holland, Isabelle. *The Journey Home.* Scholastic, 1990.

Mazer, Norma Fox. *Three Sisters.* Scholastic, 1992.

Sachs, Marilyn. *Baby Sister.* Dutton, 1986.

ABOUT MOTHERS AND DAUGHTERS:

Blume, Judy. *Tiger Eyes.* Bradbury, 1981.

Childress, Alice. *Rainbow Jordan.* Putnam, 1981.

Duncan, Lois. *Daughters of Eve.* Dell, 1979.

Ehrlich, Amy. *Where It Stops Nobody Knows.* Penguin, 1988.

Fox, Paula. *A Place Apart.* Dutton, 1982.

Greenfield, Eloise, and Lessie J. Little. *Childtimes: A Three Generation Memoir.* HarperCollins, 1979 (nonfiction).

Hest, Amy. *Love You, Soldier.* Four Winds, 1991.

Kerr, M. E. *Dinky Hocker Shoots Smack.* Harper & Row, 1972.

Kincaid, Jamaica. *Annie John.* Farrar Straus, 1989.

Mazer, Harry. *Someone's Mother Is Missing.* Delacorte, 1990.

Wickstrom, Sylvie. *Mothers Can't Get Sick.* Crown, 1989.

Ziefert, Harriet. *A New Coat for Anna.* Knopf, 1986.

Zolotow, Charlotte. *If You Listen.* HarperCollins, 1980.

————. *When I Have a Little Girl.* HarperCollins, 1988.

ABOUT FATHERS AND SONS:

Miller, Arthur. *Death of a Salesman*. Viking, 1976.

Myers, Water Dean. *It Ain't All for Nothing*. Avon, 1978.

Peck, Richard. *Father Figure*. Viking, 1976.

Townsend, John Rowe. *Downstream*. Lippincott, 1987.

Yep, Laurence. *Dragonwings*. Harper & Row, 1975.

ABOUT SURROGATE MOTHERS OR FATHERS:

Burch, Robert. *Ida Early Comes Over the Mountain*. Avon, 1980.

Childress, Alice. *Rainbow Jordan*. Putnam, 1981.

Clauser, Suzanne. *A Girl Named Sooner*. Avon, 1972.

Cleary, Beverly. *Dear Mr. Henshaw*. Dell, 1984.

Hobbs, Will. *Bearstone*. Avon, 1989.

MacLachlan, Patricia. *Sarah, Plain and Tall*. Harper, 1987.

Mazer, Norma Fox. *Downtown*. Morrow, 1984.

Paterson, Katherine. *The Great Gilly Hopkins*. Crowell, 1979.

Taylor, Theodore. *The Cay*. Avon, 1969.

Zindel, Paul. *The Pigman*. Harper & Row, 1968.

In addition to the traditional categories, Donelson and Nilsen (*Literature for Today's Young Adults*, 3rd ed., Scott Foresman, 1989) offered the unexpected: a list of stories dealing with children abandoned by sixties flower-children parents to be raised by other relatives:

Bridges, Sue Ellen. *Permanent Connections*. Harper & Row, 1987.

Brooks, Bruce. *Midnight Hour Encores*. Harper & Row, 1986.

Byars, Betsy. *The Two-Thousand Pound Goldfish*. Harper & Row, 1982.

Mazer, Norma Fox. *Downtown*. Morrow, 1984.

Paterson, Katherine. *The Great Gilly Hopkins*. Crowell, 1979.

Voigt, Cynthia. *A Solitary Blue*. Athenaeum, 1981.

TEACHERS AND KIDS, FOR ALL AGES

Not everyone likes sports. All of us don't have pesky, little brothers, but EVERYONE is an expert on one subject: school. All of us—jocks and jokers, bullies and beauties, scholars and sluff-offs—go to school, which probably explains why so many authors write about school memories and that one teacher who made a difference. Avi attributes his having become a writer to a real teacher who saved him from failing. My favorite definition of a teacher came from a legendary one. Norman Maclean (*A River Runs Through It*, University of Chicago Press, 1989), my friend, teacher, and colleague at the University of Chicago, said a good teacher is a tough guy who cares deeply about something that is hard to understand.

In too many stories, teachers sit on gilded pedestals or walk around the halls as stereotyped, stodgy sticks, but occasionally someone like Miss Nelson appears who is as right as rain. Christa McAuliffe's true story—the peppy pioneer teacher, who wanted to teach from outer space—breaks our hearts, but most of the other tales suggested here are for readers with a sense of humor. That means teachers, too, like the teacher I met who always reads *Miss Nelson* with her class early in the year so when she dresses up as Miss Swamp on Halloween, her kids will "get it."

For Young Readers

Miss Nelson Is Missing! by Harry Allard, illustrated by James Marshall (Houghton Mifflin, 1977)

ABOUT THE AUTHOR AND ILLUSTRATOR

At seven years old, James Marshall gave up drawing and seriously studied the viola. His second-grade teacher, whom he describes as a horrible woman who laughed at his early creative efforts, told him he would never be an artist. It's not surprising that Viola Swamp closely resembles that second-grade teacher.

Most people would not consider an airplane accident a lucky quirk of fate, but when Marshall flew out of his seat, he injured his hand in a way that made it impossible for him to practice the viola for long periods. Forced to give up a career which had never been right anyway, he began to teach school and to draw on weekends.

When a Houghton Mifflin vice president saw Marshall's drawings, he called him up to say he had a book for him to illustrate. "How much do I have to pay you?" Marshall asked. His first effort as a writer/illustrator was *George and Martha* (named after the characters in Albee's *Who's Afraid of Virginia Woolf*, the film version of which he was half watching on TV while he sketched), characters who have now been featured in six books. When the first book was a success, Marshall knew he had found his life's work. He died October 13, 1992 of a brain tumor at the age of fifty.

The artist met Harry Allard—who has an master's degree in French from Middlebury College, a doctorate from Yale, and has spent a lot time in Paris—in San Antonio, where they got together to speak French. Sometimes they worked on the text together. Allard often came up with titles. He would call Marshall at three in the morning, whisper, *"Miss Nelson Is Missing!"* and hang up.

Although they fought a lot about ideas, they always made up. Allard and Marshall also collaborated on a series of stories about the Stupids, as well as additional Miss Nelson books, such as *Miss Nelson Is Back* (Houghton, 1982) and *Miss Nelson Has a Field Day* (Houghton, 1985). (For more information on Marshall, see *Something About the Author*, vol. 51., ed. by Anne Commire, Gale Research Co.; obit. Oct. 15, 1992, *The New York Times*.)

Allard was born on January 27, the same day, he likes to point out, as Mozart and Lewis Carroll. A lover of animals, he has one blind, five-year-old French bulldog named Olga and one two-year-old bulldog named Monad. Of his five cats, Uncle Boris is the oldest at twenty-something.

BEFORE READING THE STORY

A discussion about *Miss Nelson* will take many twists and turns. Here is one possibility:

How many of you have a sense of humor? What touches your funny bone most? I'm delighted all of you enjoy a good joke because I would hate for anyone to be left out, and there is one rule for reading *Miss Nelson*: You must have a sense of fun.

Look at the cover. What is wrong with that classroom? Why are the walls, the kids, and the desk so close together? Do you recognize anyone in that picture? Have you ever felt like those children appear?

Predict what you think has happened. Being able to laugh at ourselves is the best way to test how jolly we are. Prepare yourselves, we are all going to find something about ourselves to laugh at in this book.

AFTER READING THE STORY

Discussion Questions
I need three volunteers to retell the story.

1. What was wrong in Miss Nelson's class and whose fault was it? Could any blame be leveled at Miss Nelson?

2. How did the situation change? How did the children feel about what happened and what did they try to do about it?

3. How does the story end? Do you think Miss Swamp will ever return? What is funny about Miss Swamp's and Detective McSmogg's names?

ACTIVITIES

1. Draw a picture showing what "might" have happened to Miss Nelson that her students didn't include.

2. Draw a picture of you in our classroom.

3. Tell your family the story of Miss Nelson. Ask your mother or father to tell you about something that happened to them at school when they were your age, or about a teacher they remember. Tomorrow, story hour will be devoted to hearing what they have told you. If they can't remember anything, make up a story.

Additional Stories for Young Readers:

The Flunking of Joshua T. Bates by Susan Shreve (Scholastic, 1985)

Joshua can't believe he's in third grade again, but then he meets Miss Goodwin—a very surprising teacher and suddenly reading is easier.

A Hippopotamus Ate the Teacher by Mike Thaler (Avon, 1981)

Ms. Jones leaned too close to the railing at the zoo, and a hippo ate her. Who will teach the class now?

Middle School Selections:

Our Sixth-Grade Sugar Babies by Eve Bunting (Lippincott, 1990)

Mrs. Oda, the sixth-grade teacher, assigns the class a most unusual project, assuring them it will build responsibility. They must dress a five-pound bag of sugar in baby clothes and watch over it for a week. Vicki and Ellie are happy with the project until a terrific seventh-grade "Thunk" (hunk) moves across the street from Vicki. Embarrassed to be seen with hers, she abandons the baby and it vanishes—maybe into cookies. A chain of deceptions leads to near tragedy.

The Cat Ate My Gym Suit by Paula Danziger (Dell 1974)

Marcy overcomes her shyness to organize a student protest on behalf of her suspended English teacher.

For Older Readers:

School Is Hell: A Cartoon Book by Matt Groening (Pantheon, 1987)

A toothy, one-eared rabbit reveals how the high spirits of the best years of our lives are flattened by, among many other things, teachers' dirty looks. A humorous look at life through mud-colored glasses for teenage comic fans.

Is That You, Miss Blue? by M.E. Kerr (Harper & Row, 1975)

M.E. Kerr claims that nearly everything, every event, in *Is That You, Miss Blue?*, happened to her when she was attending Stuart Hall, a boarding school in upstate New York . . . well, almost everything. Her mother didn't run off with a younger man, but she did stop reading her daughter's books after *Miss Blue* appeared and people started looking at her funny. In Kerr's humorous autobiography, *Me, Me, Me, Me: Not a Novel*, the boarding-school chapter is called, "There's Not a Man in This Damn Nunnery." Students who think like writers might want to read it, too, to see how authors are able to turn their real-life experience into stories.

The novel is the story of Flanders Brown's view of what she discovers about herself and life while watching the ironic situation of religious Miss Blue, who had a special relationship with Jesus, being asked to resign because her faith made teachers and students in a church-sponsored school uncomfortable.

I Touch the Future—The Story of Christa McAuliffe by Robert T. Hohler (Random House, 1987)

Christa McAuliffe, the teacher on the doomed *Challenger*, who trained with the astronauts so that she could teach from space deserves a better biography than Hohler's. However, her moving story is a natural addition to this unit.

A Potpourri of Activities and Ideas

ADOPT A WRITER FROM YOUR REGION

When kids learn that someone down the block or down the road wrote a novel, a play, or a poem, knowing not only makes them feel proud, it gives them hope. If you live in Missouri, Mark Twain is a natural choice, but Illinois has Carl Sandburg, Emily Dickinson never left Massachusetts, E. B. White's best years were spent in Maine, James Baldwin grew up in Harlem, Jack London fished for stories and oysters in California, Willa Cather's territory was Nebraska, and Walt Whitman has walked most every street and back road in New York. Go on a treasure hunt for yours. If possible, take a field trip to the writer's home, library, or neighborhood. *Walk in her footprints.*

If your writer takes center stage in both the library and the classroom, the project is easier and more fun for everyone.

Let the students work in teams to do the research:

- Team I—Biography
- Team II—History of the period
- Team III—Literary works. This group might pick a book, poem or play for the class to read together or present individual choices.
- Team IV—The arts. This group decorates the room and bulletin boards appropriately, draws a map situating the writer in relation to the school, finds music popular at the time, and locates photographs showing the fashions of the day and means of transportation.

Writing Projects:

1. Critical review
2. My Personal Impressions of the Writer
3. Ideas the Writer Gave Me for Writing about My Town, Neighborhood, State
4. A Letter to the Class in the Voice of the Writer
5. If _____ Were Living Today, I Would Call Her Up to Ask

_____

If a popular current author lives in your town, adopt her. Invite her to tea at the school. Be sure to read her books before she arrives, or it will be embarrassing.

Most kids now know S.E. Hinton's secret. She's not only a girl, but a mom living in Oklahoma City. Virginia Hamilton lives in a town with a pretty name—Yellow Springs, Ohio. Robert Cormier spends most of his time in his imagination, but he still calls Leominster, Massachusetts, home. Lou Kassem lives in the mountains of southwestern Virginia, but she often hears voices from Tennessee. Pennsylvania proudly claims Jerry Spinelli. Once Czechoslovakia was home, but now Peter Sis lives in New York City. So do Donald Crews, Ann Jonas, Avi, Walter Dean Myers, Vera Williams, Judy Blume, and Harry and Norma Mazer (for three months of the year, when it gets cold in Jamesville, New York).

If an author can't come to visit, the children might enjoy making a literary map of the United States, reflecting where their favorite authors live. They might learn a little geography in the process.

POETRY-MUSIC: FUSING RHYTHMS, WORDS, CULTURES

Poetry-music, the oldest form of poetry, originated in the oral tradition: Australian aborigine song-sticks are twelve thousand years old; Homer wrote three millennia ago, and Sappho's verse dates from 650 B.C. According to Allen Ginsberg, the most publicized effort to fuse poetry and jazz in our country took place in the late 1950s when the free verse of Jack Kerouac, Lawrence Ferlinghetti, Kenneth Rexroth, Kenneth Patchen challenged jazz musicians to create an improvised music to go beyond harmonic boundaries of 1950s jazz. But the Beats weren't the first. Langston Hughes and other African-American poets were reciting their poetry to jazz in the 1920s. (Vernon Frazer, "The Poetry-Jazz Fusion," *Poets and Writers Magazine*, March/April 1992)

Kerouac took rhythms from the music of Charlie Parker, Dizzy Gillespie, returning them to prose and poetry. The bebop jazz musicians found theirs in street-talk rhythms, the instruments talking to each other with the idiomatic rhythms of street-funk speech.

Poets like Dylan Thomas, Vachel Lindsay, Amiri Baraka, Jayne Cortez, and Sonia Sanchez fuse music and poetry with their voices by riffing (constantly repeating a musical phrase). Kerouac sometimes used jazz in the call-and-response tradition. Robert Bly has accompanied himself with a dulcimer and, since the sixties, rock musicians Bob Dylan, Frank Zappa, Lou Reed, Patti Smith have performed poetry-rock. Caribbean reggae and calypso, like American blues, were originally poetic, political commentaries. Currently, rap music attempts to reunite the spoken word and music.

Ginsberg sees a rise in poetry-music as a result of cross-cultural work of artists—brown, black, white, red, and yellow (Afro-Caribbean, Tibetan and Zen Hindu, American black blues, etc.).

After reading some of the poets, listening to recordings and discussing the cross-cultural influences, give students an opportunity to try *writing to music*. Following the session, encourage them to discuss the effect the music had on their work.

HISTORY AND LITERATURE TEAM UP

Ask the students to pick: The Most Important Decision a President Has Made in The Twentieth Century.

When a social-studies teacher and I did this several years ago with Chicago high school seniors in a team-taught gifted program, they chose President Truman's decision to drop the atom bomb. We read C.P. Snow's *The New Men* (Scribners, 1964), a novel about the conscience of a group of scientists who worked on the bomb. Musicians held a hootenanny, leading the kids in ban-the-bomb songs by Bob Dylan, Joan Baez, the Weavers. We wrote the Truman library and received material defending his decision as well as presenting John Hershey's *Hiroshima* (Knopf, 1985). The kids found, and if they were so inclined, wrote protest poetry.

The final assignment was to be a paper in which the students decided and defended their opinions on whether the president had made the right or wrong decision. Never have two teachers tried harder to weigh and balance material to present an objective view. Then I blew it.

I lived in Hyde Park, close to the campus of the University of Chicago. Near the end of our study, one day in the grocery store I met Laura Fermi (author of *Atoms in the Family*, University of New Mexico Press, 1988), a charming woman whose late husband Enrico had worked on the Manhattan Project. On a whim, I told her about the project and asked her to talk to our students. She did. Forget objectivity. In forty minutes, she enchanted and converted all the skeptics, activists, and doubters. For the final papers, the social studies teacher and I read forty-five versions of Mrs. Fermi's justification that more people would have been killed if we had continued the night raids over Japan.

Perhaps you will have better luck. Just don't invite a charismatic angel unaware.

To generate students' ideas when choosing a president's decision, you will want to mention historic events like the stock market crash in 1929 and the decision to pull out of Vietnam or periods like the Great Depression that have inspired many stories such as Steinbeck's *The Grapes of Wrath* (Viking, 1989) and *Of Mice and Men* (Random House, 1979). If your class should choose President Roosevelt's decision to close the banks, don't forget Jackie French Koller's *Nothing to Fear* (Harcourt, 1991), told from the viewpoint of Danny Garvey, a boy forced to beg for food for his family in the thirties; *As Far as Mill Springs* by Patricia Pendergraft (Philomel, 1992), about the adventures of two boys who run away when boarded out to a mean family; or Milton Meltzer's nonfiction books, *Brother, Can You Spare a Dime?* (Knopf, 1969) and *Violins and Shovels: The WPA Arts Projects* (Delacorte, 1976).

THE LAW AND ETHICS:
AN INTERDISCIPLINARY THEME FOR
GOOD READERS IN HIGH SCHOOL

Law professor Richard Weisberg's *Poethics and Other Strategies of Law and Literature* (Columbia University Press, 1992) not only presents an excellent argument for lawyers reading literature to learn ethics, but also offers a whole language curriculum too good to ignore. Besides, he is also a creative speller. With a bow toward Aristotle's *Poetics*, a discourse on poetry and drama, he combines poetry and ethics to invent "poethics" for his title and to explain his theory.

Following are selected law-related literary works he suggests:

Dickens, Charles. *Bleak House*. Bantam, 1985.

Dostoyevsky, Fyodor. *Crime and Punishment*. Bantam, 1984.

————. *The Brothers Karamazov*. Dutton, 1986.

Gogol, Nikolai V. "The Nose" in *The Complete Tales of Nikolai Gogol: 1809–1852*, edited by Leonard Kent. University of Chicago Press, 1985.

Kafka, Franz. *The Trial*. Buccaneer, 1983.

Lee, Harper. *To Kill a Mockingbird*. Warner Books, 1988.

Malamud, Bernard. *The Fixer*. Pocket Books, 1989.

Melville, Herman. *Billy Budd*. Macmillan, 1975.

Muller, Ingo. *Hitler's Justice*. Harvard University Press, 1991 (nonfiction).

Shakespeare, William. *The Merchant of Venice*. Simon & Schuster, 1982.

Small groups of students could work on different pieces of literature with a goal of presenting an interdisciplinary report to the entire class. They would include:

1. A summary of the plot.
2. The legal issue in question.
3. The historic and geographic perspective of both the setting for the story and the time the author wrote the work.

4. Current legal decisions that could have changed the outcome of the case.

RELATED ACTIVITIES:

1. Follow a trial being reported in the newspaper. Discuss the ethics of the case and the ethical behavior of the lawyers, judge, and jury.

2. Analyze the writing of a Supreme Court decision for clarity as well as for the ethical implications of the decision. For example Weisberg contends the reason *Brown v. Brown* and *Roe v. Wade* were vulnerable to revision by a later Court was because neither opinion fully expressed its central core of justice. He believes neither opinion captured in its writing "the essence of the human situation they so courageously attempted to alleviate."

3. Invite a lawyer to speak to the class. Ask him to describe and analyze the law-school training he received in ethics and in learning to write cases. Ask his opinion of Weisberg's proposal for incorporating literature into the law curriculum.

4. Arrange a fieldtrip to visit a court in session. The students might enjoy knowing that *The New York Times* book critic, Herbert Mitgang, found Weisberg's writing "turgid," better suited for a brief than a book (*The New York Times* April 13, 1992).

The Many Ways to Tell a Story

DANCING A STORY OR A CHARACTER

When I heard Cyd Charisse say she believes dancing is not about abstract movement but about characterization, Tom Sawyer, Sendak's Max and his wild things, Maniac Magee running on the railroad track, Anne of Green Gables, Sarah—plain and tall, Paddington, Charlotte Doyle, the Ugly Duckling, the Bobbsey twins, and Gatsby, began to tap, twirl, dip, strut, and sway in my head.

Many children will have seen *The Nutcracker*, at least on television, but as a warm-up to choreographing their character or story, seeing the video should inspire them all to want to cavort. Who can keep her feet on the floor when handsome toy soldiers are coming to life as dashing swains, Clara is going on spellbound journeys to romantic fairylands, or the Nutcracker is dueling with the King of the Mice?

Begin by having everyone pick a character and one scene, like Bruce Brooks' hero Jerome Foxworthy practicing his fakes in *Moves Make the Man* (Harper & Row, 1984) or Virginia Hamilton's Tomorrow Billy on his secretive night mission in *The Planet of Junior Brown* (Macmillan, 1974). Most children know how to walk like Charlie Chaplin's little tramp, which could be a beginning to understanding how to bring a character to life through silent action. After the children have worked on how to convey an emotion like shyness or bravado or fear with a movement, let them work together on a story. Picture books like Sendak's and Anthony Browne's especially lend themselves to frolic.

Look at the possibilities for the whole class to communicate Elizabeth Spurr's *The Biggest Birthday Cake in the World* (Harcourt, 1991) by dancing the characters. How would the Richest, Fattest Man in the

World move to show his heft, but also his power? The pace would speed up when all those cooks scurried to pour, sift, beat, stir, and crack 40,000 eggs. And imagine the way the cooks, the boys and the girls dived into the cake, burrowing, tunneling, smudging, sludging, licking, and sticking to make The Most Horrendous Mess in the World.

SINGING STORIES

To set the mood, play Country Western songs or ballads with a strong narrative such as "Coal Miner's Daughter," "A Boy Named Sue," "I Walk the Line," "Wind under My Wings," "Five Feet High And Rising," "The Man in Black." Let the kids retell and write the stories they hear or write song lyrics. The Rag Coat by Lauren Mills (Little, Brown, 1991), a sentimental story about a child in Appalachia who couldn't attend school because she had no coat until her mama patched one together out of scraps, was inspired by a Dolly Parton song, "The Coat of Many Colors."

Maira Kalman collaborated with David Byrne, the singer and lyricist for the rock group Talking Heads, on a book using his song "Stay Up Late" and her illustrations. Clothing designer Isaac Mizrahi has used some of her designs in his clothes, too.

When Barry Moser and I worked together on the Mark Twain project at the University of California, he was looking to the classics for inspiration, but recently he illustrated The Magic Wood (Harper-Collins, 1992) because, ever since he heard Joan Baez sing that poem on her album titled, Baptism: A Journey Through Our Time, he had wanted to illustrate the lyrics.

Then there is the non-profit "Music Mobile," open to all Boston students, ages eight through eighteen, begun by Madeliene Steczynski and Bob Grove to give students a chance to develop their creative talents, have an opportunity to discuss their problems, and come up with solutions through music—a way to communicate with their friends and family, and a way to keep kids who have nowhere else to go off the streets. The idea reminded me of the bookmobile which changed my life. One of the most telling songs composed by a group of twenty-four is called "We've Had Enough" :

> We've had enough of what's bad in
>   our lives
> We've had enough of drugs, guns
>   and knives
> Now we're going to turn it around,
> because music is something new
>   that we've found."

PUBLISHING

After partners have gone through the rehearsing, drafting, rewriting stages of a story, they are ready to publish. The partners switch roles as editor and author. The whole group picks a name for the class's publishing house. Designing a cover is the first step. Using a favorite book as a model, they draw or find an appropriate illustration. Layout comes next: where to put the title and the author's, illustrator's, and publisher's name.

To learn to write the cover copy, which not only tells highlights about the plot, but is designed to make people want to read the book, they read blurbs from stories they know.

Deciding whom to honor on the dedication page is the next important decision. Children who have begun to read like writers will always notice to whom a writer has dedicated her work. Sometimes there are surprises. Adult writer Joan Didion, who tried unsuccessfully to break a two-book contract with her publisher Simon & Schuster, wrote this dedication in *After Henry* (Simon & Schuster, 1992): "This book is dedicated to Henry Robbins and to Bret Easton Ellis, each of whom did time with its publisher." Simon & Schuster is alleged to have fired Robbins and backed out of publishing Ellis' *American Psycho* after that book's plot about a misogynist serial killer generated controversy.

Writing information about the author to go under her photograph on the back cover is good for all authors' self-esteem.

All writers are a bit nervous when they give their work to other writers and ask for a quote to use on the back cover, but most "professionals" are fair. When each author obtains two quotes, she makes them part of the back cover design using the other writer's name and title of his latest story.

When the covers are complete, the stories inserted, they are displayed around the room. Now, the children switch roles to become *reviewers*. Everyone chooses one book to review. Knowing how important their opinions will be, the critics will want to examine the form other reviewers use, making certain to include what and whom the story is about, strengths and weaknesses of the plot, characterization, or style, a line or two about the author, and about the specific audience the reviewer believes will find the book appealing (i.e., "If you like horse stories, fifth-grader Daisy Daum's *Dobbin* is a book you won't want to miss").

If other classrooms are doing the same project, the children can visit each other's rooms, view the books, check the reviews, and read each other's stories.

PREDICTING AND IMAGINING

Make up your own predicting games. Speculating on which way sentences like the following might go could give kids ideas for writing a story. Adding details to create a more vivid picture encourages them to think like writers. This exercise is also an opportunity to talk about the writing process.

1. Pretending she didn't mind at all, she waited until _____.
2. When his coat caught in the door, _____.
3. Never so embarrassed in their lives, the twins _____.
4. Carrying a _____ had been the smartest thing he had done, the day _____.

In # 1, what is the girl's name? How old is she? What has happened? What does she do? How could we change things around to make it funny? How could we add a boy to what happened?

In # 2, what color is his coat? What style? Should we make this sentence about what happens to the coat or what the boy does?

In # 3, how could we show the twins are angry? How could we show they feel guilty? How could we show if they are male or female?

In # 4, how can we indicate the boy's or man's age by what he is carrying? How can we make the story either scary or funny by our choice of what happened that day?

ROCK MUSIC AS AN INTEGRATED ART FORM: AN INDEPENDENT STUDY PROJECT

This is an "if you can't beat them, join them" suggestion, offered in memory of Paul, a handsome, shy, seventeen-year-old Chicago guitarist with a long ponytail, who for too short a period was a student in my English class in the late sixties. Paul and I hit it off. He began staying after class to tell me with touching pride about his band's weekend gigs. Then the assistant principal, whom we always suspected of having been the model for his counterpart in Bel Kaufman's *Up the Down Staircase* (Harper & Row, 1965), issued Paul an ultimatum: "Cut your hair or be expelled."

After all arguments and pleas failed, in desperation, I showed the assistant principal pictures of rebel Oliver Cromwell with his cropped hair and Charles I with his flowing locks . . . to no avail. Firmly believing a rocker with short hair could never make it, Paul, a good student, left school forever at seventeen, his ponytail and principles intact.

Rather than constantly saying, "Please, turn it down," to the kid who seems to care about nothing but loud music, here is an opportunity to put whole language philosophy into practice. Start where the student is. Plug into his interests and experience. Give him ear phones and a challenge to discover the cultural influences in the sound. Many early English rockers, like John Lennon and Keith Richards, were products of art schools. In the beginning, the rock musicians read poetry, studied Hinduism, and drew psychedelic visions in watercolors. Some of the pioneers were freaks, dreamers, and malcontents, who drew their lyrics and emotional power from the gritty rural traditions of white folk music and African American blues.

Kids seriously interested in making or enjoying rock music should be encouraged to read, to look at paintings, see foreign films, listen to jazz, country western, and classical music. Researching rock as an art form, reading and writing about the early heroes, and listening to their music and lyrics could lead the students to believe the other arts are important too.

Tips for Parents

When you ask your child what she did in school today and she says, "nothing," "played with Josie," or "skinned my knee on the slide," hold the phone call to the school. Maybe you aren't asking the right question, maybe you've put her on the spot, maybe she knows how "to get your goat." Ask about a particular story you know the class is reading, what she wrote about that day or what she drew, or if they're still working on more than/less than in math.

The emphasis in a whole language classroom is different. Keep in mind your child is *reading to learn* rather than *learning to read.*

The best way to keep abreast at school is to volunteer to become involved. Participate in the story conferences in which children talk about what they are writing and ask assistance in making it right. If you are not available during school hours, but can type or have access to typing services, help prepare the kids' work for publication.

The best way to help your child is to be supportive, interested, there, and not connect learning with punishment.

Reading

Encourage your child to read EVERYTHING—the cereal box, street signs, addresses on envelopes, names on mailboxes, and directions for games, as well as books, newspapers, and magazines. Inundate her with print.

Good readers take chances, risk being wrong, in order to find the meaning. They guess at words they don't know or just skip them until they find the gist of what they're reading.

Read independently and with your children, setting an example that reading and discussing books and ideas is an important value in your family.

Make a game out of having your child read aloud to entertain you while you do chores. Encourage him to relate family lore to the stories he reads. You tell him stories; ask him to tell you tales, those he has read and especially those he makes up. Suggest he sing, act out, or draw stories, too.

It's best not to show concern if your child finds words in his reading you would rather he didn't have in his vocabulary. He sees and hears worse in the street. Having an opportunity to discuss connotations of words at home prevents them from becoming tempting forbidden fruit. Also, if you haven't been able to tackle sex education, an intelligent book that does is better than having your child pick up dangerous misconceptions in the school bathroom. Believing he can trust you to discuss his concerns and ideas sensibly is one of the best beliefs you can instill in your child.

Writing

Let your child join in on your writing activities like making grocery lists. Before she can write, encourage her to make symbols for cookies, cereal, carrots. When you write to Granny, discuss the process. "We will tell her about the new car. Now what will she want to know?" "The color, right. How would you describe that shade of blue? That Daddy said it cost an arm and a leg? Oh, okay if you think that will make Granny giggle."

The Library

Begin to take your child—even toddlers—on weekly trips to the library. Most libraries have toddler and/or preschool story programs. Some even have infant or lapsit sessions for rhymes, songs and finger-plays. When you visit, pick out books for both of you. Make it a fun junket the child looks forward to.

See that your children have their own library cards as soon as possible. Most libraries are open in the evening and will issue a card to children who can print their names, if parents will countersign.

Ask the librarian to introduce you to journals like *Horn Book, School Library Journal, Booklist,* and *Cricket* that give reviews of children's literature. *The Alan Review,* published three times a year, is a good source for young adult critiques. Books to help you and your child select books she will enjoy include:

Hearne, Betsy. *Choosing Books for Children*. Delacorte, 1990.
Kimmel, Margaret, and Elizabeth Segal. *For Reading Out Loud*. Dell, 1983.
Larrick, Nancy. *A Parent's Guide to Children's Reading*. Pocket Books, 1983.
Trelease, Jim. *The Read-Aloud Handbook*. Penguin, 1983.

Math

Help your children learn to count by counting *real things* like cousins and Cheerios, beads, buttons, books, and beans.

Understanding the practical relationships of objects and movements in a pattern helps children to master mathematical concepts. Make money patterns with coins: penny, penny, nickel; then one cent, one cent, five cents. Ask the children to make patterns and tell you the name of the coin and what it's worth, establishing the relationship between the names of the coins and their values.

Talk about shapes of the mixing bowl, the square cake pan, triangle and diamond shaped kites.

Geography

Have maps and an atlas in the house. Ask your child to trace routes for real and imagined trips, paying attention to cities, states, and rivers along the way. When foreign countries and leaders are in the news, make a point of finding the country in the atlas, figure out how far away it is from where you live. She'll have a geography and math lesson unaware.

Science

Encourage your children to plant seeds, tend the flowers or vegetables through the different stages.

Take a walk in the woods to identify wildflowers, leaves, trees, and plants.

Give her safe gadgets to take apart and put back together, like a discarded flashlight.

IV. WHOLE LANGUAGE SUCCESS STORIES

Whole Language Activities That Worked for Others

T rying a new teaching method, like breaking in a new pair of shoes, takes time to feel comfortable. The generous teachers and librarians featured below, not only offer suggestions and ideas they hope you can use, but tell how they became whole language believers and practitioners.

Sara Miller, a librarian at Rye (N.Y.) Country Day School, admits that the first time she was asked to assist, she got a bit carried away. She was a librarian in another school when the principal, after hearing about whole language, decided the third grade teachers would try it. "How?" "What is it exactly?" the dismayed teachers asked. He didn't know much about it, but the librarian would help them, he promised.

Delighted with the opportunity to be involved in the planning of a theme to integrate the disciplines, Miller suggested they build their curriculum around animals, so that using folklore, natural science, and math would be a realistic fit. The teachers agreed until Miller pulled three hundred books from the shelves, booktalking them with the rapidity of an automatic rifle.

Taking a breath, she noticed the teachers were in shock. "That was the day I made *focus* a key word in my planning," she said. The teachers left with twenty books each. They came back to talk about what worked and what didn't, and to discuss how they were going to explain a literature-based curriculum to parents who were expecting basal readers, spelling lists, and workbooks.

The following tells the tales of others from coast to coast, who made it work very well.

THEMES FOR KINDERGARTEN

When Dana Brown earned her elementary education degree at Eastern Illinois University in 1989, she had not had any courses preparing her to be a whole language teacher, but as so many other creative educators, she evolved into the approach. The theory and the practices she read in the literature and picked up from fellow teachers worked for her kids and, with every day offering a different challenge, she enjoyed her role more. Not having years of experience as a traditional teacher to forget also made the change easier.

Brown's kindergarten class at the John Muir Elementary School in Glendale, California, consists of 90–95 percent Armenian children for whom English is a second language. With the acquisition of language taking a bit more time, her aim is to make it something the children enjoy, like singing their numbers and colors and writing their Beautiful Word Books. Starting with A and working through the alphabet, they make books in the shape of the letter, filling it with beautiful words starting with A like "apple," "ankle," "acorn," "April," "apron." The next step is to illustrate the word, fit the pages together, and sign the book as written and illustrated by _____. Brown's students are thinking of themselves as authors before they can write a sentence.

Each month the class works on a different theme. Arriving in September, the children find the school and the people look big and strange, but there is someone familiar on the bulletin board. Why, it's the Gingerbread Man. But lo and behold, he runs away! Where to find him? First, they go to the principal's office. The kids meet the principal, who seems like a very nice person, but he hasn't seen the Gingerbread Man. "Why don't you look in the library?" the principal suggests. So off they go. The librarian is as friendly as the principal. She invites them to come back to hear a story and to look at the books, but she is terribly sorry about the Gingerbread Man. That rascal didn't come to the library either, but they might find him in the cafeteria. After they have toured the entire school from the bathrooms to the playground and made friends with many people, they go back to their classroom. And much to their delight, the Gingerbread Man has returned. After their search for the Gingerbread Man, the children feel more at home in their new school, and they are launched into their first theme. They will draw, sing, read, act out, and tell stories about the Gingerbread Man. Finally, they will eat him.

The Gingerbread Man is tasty, monsters and penguins are fascinating, but everyone's favorite is the Teddy-Bear Unit. Don Freeman's A

Pocket for Corduroy is like one bite of popcorn. It only makes you hungry for more. Reading *The Three Bears* is a pleasure, but putting on a play about Goldilocks' intrusion in their house is even more fun, especially when you get to wear the bear masks.

Looking around the room, the class decides they really should have some new art work to display. Why not do a whopper? A butcher-paper mural to cover an entire wall as some of the children have seen at church or in art galleries. Why not sponge paint the three bears' house? They could have a yard with lots of grass and Mama Bear would like some flowers. How about a rope swing for Baby Bear? Where will they put it? Of course, they must add a tree. Armed with their sponges, a class of young artists set to work with the vim of Michelangelo in the Sistine Chapel.

In a whole language classroom, however, children never practice only one of the arts. These kindergartners also think like writers and illustrators. After all, they publish, too. When they read a bear book, they pay attention to who wrote it and who drew the pictures for the story, and it's even better when they can find out something about the author. As fellow writers, they want to know where Freeman got his idea for Corduroy, and why none of the different illustrators have made the bears and Goldilocks look the same. Brown's students' books look just like what they are, bear books. They have cut out three good-sized bears. Their stories fit into the tummies. Having read many picture books, they know you can be an author without words. Pictures will tell their story. On one page, they illustrate the three bears' house, another has three bowls of porridge, the last one has three beds and just guess who is sleeping in one of the beds?

Every day during this unit Ms. Brown reads a story about bears from one of the books in the class library—Berenstein's bears, Paddington— they are all there. When the children finish the books they've written, where do their creations go? In the classroom library with Bill Peet's *Big Bad Bruce*, the Beautiful Word Books, and all the other bear books, of course, so they can read their own stories again and again.

Math is not about numbers; it's about bears. They count, add to, and take away manipulative bears. The teacher does bear math, too (*modeling*). She puts footprints on the overhead (the bears made the tracks): one is red; one is yellow; the next one is red . . . they make a pattern. After the children have had a go at making patterns on their papers, they add the feet that made those prints, and before you know it, they have a bear running off to the movies.

Almost all children wish they had one of those great big, expensive teddy bears they've seen in the stores, so why not make their own? From butcher paper, each child cuts two bears, as big as she is. Brown staples them together, leaving the top open until they are stuffed full of paper. The class size suddenly doubles. Now there are as many bears as children.

When Brown was a child, her favorite book was *Going on a Bear Hunt.* She saves for last the excellent version of that picture book written by Michael Rosen with illustrations by Helen Oxenbury (Macmillan, 1989). The children's hand gestures create the action right down to the moment they tiptoe into the cave . . . see the bear . . . run home fast as they can to crawl under the covers!

What more perfect way to end the month, than to have a Teddy Bear Sleepover? The children come to school in their pj's and they bring guests, their teddy bears. If someone doesn't have one, not to worry, Miss Brown has extras. After she reads a bedtime story, they have milk and cookies before snuggling in with their bears for a nice nap.

SOCIAL-STUDIES-BASED, INTEGRATED CURRICULUM FOR FIRST GRADE

Neighborhoods and Jobs

Anyone who has given up on education or New York City should visit PS 87, a racially balanced elementary school on the Upper West Side of Manhattan. In my opinion, school architects, especially in New York, must go to mole training. What else explains the dark and dreary halls? At PS 87, things begin to brighten up the moment principal Jane Hand starts to cheerlead for her kids, her parents, her teachers, the neighborhood, and one of the more innovative whole language curricula I've ever seen. Hand, a Piaget champion and a former whole language kindergarten teacher in the South Bronx, knows what she is talking about. So do her teachers, most of them products of Columbia Teachers College or The Bank Street School where the whole language philosophy predominates in teacher training.

Picking what to spotlight here was most difficult. But even though the third-grade block-printed, folded, Haiku poetry books, an outgrowth of a unit on Japan, and the kindergartners' cookbook for breads from around the world (which they had also baked) held intrigue, I finally chose the first-grade social studies Neighborhood & Jobs unit, because of how completely the teachers had integrated the curriculum and built on the children's experience by using their home turf.

The three-and-one-half month project, originally designed by teacher Paul Schwartz, who has moved into administration, goes through major updating to keep up with the changing neighborhood and the children's interests. When I visited, five first grade, heterogeneous classes taught by Elissa Grayer, Rebecca White, Jacqui Getz, Christiania Santiago, and Starrett Pierson had adopted for study a block of Broadway, a street three blocks from the school.

For homework, the children concentrated on the block where they lived. They made maps of their bedrooms, drew pictures of their buildings, wrote their observations of the street and their neighbors.

As teacher Elissa Grayer said, "At this age, kids are interested in themselves and their neighborhoods. We simply start where they are and take them as far as they can go."

Students help to generate the curriculum, sometimes changing it, like the time the teachers planned a scientific unit on water until they discovered what the kids really wanted to know was how the water got from the reservoirs to their tap. According to teacher Rebecca White, this turned out to be one of the most interesting units of the year because the teachers learned as much as the children. White claims still to be giving mini-lessons on the subject to her dinner guests.

The kids responded to: "What do you know and what do you want to know about your neighborhood?" and "What kind of jobs do people have here?" with things like:

- Who built the buildings?
- How tall are they?

- Who turns the street lights on and off?
- Where do the manholes go?
- Who paints the lines on the street?
- How does the merchandise get to the stores?
- Who times the stop lights?

Following is the teacher-generated curriculum web, incorporating the students' input:

Language Arts

Reading—street signs, maps, prices, labeled goods, books, cooking recipes, trip sheets, charts.

Writing—labeling murals, drawings, and paintings; poems; stories; letters, trip observations.

Communication/Organization—interviewing, categorizing, group planning, problem solving.

Math—measuring, mapping/grids, counting, patterns, addresses (odd/even), money/prices, addition/subtraction.

Art—texture rubbings of sidewalks, plaques, walls, tree trunks, manhole covers; mural (multimedia): "Jobs in Our Neighborhood" and "Stores in Our Neighborhood"; paint, clay, crayon representations of buildings, workers, traffic, signs.

Science—plants: trees/shrubs; animals: squirrels, birds, cats/dogs, horses, cockroaches, mice, and rats; Materials (man-made and natural): concrete, rock/stone, wood, brick; lights/electricity; heat; transportation; cooking (various ethnic specialties).

The first neighborhood walks were to do rubbings, observe shapes of windows on the brownstone-lined streets leading to Broadway, think about jobs in the area, count fireplugs, stoplights, signs. The children carried trip boards to record what they saw. Back in the classroom, the teachers modeled how to use the information to write a story that flowed.

After working on interviewing skills and generating appropriate questions, by using parent resources, the children were able to question an actor and musician who came to school and to plan trips to places that included: the fire station, library, sports writer's office (a parent), neighborhood stores and restaurants, a lab technician's office, behind the scenes at the Museum of Natural History. The children did their interviews in groups of four. The remainder of the class joined other teachers' groups. Teachers at PS 87 teach to learn, and they work as a team.

They also pool their literary resources by giving each other lists of related books they have in their individual rooms. Following is a selected list of the choices for neighborhoods and jobs:

Aesop. *City Mouse, Country Mouse.* Putnam, 1985.

Aitken, Amy. *Ruby!* Bradbury Press, 1979.

Arnold, Caroline. *What Is a Comunity?* Watts, 1982.

Farber, Norma. *I Found Them in the Yellow Pages.* Little, Brown, 1973.

Florian, Douglas. *People Working.* Crowell, 1983.

————. *City Street.* Greenwillow, 1990.

Henkes, Kevin. *Once Around the Block.* Greenwillow, 1987.

Hoban, Tana. *I Read Signs.* Greenwillow, 1983.

Isadora, Rachel. *City Seen from A to Z.* Greenwillow, 1983.

Munro, Roxie. *The Inside-Outside Book of New York City.* Putnam, 1985.

Raskin, Ellen. *Nothing Ever Happens on My Block.* Macmillan, 1989.

Robbins, Ken. *City/Country.* Viking, 1985.

Rockwell, Anne. *Gogo's Payday.* Doubleday, 1978.

————. *When We Grow Up.* Dutton, 1981.

Rosenblum, Richard. *My Block.* Macmillan, 1988.

Scarry, Richard. *What Do People Do All Day.* Random House, 1968.

Stevenson, James. *Grandpa's Great City Tour.* Greenwillow, 1983.

Waber, Bernard. *The House on East 88th Street.* Houghton Mifflin, 1973.

Watanabe, Shigeo. *I Can Take a Walk.* Philomel, 1983.

Zion, Gene. *Dear Garbage Man.* Harper, 1988.

Although the list is impressive, the books the kids liked best were the ones they wrote themselves based on their observations and interviews. After they worked on achieving a narrative flow for their ideas, getting help from each other as well as from the teacher, they did the illustrations. Parent volunteers helped out with the typing. All books were published. The students read their own and the other kids' stories over and over again.

The unit culminated in a major challenge. After measuring the buildings, the length and width of the block, the sidewalks, and the island in the middle of the street, the children drew a map to scale showing both sides of their Broadway block, including illustrated storefronts, like a window full of eyeglasses and paperdoll figures of the people who run the businesses. The map must be large enough for a large group of children to work on it at one time and to gather around it for discussion. PS 87 teachers used centimeter graph paper one meter wide and twelve meters long.

Finally, everyone contributed to writing, illustrating, and publishing a fat guide to the street. Pairs of children adopted a store. With some help from the teacher, they decided what they wanted to know about the shop and the people. After a trip to observe and interview, they wrote and illustrated a story to include in the guide. The collected stories have construction paper covers and are held together with large metal rings.

This school has always involved the community in their pursuits, this year more than ever. With a grant from the chamber of commerce, PS 87 will publish a real newspaper covering their block study. Each class will have a page written by the children. The professionally printed paper will be distributed to children, parents, and all the businesses in the neighborhood.

FIRST-GRADE ENTREPRENEURS

As a result of their social studies, many of the children at PS 87 have already accumulated job experience fit for a resume. Christiania Santiago's first graders opened a restaurant where they cooked and sold spaghetti, English muffin pizzas, bagels and cream cheese—things they could make on a hot plate and in a crock pot or store in ice chests and a portable refrigerator. The kids filled out job applications, had a work schedule, alternating their roles as cook, waiter, cashier, busboy/girl, etc. Parents contributed the first supplies, but, to learn about money and running a business, in the beginning, they reinvested the profits to expand their menu. When the restaurant closed, these enterprising business people contributed ninety-six dollars to Meals on Wheels.

When they studied fruit markets, it began with a trip to an apple orchard, but by the time they finished the unit, the kids had opened a fruit and vegetable market in the hall at PS 87 (a parent went to a wholesale market for supplies each morning), for which they not only designed artistic grocery bags, wrote inspired poetry about string beans, converted other students to buy fruit and vegetables for snacks, but also made eighty-seven dollars' profit to contribute to a homeless shelter.

The day I visited, Jacqui Getz's and Elissa Grayer's classes had opened a shoe store, measuring customers' feet with a device they had invented out of unifex cubes. When they weren't selling shoes contributed by parents, they were working on a feet-and-shoes theme. (Would I kid in a serious book like this?) The kids were very busy drawing a monster with seven feet, counting the cumulative toes in the room by 5's and 10's, reading Polly Chase Boyden's poem "Mud"; Margaret Hillert's "About Feet"; May Justus' "The Rain Has Silver Sandals"; and Anon's "Shoes." They had plans to write a book of directions on how to tie a shoe, as well as to design the perfect shoe and read fairy tales about shoes like Cinderella's.

Bobbi Katz had written this poem he calls "Spring Is":

Spring is when
   the morning sputters like
bacon
   and
     your
       sneakers
         run
           down
             the
               stairs
So fast you can hardly keep up with them,
   and
     spring is when your scrambled eggs
       jump
        off
          the
            plate
And turn into a million daffodils
   trembling in the sunshine.

However, PS 87 is not a mini-business school. They also take advantage of the rich cultural resources in the neighborhood. Located within walking distance of The Metropolitan Museum, The Children's Museum and down the block from The Museum of Natural History, one of their more successful studies was a museum theme. I read a terrific pattern book called *In a Dark Dark Museum*, a takeoff from *In a Dark Dark Wood*.

Everywhere I looked, I saw examples of creative, humorous, and imaginative work by kids. I especially liked a rewriting of Red Riding Hood stretched across one wall in which two little girls, on the way to Grandma's house, met an alligator who ended up as Grandma's wallpaper.

Granted PS 87 happens to sit in a rich environment, but wherever you live, kids will be interested in the world they inhabit. As Elissa Grayer said, "I suppose if we lived in the middle of a cornfield, we would do a grain theme." "Sure," Starrett Pierson chimed in, "Like . . .", and they were off, the principal too, throwing out outrageous and interesting ideas, laughing, taking turns hugging the child who came in needing one. The next time someone tells me they have to move out of the city for the good of the children, I'll remember that scene.

PRESERVING NATIVE CULTURE IN THE FIRST GRADE

In another time and another place, after studying butterflies, pumpkins, and strawberries, Marian Elliott took her class on field trips to the truck farms behind her Long Island Montessori school. Then she went to Alaska and started a new life and a new family in a remote cabin in the wilderness. When her son started to school, getting him there, a twenty-mile snowmobile trip down river (which is frozen most of the time), began to be too much of a challenge in temperatures that often fell ten degrees below zero. The family moved to town and Elliott began teaching at the Mountain View Elementary School in Anchorage. Moving from the Montessori Method to whole language was as smooth as a ski trail, she said.

Her students—Native Eskimo, Aleut, Athabascan (related to the

Apache and Navaho tribes), South East Tlinket, Haida, and others—
are considered "at risk." The exorbitant drop-out rate and all related
social problems these children experience are often attributed to their
losing touch with their culture. What does a whole language teacher
do? Plug into the power of what kids know and are interested in, of
course. Students at New York's PS 87 adopt a block of Broadway;
Elliott's kids' favorite theme is the Iditarod Races, where dog teams
race one thousand miles across the wilderness in ten days.

These dogsled races, named after the Iditarod Trail, were begun to
pay tribute to the heroic teams who delivered serum to Nome when
the city had a diphtheria epidemic in 1925. Elliott was disappointed
to learn I didn't know about the statue in Central Park for Balto, the
lead dog for the original team. Her children take pride in a photograph of it that hangs in their classroom and read stories about him
and other brave dogs. They especially like stories like *The Bravest Dog
Ever: The True Story of Balto* by Natalie Standiford (Random House,
1989) and *Kiana's Iditarod* by Shirley Gill (Four Winds, 1984).

Before the big event, Athabascan Emmit Peters comes to class to
tell the kids about his dogs, equipment, the dangers on the trail.
When the races begin, Elliott makes a huge map of Alaska, where
they track the teams' progress each day. Every morning they call a
hotline and search the paper, especially eager to follow Peters and his
dogs.

The children have come to Anchorage from remote villages all
over the state. When the teams make a stop in their hometowns, the
kids tell the others their memories and about their relatives left behind. One of the stops was Shaktoolik, whose name—to everyone's
delight—a culturally shy child finally found courage to tell the teacher she wasn't pronouncing properly.

The kids tell stories, write—pretending to be one of the racers—
draw pictures of the dogs, the drivers, the scenes, but the theme is
especially good for math work. They count miles, booties for the dogs,
figure speeds and how much the food on the sleds weighs.

Even the shy little girls say, "In Alaska, men are men and women
win the Iditarod." Libby Riddeles was the first woman to win, and
Susan Butcher, another winner, was invited to the White House.

When the kids are older, they will read Scott O'Dell's *Black Star,*

Bright Dawn (Fawcett, 1989) about a young native girl who enters the race, caught between her culture and her need to be a modern woman, and of course, they will explore a mystic wolves theme built around *Julie of the Wolves* by Jean C. George (HarperCollins, 1972).

Native children losing their culture are having a hard time finding their purpose in life, Elliott says. Her goal is to build their self-esteem by validating that culture.

INTEGRATING THE DISCIPLINES IN THE SECOND GRADE

The children in Dick Koblitz's, second-grade class at the Dorris School in Collinsville, Illinois, read and write all day long. By integrating the disciplines, he is able to schedule longer blocks of time, sixty to ninety minutes, to complete "whole" projects and to give longer periods for independent reading and writing. By mid-year his seven-year-olds can read for an hour without squirming. Modeling behavior as well as instruction, he reads when the children do. If the kids do not come from homes where parents read and books are treasured, at least at school they have a respected adult who enjoys books, and shares his discoveries with the class. He writes and does research with the class also. With twenty-four members in the group, when they decided to investigate all of the states, it worked perfectly. Everyone chose two states, including Dr. Koblitz, which allowed them to cover the map from Alaska to Alabama.

To save the time usually spent with housekeeping chores like taking attendance, the lunch count, and putting events on the calendar, for the first few days he also models how those tasks are done. Then the kids take over. Not only does he save valuable time, but also gives the children responsibility, accomplishing another whole language goal.

Some stories, like Pat Hutchin's *The Doorbell Rang* (Greenwillow, 1986), fit with math exercises, but finding literature to mesh with the other disciplines like art, science, and social studies is easier. However, Koblitz's kids write their math, usually in complete sentences such as the day they worked on measuring everything they could find in their classroom in every possible way. Carrying paper and pencil on their rounds, they wrote things like: "My science book is three crayons long," "Six centimeters is the length of my lunch box," and I take twelve steps from the door to the table."

Always alert for "meaningful" activities, Koblitz capitalized on his students' avid interest in the 1992 Winter Olympic Games in France for reading, writing, geography, and math activities. They learned to understand the concepts of more than/less than, to read tables, to make and interpret bar graphs. By taking information from the newspaper each morning, they made graphs to show gold, silver, and bronze medal winners, while counting and comparing the number of winning contestants from the different countries which they had located on the world map.

Koblitz has given up on daily math worksheets and workbooks, preferring to use educational tools known as manipulatives, such as unifix and pattern blocks, geoboards, cubes, and patterns, but he does do an occasional worksheet, like a quiz, to test such math basics as borrowing and carrying. He is a strong advocate of what Yetta Goodman, author of several books on whole language, calls kidwatching—when the teacher observes a student directly and informally in order to support his or her learning. The worksheet is only one of many ways Koblitz finds the child who needs individual attention.

A favorite activity with the children is literature study. The kids choose a book. The entire class reads one or two chapters each day. In literature groups, they discuss what they have read and sometimes someone illustrates what they have discussed. When I spoke with Koblitz, they were reading The Wizard of Oz by Frank Baum (Ballantine, 1986). When they finished, the plan was to use their illustrations and write a text for a big book—their version of the classic story.

"We read books like The Wizard of Oz because it is easier to fit the pieces of a puzzle together," Koblitz says, "when you begin by seeing what the whole picture looks like." The puzzle is a whole language metaphor—one that he has borrowed from Australian teacher Andrea Butler, who is now a consultant in the U.S., for starting with the whole work and moving to the parts. His students read whole poems, whole books, see the complete picture before they begin to look at the sentences, the words that fit together to make the story.

Koblitz so firmly believes in whole language, he has traveled to the source, observing and working with teachers in New Zealand and Australia.

INTEGRATING LANGUAGE ARTS, SCIENCE, AND SOCIAL STUDIES IN A FOURTH-GRADE WRITER'S WORKSHOP

When I asked Hilda Parfrey, librarian at the Carl Sandburg School in Madison, Wisconsin, how she supported whole language teachers, she immediately mentioned Cheryl Bower's writers' workshop, where by the end of the year, her fourth-graders are using the library for their research papers with the dedication of doctoral candidates working on dissertations.

Presently, Bower sets aside at least two, one-hour writing sessions per week, but with the kids, who feel good about themselves and their work, clamoring for more time to write, she is planning to integrate the idea with other subject areas.

Using the process approach to writing (choose a topic, web ideas, rough draft, revise, edit, final copy, publish), Bower begins each session with a mini-lesson which teaches a needed skill, determined by what she has observed from the children's work. To keep track of what each student is working on, she draws a checklist and in the beginning, moves around the room to make certain every child is clear about her purpose for the session. Silent writing time follows with everyone working independently, usually at different steps in the process. Bower writes too.

Writer's work time is the next step. The kids take the responsibility of deciding if they will continue to work independently, ask students in their cooperative group questions, or conference with the teacher. (Thinking Bower was being a creative grammarian, I checked the dictionary. Conference does, indeed, have a verb form.) She also encourages the children to conference with their peers and has used parent volunteers to help with the conferencing.

The workshop period ends with a voluntary sharing time. The kids decide if they are ready to present their work. As the authors, they also can determine if they want feedback from their classmates.

The process is ongoing, allowing each child to work at her own pace. When an author has completed all steps, the process begins again with the student selecting her new topic and the form. She might choose to write a story, a newspaper article, a letter, a report on a historical figure or event, or an experiment from science.

The final stage is a required research paper, using the same process-writing format. Bower does mini-lessons on research skills necessary to complete the project. The kids select a topic, find resources, think of questions to answer, read and take notes, organize an outline, write a rough draft, revise and edit with peers, write a final copy, make note cards, and plan an oral report complete with audio-visuals. The joke at the University of Chicago used to be how the campus was haunted by ABD's (All But Dissertation), Pirandello-type characters in search of topics. With this kind of background in the fourth grade, I don't think Bower's students will ever have to join the ABD rank.

FIFTH GRADERS LEAD THEIR TEACHER
TO WHOLE LANGUAGE

When Trish Richardson, fifth-grade teacher at The Sinking Fork Elementary School in Hopkinsville, Kentucky, told me the district and the state mandate skills, such as requiring that fifth graders recognize similes and metaphors, I wondered why the children didn't just listen to their teacher talk.

"By the time my husband finished law school, I was so sick of living on casseroles," she said, "at first, I had no taste for whole language. Mixing everything together that way just sounded like another casserole mess to me."

Then, one day, after reading Elizabeth George Speare's *Sign of the Beaver* (Dell, 1984) (the *whole* book), the sliver of the story in her basal reader just seemed like too thin a slice. Taking a bold step, Richardson had the class read the entire book. The story was a hit, but the historical research happened serendipitously. First, she noticed the encyclopedias were out of order. Some kids had been sneaking around to look up things about the Indians in Maine, so she brought more materials from the library and the whole class put the story into historical perspective. By the time they read Speare's *The Witch of Blackbird Pond* (Dell, 1978), she knew to be prepared to go back to Salem for the witch hunts and the trials.

When they read Lynne Reid Banks' *Indian in a Cupboard* (Avon, 1986), it was English history they had a need to know. Roald Dahl's *James and the Giant Peach* (Penguin, 1988) and *Charlie and the Chocolate Factory* (Penguin, 1988) inspired the children to try their hand at poetry. Both British born, these writers also motivated the kids to do a comparative study of British and American words like "cookie" versus "biscuit," "lift" versus "elevator," and to impress their friends and families with their cosmopolitan vocabularies.

Richardson was secretly delighted when her students ignored her suggestion that they not read ahead. There were other ways to prac-tice predicting. But it was the infamous troublemaker in the back of the room who really converted Richardson. Most of her students were reading more, but when even the squirmy boy had gone on to read several of Dahl's books, she was flabbergasted. Then, one day, to his teacher's total amazement, he volunteered and began to explain the themes of good/evil, rich/poor he had found in the stories. That did it. Her basal readers have retired.

"How about those mandated reading skills?" I asked.

"Oh, we find them in the literature like *Old Yeller*, *Island of the Blue Dolphins*. See how the authors use them and then the kids practice the skill in their work," she said. "Learning to read is like riding a bike. You wouldn't just hand a child the handlebars and expect him to peddle down the road, now, would you?"

READER/WRITER WORKSHOP FOR SIXTH GRADE

Lynn Winslow at Central Middle School in Greenwich, Connecticut, does not need to hang out a shingle. One glance in her classroom tells you kids read here. Winslow, teacher and sixth-grade facilitator at Central Middle School in Greenwich, Connecticut, has *five hundred* eclectic volumes on her shelves.

Quality is the quest. Winslow doesn't check the suggested reading level when she adds a book to her classroom library or suggests a title to a student, but she has an antenna for one that is well-written, like Patricia MacLachlan's *Journey*, new when we spoke. Books on needlepoint, nature, dance, sit next to fiction, nonfiction for all ages, picture books, best sellers. This collection spreads across the disciplines. Any child, no matter how whimsical her taste, can find something interesting.

At the beginning of the marking period, the kids set goals for themselves, which at the start are usually quantitative, like "I will write twenty stories" or "I will read twenty hours each week." When I spoke to her in the spring, the goals had become qualitative, like the child who wrote, "I will chart four ways an author develops character," or the one who said, "I will work on strengthening the conflict in my stories." My favorite came from the young man who wrote Winslow a letter: "Here it is April, and can you believe, I'm still confused about the difference between the antagonist and the conflict?"

Two hours of each day her sixth graders spend in a Reader/Writer Workshop, where, as with setting the goals, they continue to take responsibility for their own learning. Winslow divides the time in different ways, but she always leaves at least thirty minutes for the students to concentrate on their choice—writing or reading.

Somedays she will do a mini-lesson on a problem she has seen occurring in the kids' writing like punctuating a compound sentence, or maybe the instruction will be on sticking with the same verb tense in a story. They could be reading or writing independently, but the whole class also reads core books like *Alice in Wonderland*. Recently, they tackled Forrest Carter's *The Education of Little Tree* (University of New Mexico Press, 1986), but Winslow, not tied to reading levels, introduced it with a picture book by Cynthia Rylant and Barry Moser, *Appalachia: The Voices of Sleeping Birds* (Harcourt, 1991).

These sixth graders read like writers and write like readers. After finishing a core novel, the young writers often elect to spend their free writing time practicing a technique they picked up from the author. Jacquie Gordon's *Give Me One Wish* (Norton, 1988) is popular because they like to try her cliff-hanger chapter endings. In the beginning, they looked at Hemingway's *Old Man and the Sea* (Macmillan, 1984) in a traditional way, paying attention to how he developed characters, created the atmosphere and setting, but the concept of the interior monologue was brand new to them. They were familiar with dialogue and dialect, but the kids were intrigued when Winslow did a mini-lesson on the technique Hemingway used of having characters carry on conversations with themselves. Following the lesson, some children did free associating, talking over problems with themselves in their writing. Others tried the method to develop characters in their stories.

During independent writing time, the kids could be writing in their journals, to other kids, or keeping up their literature log. Once a week they are required to write to the teacher, including comments from the log where they have responded to the authors they've read, like a note to Rachel Vail: "You should write more books because you know right where kids are." One of Winslow's favorites came from Billy, whose responses after reading *Boy* by Roald Dahl went like this:

"Dear Mrs. 'Win,' I just read *Boy*, and I would have done it so differently. I would have started the story much earlier, but then who am I, Billy Callahan, to second guess Roald Dahl?"

In addition to a creative and enthusiastic teacher, another asset to this program is twenty-five Apple computers. Winslow gives a keyboarding and computer course to all of these TV-generation children for whom this skill is a piece of cake. Writing on a computer makes revisions easier for everyone, but this miracle machine that makes the work look good is a special motivator for students with learning disabilities who have serious spelling or handwriting difficulties.

All of the writers want their work to look first rate because they are already submitting stories and essays to magazines. Recently a boy with a bushel of red hair and a face full of freckles read that a child who submitted to *Ebony Junior* had a good chance to be published. Handing his story to Winslow, he asked hopefully, "Do you think I have a chance of being accepted even though I'm not black?"

A THEME FOR THE "WHOLE" JUNIOR HIGH

Community of Learners

After meeting a few whole language teachers and librarians thrilled with what they're doing, wherever I went I expected to meet enthusiastic teachers, but nothing prepared me for the crackling excitement of *ROARING TWENTIES WEEK* at the Vandalia, Illinois, Junior High School (sixth, seventh, and eighth grades). For one week, with gusto, everyone—the coach, the kids, the principal, the teachers, the cooks, the parents, members of the community—went back in time to the Jazz Age. If learning could always be such a pleasure for the young and the old, we would be a nation of intellectual wizards.

Opening the front door, I faced an eight-foot-long bulletin board featuring a couple dancing the Charleston, a cut-and-paste design from the eighth grade art class. Two weeks prior to the event, the subject of the bulletin board changed every four days. Babe Ruth wearing Yankee pinstripes as he hit his sixtieth homerun, the Spirit of St. Louis, a mask of King Tut, Albert Einstein, and a Model T had been on display. On a side wall, debonair Rudolph Valentino tangoed on a poster with an elegant lady wearing a headband with a feather. Flapper dresses, beaded bags, skimmers (loaned by a woman in the community) filled the coat closet. Every classroom had photographs of Model T's, Pierce Arrows, Packards, bi-winged planes, twenties politicians, artists, actors, and athletes. Strains of the "Charleston" bounced from a tape recorder in the gym where sixteen kids were practicing that dance to a lively 4/4 beat.

When principal Bill LaDage appointed a committee—Stoy Daume, art; Nancy Mecadon, special education; Debbie Hobbie, social studies and health; Norma Holtcamp, language arts—to find a theme the whole school could explore across the disciplines, what he got was a commitment that went beyond his hope and expectation. Torn between the Roaring Twenties and the Western Movement, they decided to save the cowboys for the next year. I plan to return as Belle Starr.

Goals

First the committee generated three main goals to distribute to the faculty:

1. Through your curriculum, teach about a *person* who lived in the 1920s.
2. Through your curriculum, teach about a 1920s *trend* which impacted at that time or today.

- The commitment to business and business values became an important part of the American way of life.
- The rising standard of living led to a better life for more people.
- United States isolationism gained popularity.
- Oil replaced coal as the main energy source.
- Urbanism within the U.S. grew while rural living declined.
- Technological advances (automobile, radio, electricity, movies, etc.) led to social changes.
- Scientific discoveries expanded life expectancy.
- The fine arts reflect the life and times of the 1920s.
- The lack of an income tax made unchecked wealth possible.
- Sports, recreation, and leisure time became an economic issue.
- The 1920s was the first decade that existed for the "now," not the future.

3. Through your curriculum, teach about an important *event* of the 1920s which impacted on society in that time or today.

- Immigrants, once again, rushed to the U.S. shores resulting in new immigration laws.
- The demobilization after World War I put the economy under heavy pressure.
- Economic nationalism rose within the U.S. resulting in higher tariffs.
- Women began to obtain limited liberation which caused social changes.
- Prohibition was passed resulting in the rise of organized crime.
- Labor unions began to grow.
- U.S. tax reforms were passed.
- Communism grew with a resulting anti-red attitude in the U.S.
- The Ku Klux Klan gained strength.
- The decade ended with the stock-market crash.
- Discovery of King Tut's Tomb in 1922 created a high interest in the Egyptian style and culture.
- Major issues of constitutional rights were tested in the courts.

Schedule

As the faculty began to plan, Daume prepared a promotion video. To motivate the students, with "Rhapsody In Blue" as background music, he showed photographs introducing events and people of the time, most of them new to the children. After the festivities, he showed it again, to reinforce and to give the kids a chance to build their self-esteem by seeing how much they had learned.

Since every teacher planned special courses of study and activities, LaDage staggered all school events across the five days so that all teachers would meet their regular classes at least four days. Monday, when the kids got off the bus, they were greeted by teachers dressed in costumes sitting in a 1927 roadster owned by a man in the community who was also dressed in the style of the twenties. Tuesday morning 8:30–10:00, everyone saw the movie, *Cheaper By The Dozen*; Thursday, 10:00–11:40, the movie, *Spirit of St. Louis*; and Friday, 1:04–3:15, they entered a lyceum where the band played "Gaslight Gaieties," a George M. Cohen medley of "Hello My Baby," "You Tell Me Your Dream," "Mary's a Grand Old Name" and "Give My Regards To Broadway." The chorus sang twenties' favorites, like "Don't Sit Under The Apple Tree With Anyone Else But Me." In costumes, students presented skits about gangsters of the 1920s, danced the Charleston, and impersonated famous people of the time. I met a Charlie Chaplin, an Einstein, an Amelia Erhardt, and much to my delight, a Virginia Woolf.

On the following Monday all students wrote across the disciplines about the week's experiences.

Curriculum and Activities

In language arts, literary selections included: short stories written or set in the twenties such as "The Ransom of Red Chief," and "Underground Ordeal," based on the real story of Floyd Collins, who was trapped in a cave, and the poem, "Casey At The Bat." The sixth and seventh graders all read *Cheaper by the Dozen* by Frank B. Gilbreth (Bantam, 1984) before seeing the movie.

The seventh graders made a time-line banner, posting it in the cafeteria where kids could check out the daily additions during their lunch break. Each day, as they learned more about the women's movement, prohibition, automobiles, the Ku Klux Klan, the fads, fashion, and entertainment of the decade, the class added pictures, dates, and signs under the appropriate year.

The eighth graders studied the background of *Inherit the Wind* before they saw the movie, but why should Hollywood actors have all the fun? While one teacher's group reenacted scenes, another class, armed with placards and a drum, picketed the performance singing "Give Me the Old Time Religion."

The older kids were also introduced to Scott Fitzgerald, his flapper wife, Zelda, and his chronicles of the Jazz Age.

When the math teacher found a textbook published in the twenties, the students had a taste of the problems their grandparents sweated over. When Grandma added two and two, her answer was still four, but the language in the word problems was a bit different. "If Lem sold Luke a three-year-old cow that he had raised from a calf for twenty-five dollars, but he had spent fifty cents a month on feed, and he had sold fifteen dollars' worth of milk from her, what was Lem's profit?"

Math might be noted as the most factual discipline, but a bunch of seventh graders did some dreaming about getting rich when they learned how to read the stock-market quotes in *The Wall Street Journal*. Then, just when they were calculating how long it would take to buy a share of Good Humor or Nike with five-dollar-a-week allowances, they learned about the 1929 crash and had some second thoughts.

Determining what caused the crash led them to the "buy now, pay later" concept which was a new and abused phenomenon in the twenties. In conjunction, they learned how to write checks and the difference between a checking and savings account. In math class they figured the deceptive costs of items bought on five-dollars-down and five-dollars-a-month installment purchase plans. In social studies, they went on to learn how, as a result, the "roar" of the twenties turned to a whimper in the Great Depression of the thirties.

When a woman in the community donated a 1927 Sears Roebuck catalogue, the eighth-grade math teachers realized they had struck pay dirt. To get the kids' attention, they started with the pages showing tennis shoes. Comparing the six-dollar, top-of-the-line prices to their one-hundred-dollar pump-ups almost convinced the students they lived in the wrong age—until they began to calculate comparative salaries, cost of living, and inflation. They learned a great deal about percentages unaware.

Great scientific and technological progress was made in this period. Famous scientists like Madam Curie and Einstein did much of their important work during the twenties. Walt Disney made a significant contribution to applied technology. In the lab and classroom the science classes learned about the miraculous discovery of penicillin, insulin, the ability to identify blood types and to test IQ's. They discussed advances in aviation, rocketry, polygraph tests, and came to understand scientific aptitude tests through hands-on experience.

The art students were so busy, they needed to form an assembly line as Henry Ford had done in the twenties. They were not only decorating the school, but each group also had a twenties project, and they were learning about famous artists like Georgia O'Keeffe and Louise Nevelson, who did their best work at that time.

The discovery of King Tut's Tomb in 1922 had inspired the sixth graders' study of a hieroglyphic alphabet. The children were all writing, or perhaps drawing is a better word, their names using a bird for an "A," a man's foot for a "B," etc. They wrote their symbols in a vertical line as had the Egyptian and then put their emblems inside a cartouche, an oval symbol of protection or safety. When I visited, one artist and several young supervisors (carrying out their own idea) were making a cartouche to present at the lyceum to Principal LaDage, "because he was cool."

The seventh graders were preparing entries for a gallery show of their surrealistic pictures. Surrealism, dedicated to the expression of imagination as revealed in dreams, free of the conscious control of reason and convention, was founded in 1924 in France and affected literature and films as well as painting and sculpture. Salvador Dali, Max Ernst, and Joan Miró were some of the artists of the period the students were studying.

Eighth graders trusted fate as they drew their art assignment out of a fishbowl. One boy's slip said, "coffeepot." A girl drew "lamp." They were learning about art deco. Their task was to design the object they had selected in the art-deco style.

During Roaring Twenties Week, forget about the three-point shot.

In gym, the kids played basketball by the 1920s' rules and practiced for a demonstration game they would put on for their classmates. They also saw videos of sports heroes of the day like Ty Cobb, Jack Dempsey, Red Grange.

One small section of the gym was taken over by the home economics students. They transformed it into a speakeasy, with black-and-white murals painted on moveable panels depicting the fashions and trends of the day. Men sported bow ties, skimmers, and two-toned shoes. Women with bobbed hair wore short skirts, long beads, and lots of bracelets. Students entered through a green door, of course, but only if "Scarface" Al Capone, in costume, who answered their knock, liked the way they looked. Admission was only granted to those in costume. No bootlegged liquor was served, but the kids paid twenties' prices for the Cokes and cookies.

Not to worry about children being corrupted by the allure of the speakeasy. The material in most classes overlapped, especially the adverse social effects of prohibition, bootlegging, the rise in organized crime. Health teachers used the theme as a means of discussing the detrimental consequences of alcohol on the body, on the society as a whole, and Carrie Nation's temperance movement.

"Give us a year, not a week" was the plea of the social studies teachers who began with a map showing the world as it was in 1920. Their goal was to give an overview of 1920 historical events like the women's movement led by Susan B. Anthony, prohibition, the advent of the automobile and movies, the rise of the Ku Klux Klan, the Scopes Trial, the Great Depression, to present the famous people of the time. . . .'We stopped, but we would never finish," Hobbie said. "Our hope is that students will continue independently to follow interests they've discovered this week."

Young singers leaving chorus still humming the twenties' songs aren't apt to stop in a week. Remember "Varsity Drag," "Chicago, Chicago," "Birds Do It, Bees Do It," "Yes, Sir She's My Baby," "How Dry I Am," "Bye Bye Blackbird," "Hail, Hail, the Gang's All Here"?

The students in special education classes had heard about King Tut's Tomb, Charles Lindbergh, Al Capone, Amelia Erhardt, Langston Hughes, and many famous people, but they were especially intrigued with Walt Disney's creation of Mickey and Minnie Mouse,

Donald Duck, Pluto, Porky and Petunia Pig. They had learned to write checks and heard about the problems that buying on credit had caused for people in the twenties. The skit they were to perform in the lyceum was ready, and they were working on a problem. Given a 1920s salary, they were trying to decide how to spend it on the goods, services, recreation, etc., of that era.

Family Involvement

A whole language approach to language, learning, and literacy like the Vandalia Roaring Twenties theme spills out into the home and community, enriching everyone's lives. Mothers and daughters sewed together working on costumes to wear in lyceum skits or to represent a twenties personality. A grandmother donated her *Good Old Days* magazines for research. Families dug through their trunks and their memories. Perhaps most important was the burst of communication among the generations. Kids talked to their grandparents about what it was like to live when thirty miles an hour in an automobile was moving at a good clip and movies didn't talk.

My eighty-five-year-old mother lives in this community. When Chris, a seventh grader, came to talk to her, she told him about her boyfriend who was a "scab" who crossed union picket lines and how, wherever they went, there was a fight. One night at a pie supper, to harass her boyfriend, the union men bid Mother's pie up until her friend had to pay fifty dollars, more than a month's wages. When Chris begged for more stories, it made both their days.

Observing this school, where students, teachers, and administrators were excited about learning and working as a team to make it happen, made mine. They and I hope you steal their ideas and make it happen in your school.

FOXFIRE: PRESERVING THE HILL COUNTRY CULTURE IN HIGH SCHOOL

I'm blessed with enough interesting cousins to fill Yankee Stadium. The one who married a Kentucky doctor, among other things learned to play the dulcimer and became enamored with the culture and crafts of Appalachia. She discovered Eliot Wigginton and the work he and his high school students—with the help of community people like Luther Rickman and Aunt Arie, in Rabun Gap, Georgia—were doing long before Jessica Tandy and Hume Cronyn brought *Foxfire* to Broad- way. To acquire the dramatic rights for the stories that came out of Rabun Gap students' *Foxfire* magazine and books, the actors and playwright Susan Cooper had to go to Georgia to explain to a group of stern-eyed youngsters that they were not out to frame their cherished old people in another version of "L'il Abner."

According to Wigginton, the majority of his ninth-grade students, who will later collect and write the stories and oral history, arrive in his classroom decorated with regional artifacts (quilts, baskets, hand-made tools and toys, etc.) "as restless as a roomful of weasels" with language art skills below the national norm, a dislike for English, and a resistance to the didactic approach to writing. He arrives with a state mandate to teach "enabling skills."

Wigginton has recorded this astonishing story of how these at-risk students have started a magazine, published books, built log cabins in *Sometimes a Shining Moment: The Foxfire Experience* (Doubleday, 1986). Here we will look at what whole language educators can glean from this creative teacher's and his students' brilliant decision to collect folklore and oral history from their elders.

First step: throw out the grammar texts and workbooks. To find out where the ninth-grade students are, the first day Wigginton asks them to pretend he is a stranger knowing nothing about the Appalachian region—its geographic location, history, people, culture, or tradi-tions. Their job is to tell him what is unique or different about where they live. He learns what skills they need, continues to work on correcting them within the context of their continuous writing, and that is about as traditional as it gets. They move on to how to operate a tape recorder, how to transcribe from a tape, how to operate a camera. They take historic field trips to learn how their ancestors acquired land in a lottery, how they constructed their log cabins with the handmade tools the students have been studying in class.

Since they will soon be collecting stories that will be published, they work on learning to describe someone as accurately as area writers, like

Thomas Wolfe, have done. They concentrate on features, body language, accessories, mannerisms, descriptive verbs, figurative language—especially similes used in their county, like "straight as a rifle barrel," "ugly as a mudfence." The things the camera leaves out are what writers for *Foxfire* put in. The writers are the eyes and the ears for their readers.

They also look at the difference between ridicule and humor and at cultural stereotypes, their own and others, like "nigger," "hick," "hillbilly," and "damned yankees."

The young writers work equally hard learning to describe a place. When you're telling a real audience about a place and people you are proud of, you want to get it right. The number of people who still ask about Aunt Arie is evidence that they have.

When she was in her eighties, Wigginton and his students met Aunt Arie, reported to have the most beautiful smile they had ever seen on the face of a woman, living alone on the side of a mountain in an unchinked log house with stone chimneys and a tin roof. The first day they found her out back scraping the hair and bristles from the severed head of a huge hog. When Wigginton, with images of *Lord of the Flies* dancing in his head, reluctantly agreed to help remove the eyes, she patted him on the back, talking him through the ordeal. A student recorded the conversation which became the focal point of *The Foxfire Book* (distributed by Dutton, 1972), and they all began friendships with Aunt Arie, lasting until her death.

Wigginton has created and edited a series of nine *Foxfire* books written by his students. The following describes the contents of the first one: Hog dressing, log cabin building, mountain crafts and foods, planting by the signs, snake lore, hunting tales, faith healing, moonshining, and other affairs of plain living.

Call it building their self-esteem if you prefer, but helping children to be proud of who they are and where they come from, be it the Upper West Side of Manhattan, Shaktoolik, Alaska, or Rabun Gap, Georgia: is the starting point for helping them to become literate.

Whole Language Approaches That Work

THE LIBRARIAN AS CATALYST
FOR WHOLE LANGUAGE PROJECTS

Sandra Stroner Sivulich, Librarian at the West Nyack Elementary School in West Nyack, New York, began her career as a public librarian, a group who, she says, have been thinking thematically forever. In the sixties, she did freelance work for *The Encyclopedia Britannica* Learning Corporation, an exercise that began to prepare her for whole language before any of us, including Sivulich, had heard the term. Although teachers might still have been teaching reading with phonics or single-word flashcards, in a project called "Language Experience in Reading" she provided annotated bibliographies linking themes, books, and activities, much as whole language teachers and librarians do today.

Following are whole language approaches to books Sivulich begins in the library today, either storytelling or dramatically reading aloud. Unfortunately, she sees the children for only thirty-five minutes per week while their teacher has his planning period—and she must also check out books then. If the schedule allowed time for the teacher to remain with the class, he would have a better sense of how to build on what Sivulich has begun, instead of the catch-as-catch-can conversations they now have.

Four Fur Feet by Margaret Wise Brown (Wm. R. Scott, 1961)

Since the artist never lets them see the animal who walks around the world, Sivulich tells the children they will simply have to imagine what he looks like. "I will draw him," she says, "but you must tell me how. How big are his ears? How many eyes does he have? Does he have a tail to wag?" (Or the children draw their own version.)

"Now this poor creature needs a language. How shall we have him speak?" (Kids have come up with color language such as red=hello, blue=I'm hungry. Another group has had him speak through music, while some other children have invented a sign language for their creation.) Writing or acting out stories in the animal's language is a good classroom follow-up to the story.

Mr. Tamarin's Tree by Kathryn Ernst (Crown, 1976)

Mr. Tamarin's cutting down his trees starts a lively discussion about what the world would be like without trees, which provides a natural lead into a connection with science and ecology activities for the teacher.

Alexander, Who Used to Be Rich Last Sunday by Judith Viorst (Atheneum, 1978)

Teachers who are always looking for math tie-ins will love this story that Sivulich ends with having the kids track what happens to Alexander's money. Teachers continue with a change-making activity.

Three Wishes by Charles Perrault (Troll, 1981) and
Pizza for Breakfast by Maryann Kovalski (Morrow, 1991)

These books—one modern, the other traditional folk lore, but with the same theme—give children an opportunity to contrast and compare, as well as come to understand an important literary element. Sivulich reads *Three Wishes* the first week and on the following visit, presents *Pizza for Breakfast*.

Sivulich's strategy for telling any story is to observe the three L's: 1. like your story, 2. learn your story, and 3. live your story.

TEACHERS AS READERS PROJECT

When basal readers were replaced by a literature-based curriculum, many teachers felt they needed to catch up on the many fine books that would be assets to their whole language program. Everyone has pitched in. Librarians give workshops and booktalks. Publishers invite teachers to presentations of their new titles.

One of the more successful approaches is the Teachers as Readers Project sponsored by the Association of American Publishers in conjunction with the International Reading Association and the American Library Association. Teachers, principals, librarians, and parents meet regularly to discuss children's books, reviews, and professional literature. As students do, participants learn more about authors, keep response journals. These teachers realize you have to have been there to get it.

For more information, contact Mary Sue Dillingofski, AAP Reading Initiative, 220 E. 23rd. St., N.Y., N.Y. 10010. Telephone: (212) 689–8920.

MAKING CONNECTIONS

"If you give a moose a muffin, he'll ask for blueberry jam . . . " and before you know it, he'll want more muffins and . . . you know how it goes.

The story serves as a metaphor for learning for lively Peg O'Sullivan, storyteller, creative dramatist, and literature consultant in Fairfield County, Connecticut. "Making connections is how we—young and old—learn, how we acquire knowledge," O'Sullivan says. "When we go to a museum, we don't look only at one facet of a picture. The form, the color, the subject, the time, the artist's point of view, connect to make meaning of the canvas. Our minds make the same kinds of leaps, the same associations when we read or hear a story."

There is nothing that can't be taught around a story, according to O'Sullivan, who models her approach in classrooms where teachers want to know how to implement whole language practices. Hiring people to do modeling costs more initially, but she feels it works better when a teacher asks for her services. Then there is a commitment from someone who will touch hundreds of children's lives. Workshops, which O'Sullivan also does, can be a bust, she says, if teachers go because they are sent, not because they feel a need to know and to implement whole language.

Here is how she operates:

Working with a kindergarten teacher, they begin by brainstorming ideas for possible themes. (With older classes, she will use the same process with the students.) After choosing "growth," they began to make connections with things that grow—like children—physically and emotionally, and in nature—plants, animals, caterpillars to butterflies, etc. O'Sullivan's goal is to broaden a theme, considering all of the best possibilities before narrowing down the curriculum decisions. Whole language is making connections. Everything takes you someplace else. It's like giving a moose a muffin. . . .

The next stop is the library to pick good books to develop the growth theme. O'Sullivan collects a basketful of books to leave in the classroom for browsing. She chooses a story that is tellable or that she can present dramatically. Half way through the story—when there is a problem to solve—she stops, leaving the teacher and the kids to work on possible solutions before finishing the story.

One of her favorite themes for second graders is that of smaller (persons, objects, forces) overcoming greater ones. The library is filled with possibilities where this story is like that one. These include *The Name of the Tree* by Celia Lottridge (Macmillan, 1990), *How Rabbit Stole the Fire* by Joanna Troughton (Bedrick Books, 1986), and the many, many versions of "Hansel & Gretel" that she will sometimes give students to compare.

For a book to introduce the study, she especially likes *The Emperor and the Kite* (Philomel, 1988), Jane Yolen's retelling of a Chinese folktale about the little princess who was so tiny no one noticed her. When the Emperor is captured and locked away, no one knows where he is except the tiny princess because, being so small, she was not noticed by his abductors. As usual, everyone notices her older and bigger brothers and sisters who weep and wail for the Emperor, while each day the diminutive princess, whom no one notices, flies her kite, carrying food and drink, to the tower where the Emperor is being held. But of course, he must be rescued. What to do? O'Sullivan stops at this point . . . wouldn't you know it? Now the children must find a way to save him.

When kids begin to give their ideas (she encourages them to use their own creative powers rather than magic), O'Sullivan does "solution valuing" by asking, "Will this work? What can we do to make this work?" Then they go back to finish the story.

At this point, the kids have only heard the story. They draw pictures from the images the teller put in their heads before they see the illustrations in the book. Looking at their drawings she begins to ask them to think like a writer, explaining how they can tell a story with their pictures: "What kind of day is it? Who else is in the picture with the little princess?"

Continuing to think like writers and to make connections, they do cinquains. I had to be reminded of the formula. In case you've forgotten, too: a noun goes on the first line; second line, an adjective; third line, the verb; fourth line, adverbs; fifth line, synonyms for the noun on the first line. Inspired by the little princess, the children draw their cinquains in shapes of kites. The words flying on their kites become their spelling words, and that leads to a mini-lesson on synonyms for "small," and in art they make kites, which means they must have a kite-flying day . . . because when you give a moose a muffin. . . .

WHOLE LANGUAGE STORYTELLING

Retelling stories, the kids' own and others, plays an important role in a whole language classroom. Marcia Bowers, who writes "The Storyteller's Corner" for *The Journal of the Children's Literature Council of Pennsylvania* (The Children's Literature Council of Pennsylvania, vol. 5, no. 1, 1991) caught my attention when she suggested there is not only an art to doing it well, but skills children should be given early on.

We know that children who begin to think of themselves as writers, even before they can write, want to know where authors find their ideas for stories. In her storytelling sessions, Bowers begins by asking kids where stories come from, leads them to discovering that before they get into books, stories reside in people, and there are many untold stories just itching to be told (see the Foxfire stories, pp. 191–193). She hints that some of them reside in the kids sitting in front of her.

Bowers explains a good starting point for telling stories is to start with what we know. But retelling a story and making it interesting is not as easy as it seems. First, it must reside in both the head and the heart. In our heads, we hold the pictorial understanding of a story—the idea and the language—but the emotional understanding is in our hearts. To grab the interest of listeners, a storyteller has to draw from personal experience. She has to daydream, reminisce, collect images, and let those images and memories grow into the story. Here are Bowers' suggestions for helping your students learn how:

- Have storytelling role-modeled by a "master teller," who might be as close as the library.
- Develop group storytelling sessions that offer a safe environment conducive to gaining creative experience and risk-taking.
- Build a resource library of storytelling materials.

The "master" will inspire rookies when she brings a story to life in her own inimitable style. If they start out copying her, that's okay. As they progress they will begin to dip into their own emotional responses. A story "washes" through a teller and will, in time, emerge in his or her own voice.

A role model will talk about her research—reading, writing, trial and error process. She will explain how she learned from mistakes as well as successes in front of a group.

As she demonstrates, children will notice that particular look and demeanor—*the storyteller's trance*—acquired from her ability to look inward at the imagined while, simultaneously, looking outward to the audience, paying attention to both.

Drawing from private emotional and imagined experience, pointing to the creative interchange between listener and storyteller, the teller demonstrates how to make a known story new. Most important, she shows the freedom and pleasure in creativity.

I especially like the idea of stressing how the listener is part of the creative process. It is good training for more than storytelling. Before

James Earl Jones had become quite so famous, and interracial romance and marriage had gained wide-range acceptance, I took a high school class to see him play *Othello* at the Goodman Theater in Chicago. A white Goodman student was playing Desdemona. When Jones kissed her, many in the youth-filled audience giggled nervously.

Stepping to the apron, Jones talked to the kids two or three minutes about the unwritten agreement between the actors and the audience, who were all a part of the creative experience. When he went back into character, I would gamble on his having created a group of kids, that no matter what other mischief they might have found since then, they will always behave themselves in a theater audience.

Bowers also has a sensational idea for developing a storytelling environment. She says storytellers create rituals of *calling the audience over into story*. Hers begins with a chant (from *Storytelling Process and Practice* by Norma J. Livo and Sandra Reitz. Libraries Unlimited, 1986):

A story, a story, let it come,
    let it go
A story, a story, let it come,
  let it go

She also carries a *story stone*, richly waxed from first time storytellers' sweaty palms. Children see the stone as a talisman and think the story stone holds the stories. Bowers says perhaps it does. The rule is the one holding the stone is the storyteller. The other children are listeners until one of them receives the stone and must begin looking in her head for the words to tell the tale. While the teller searches, the others chant. This is to block judgment of the story just told, which can kill risk taking.

Being very practical as well as creative, the box containing the tools of her trade is another part of her ritual. The box is the *storyteller's seat*. When the teller passes the stone, he also gives up his box seat.

To help kids find stories, Bower will often start off with something from the traditional literature like trickster tales, following with a personal story about being a trickster. Then the children are offered an opportunity to tell about a time when they were tricksters.

Each story is a gift, not to be corrected, approved or disapproved. Kids seeing the expressions on their peers' faces can't help but self-evaluate. Bower simply asks the tellers for suggestions they might wish to offer future storytellers.

The following are resources Bowers suggests:

Barton, Bob. *Tell Me Another: Storytelling and Reading Aloud at Home, at School, and in the Community.* Markham, Ontario: Pembroke Publishers, Inc., 1986.

————. *Stories in the Classroom: Storytelling, Reading Aloud, and Role Playing with Children.* Markham, Ontario: Pembroke Publishers, Inc., 1990.

Collins, Chase. *Tell Me a Story: Creative Bedtime Tales Your Children Will Dream On.* Houghton Mifflin, 1992.

Griffin, Barbara Budge. *Students as Storytellers: The Long and Short of Learning a Story.* Barbara Griffin, 10 South Keeneway Drive, Medford, Oregon 97504, 1989.

————. *Student Storyfest: How to Organize a Storytelling Festival.* Barbara Griffin, 10 South Keeneway Drive, Medford, Oregon 97504, 1989.

————. *Storyteller's Journal: A Guidebook for Research and Learning.* Barbara Griffin, 10 South Keeneway Drive, Medford, Oregon 97504, 1990.

Hamilton, Martha, and Mitch Weiss. *Children Tell Stories: A Teaching Guide.* New York: Richard C. Owen Publisher, Inc., 1990.

Livo, Norma J., and Sandra A. Reitz. *Storytelling Activities.* Libraries Unlimited, 1987.

————. *Storytelling: Process and Practice.* Libraries Unlimited, 1986.

Moore, Robin. *Awakening the Hidden Storyteller: How to Build a Storytelling Tradition in Your Family.* Boston: Shambhala, 1991.

Here is a list of books with very short stories Bower suggests for retelling:

DeSpain, Pleasant. *Twenty-two Splendid Tales to Tell from Around the World.* Vol. I and Vol. II. Seattle: Merrill Court Press, 1979.

MacDonald, Margaret Read. *Twenty Tellable Tales: Audience Participation Folktales for the Beginning Storyteller.* Bronx: The H.W. Wilson Company, 1986.

————. *When the Lights Go Out: Twenty Scary Stories to Tell.* Bronx: H.W. Wilson, 1988.

Russell, William F. *Classic Myths to Read Aloud*. New York: Crown, 1989.

San Souci, Robert D. *Thirty Chilling Tales: Short and Shivery*. New York: Dell, 1987.

Young, Judy Dockrey, and Richard. *Favorite Scary Stories of American Children*. Little Rock: August House, 1990.

MAKE UP STORIES TO TEACH HISTORY

Someone wise once told me history was what happened and literature was how people felt about it. Judith Black, a professional storyteller who lives in Marblehead, Massachusetts, works from that premise when she gives suggestions to storytellers on how to create a story out of a historical event, such as Rosie becoming a riveter when the men went to war in 1941. I think her ideas would work just as well with kids.

Begin with research, Black advises. A good story takes from the realities of a place, time, and people and then imbues them with human detail to animate the material. She suggests a story line, defined and structured by an event. The tale must be filled with details of the era, place, and person being fictionalized. The social, political, economic, and philosophical temperament of a time and place defines an act of courage, humanity, deceit, or bravery, such as Rosa Parks' sitting in the front seat of a bus in Montgomery, Alabama. Knowing the low social, political, and economic status of women in the 1860s vitalizes the story of a woman who successfully spied for the Confederacy, revealing the battle plans for Bull Run.

Details of the physical world to add depth to your story can be found from old photographs, newspapers, historical societies, recorded interviews. Black suggests collecting more information than you will actually use, but, like an actor building a character, your final story will be supported by this knowledge.

As an example, Black uses the Bread and Roses strike of 1912. After she has the *who, what, where,* and *when,* she makes the story add the *why.*

When she has an outline of the strike events, she thinks about her audience. The trick is to present a character with whom they can identify. She tells about leaving juvenile offenders in tears at an adolescent lockup in Tauntan, Massachusetts, when she told a story about a father deserting his son and the boy's heroic effort to prove himself. On many levels, this had been the delinquents' story—parental rejection and the endless road to finding acceptance.

Making her strike story work for middle-class adolescents, Black builds the tale around a fourteen-year-old girl who overhears an actual event of the strike when the mill owners plot with the town mayor to frame two Wobbly organizers for a bombing.

Black says that once you've created a sympathetic character whose life reflects the times in which she lived you have the beginning of historic drama, an exciting way to present history, challenge your skills as a researcher and a maker of tales.

Why not try the exercise with your students, too? Perhaps, you go first, explaining the process as you build the tale:

- Know your era, character, and the details of the event.
- Use human details mixed with authenticity found through research.
- Tell how your character lived through a specific time/place/event.
- Conclude with how your character resolved his needs, wishes, and conflict.

BOOKS TO SUPPORT THE PROJECT:

Many authors have chosen family legend, an era, a historical sight, event, or person as the grist for their stories. To tell Ben Franklin's story, Don Lawson even enlists help from Franklin's intimate friend and advisor Amos the Mouse (*Ben and Me*, Dell, 1973).

Some other stories set against the backdrop of history are:

Conrad, Pam. *The Journal of the Ship's Boy*. Boyd Mills Press, 1991.
    Columbus.
Cormier, Robert. *I Am the Cheese*. Knopf, 1977.
    Witness Protection Program.
Fox, Paula. *The Slave Dancer*. Dell, 1974.
    Slave-ship life.

Fritz, Jean. *The Double Life of Pocahontas*. Putnam, 1983.

Garland, Sherry. *Song of the Buffalo Boy*. Harcourt, 1992.
Vietnam, 1973.

Greene, Bette. *Summer of My German Soldier*. Dial, 1973.
World War II.

Hansen, Joyce. *Which Way Freedom*. Avon, 1986.
———. *Out From This Place*. Avon, 1988.
Civil War.

Hunt, Irene. *Across Five Aprils*. Berkley, 1987.
Civil War.

Kassem, Lou. *Listen for Rachel*. Avon, 1986.
Civil War.
———. *A Haunting in Williamsburg*. Avon, 1990.
Colonial days.

Koller, Jackie French. *Nothing to Fear*. Harcourt, 1991.
The Great Depression.

Mazer, Harry. *The Last Mission*. Delacorte, 1978.
World War II.

Mazer, Norma Fox. *Downtown*. Avon, 1984.
The sixties.

O'Dell, Scott. *Sing Down the Moon*. Dell, 1976.
Navajos' forced migration.

Rappaport, Doreen. *Trouble at the Mines*. Bantam, 1989.
Pennsylvania coal miners' strike of 1898.

Reeder, Carolyn. *Shades of Gray*. Avon, 1991.
Civil War.

Richter, Hans Peter. *Frederich*. Viking Penguin, 1987.
Germany and the Holocaust.

Rostkowski, Margaret I. *After the Dancing Days*. Harper & Row, 1986.
World War I.

Say, Allen. *The Bicycle Man*. Houghton Mifflin, 1982.
Japan after World War II.

Schlein, Miriam. *I Sailed with Columbus*. HarperCollins, 1992.

Treviño, Elizaeth Borton de. *I, Juan de Pareja*. Farrar Strauss, 1966.

The painter Valesques.

Yep, Laurence. *Dragonwings*. HarperCollins, 1975.

Early Chinese immigrants in California.

"CO-CRELATING," RESCUING CHILDREN AT RISK

Co-crelating, a made up word combining co-creating and relating, was coined by Mara Capy, Ed.D., A.D.T.R., recently deceased, who was a registered dance therapist and trained teachers and expressive arts therapists at Leslie College in Cambridge, Massachusetts. Co-crelating is a method calling upon the storyteller to play her historic role as educator, healer, and artist, with an emphasis here on healing. The idea is much better than the hard-to-say term.

Whole language draws on the new and the not so new. It sounds to me as if villages in Africa accepted the philosophy and used some of the techniques long before educators coined the phrase. As her model for helping troubled children, Capy used African storytelling, praised for motivating the young and developing their self-esteem while affirming their creative spirit. An African storyteller lived among the people, knew their problems. When a child was at risk emotionally or in the community, the teller of tales told a traditional story reflecting the problem. Everybody listened. She encouraged the child and the listeners to join in. They acted out the story, used music and chants to breath life into the tale.

When the child added to the story, the audience praised him while the storyteller wove his gift into the fabric of the story. The events of the story remained basically the same, but together, the child and the storyteller embellished it so the child could live in the story, move through struggles toward psychic health. The idea was to release the emotional tension and rechannel behavior interfering with the child's progress.

When working with troubled children in your schools, Capy suggested that you build from the model, but rather than using traditional stories, she recommended allowing the child to improvise a story built on a fantasy. The adult may help the child mold the storyline, but the kid is in charge. Living through the tale while telling it, the child unconsciously projects her fears, hopes, and dreams into the safe boundaries of the story. The child might ask the audience to chant, clap, dance or sing with her, making them part of her fantasy.

At the climax of the story, something has to change. The child and the storyteller work together to find a resolution by which the child's hopes and dreams are accomplished. Through play, this child in pain, who needs to speak and be heard, has confronted her fears and created a story given as a welcomed gift to her community. Her creativity has built trust and acceptance. With a little help from the storyteller, she has become a hero.

As references, consult Odette Blum, *African Dances and Games* (New York: Selva, 1969) and Pearl Primus, "Life Crises: 'Dance from Birth to Death,'" *American Dance Therapy Associon Proceedings* (Philadelphia: American Dance Therapy Association, 1969).

Fish for Ideas

Following is a potpourri of individual ideas collected from whole language teachers. Dip in to supplement your plans.

PRACTICAL "HOW-TO'S" FOR USING LITERATURE

The following are selected from suggestions of Barbara Goldenhersh, M.S.Ed. Educational Consultant, Belleville, Illinois:

1. *Literary Journals.* Have students pretend to be a character in the story. They each write a diary account of one day in their life as this character. They must think, feel, act, talk, and write as though they REALLY are the character.
2. *Imaginary Journeys.* Prepare students for new materials as well as reinforce what they have already learned by taking imaginary journeys. Immerse the students in the settings and characteristics.
3. *The Same or Different?* Encourage children to see how change in setting alters the story by putting the main character into a new setting or time. How will the changes alter the story?
4. *The Reading Chain.* Encourage your students to complete a "link" for each book they read. Have them write their name, title of the book and author on each strip of paper. Form it into a chain. This can be done using inchworm segments, footprints, etc. The chain can become a schoolwide experience by linking it from classroom to classroom or to the principal's office.
5. *Character Report Cards.* Have students create report cards for characters from the books they read.

6. *Sequel.* Ask students to create a sequel to a story they have read. Present these ideas to the class for feedback.

7. *Survey.* The children conduct a survey of five people to find their three favorite children's books. Students will record responses, bring their lists together, and graph their results to compile a class list of community favorites.

8. *The Most!* Decide who is the most humorous, frightening, bizarre, intelligent, attractive, courageous, honest, heroic, unselfish, greedy, or kind character you have met in your reading. Support your choice with descriptions and examples of behavior from the story.

9. *Dear Abby.* Each student assumes the role of a character in a recently read story. He or she then writes a letter to Abby asking for advice to solve a problem. Letters are collected and distributed to other class members who assume the role of Abby to write advice to the character.

10. *The "Oscars."* Coordinate an awards show for reading material. The group selects categories for awards such as Best Animal Story, Best Poem, Best Illustration, Best Nonfiction, Most Humorous, Most Likely to Be Read Again, etc. The children vote, tabulate the results, prepare the awards, and host the show. You might want to create a name for your award, perhaps modeling it after a school mascot.

11. *Guest Reader.* Each week invite a guest to read to your class. The guest could be from a child's family, the school staff, local office holder, community member—even the mayor or local judge. This is a way to show your students that people love to read.

12. *Literary Interview.* After reading a story, pair the students for literary interviews. One child will be a character from the story. The interviewer will interview the character for a mock TV or radio show. The interviewers are responsible for creating meaningful questions and can even design sets. The character responds from his limited viewpoint. He can wear a costume, if appropriate.

ESL STUDENTS TEACHING TEACHERS

In 1992, New York Chancellor of Eduction Joseph A. Fernandez reported that in a three-year period, 120,000 immigrant children from 167 countries had entered New York City public schools ("Students Teaching Teachers," Maria Newman, *The New York Times*, April 16, 1992). To accommodate the students something had to be done. Here is one pilot program.

At Theodore Roosevelt High School in Bronx, New York, sixteen Hispanic and Vietnamese teenagers and sixteen teachers are the players in a rare exercise of role reversal intended to narrow the chasms of language and culture that separate so many of New York City's young immigrants and their teachers. Since the program began two years ago, approximately 100 staff members have volunteered for classes.

The plan uses students as teachers in their native language. The mission is not to train teachers to qualify as English as a Second Language (ESL) teachers, nor is there the expectation that, by spending two hours per week for ten weeks, the staff will become fluent in Vietnamese or Spanish. Rather, the program merely wants to help students and staff to understand each other better. Humbled teachers say they now have a better understanding of what kids go through learning English. On open-school night, teachers are also able to speak with parents at least in a very simple dialogue, having gained a basic appreciation for the language.

The program builds self-esteem for the student teachers, who are selected on the basis of their academic records, and is an incentive for those who would like to be teachers.

Adult Literacy and Whole Language Programs

ELECTRONIC MAIL

The whole language approach is such a logical way to learn, it works at any age. At night, when his wife and children sleep, words come to Sonny Carbone, sixty-year-old New York City construction worker who bought his first book the other day. He carries a notebook on the job to capture the words in his head. For most of his life, words were things that other people wrote and read, until he learned to read by writing to his teacher, Ann Heininger, in an electronic mail duet.

Heininger's employer, the accounting firm Coopers and Lybrand, donated computers and easy-to-use software to Literacy Volunteers of New York City, where she has worked for several years, and that made all the difference. The group meets in person twice a week, sitting at a table surrounded by Boggle games, books, and printouts of their writing that grows out of their lives. Heininger talks about tone, varying sentence length, rhythm, and encourages them to write more, to dig deep.

"As adults, we're so afraid of writing. The computer is a process to loosen them up. They draw on their own experience, make up their own stories, and then they get better at reading other peoples'," said Heininger.

The U.S. Department of Education estimates that one in five American adults is functionally illiterate, not reading well enough to fill out forms, read letters children bring home from school or take telephone messages.

Mr. Carbone looks back at his days of illiteracy with wonder and sorrow. "Before, your mind's asleep . . . where you're writing and reading, your mind hears everything and puts everything together," he says. ("Linked [at Last] by the Word," Susan Chira, *The New York Times*, 25 Mar. 1992)

A FAMILY LITERACY PROGRAM

Look at what they are doing to wake up minds and solve problems at the National Center for Family Literacy in Louisville, Kentucky.

The staff work from *A Strengths Model for Learning*, a manual focusing on the healthy traits of families, even those considered "at risk." When parents enter the program with their children, they often lack the self-esteem necessary to think of themselves as "first teachers," but the instructors begin by pointing to their *courage*. Without it, they wouldn't have come. The goal is to build on parents' diverse knowledge and beliefs, to affirm what they do well, and to encourage them to do even better.

Once a family identifies its strengths and healthy traits, they form the core of a family support plan designed to mobilize resources to help meet their needs for improved literacy as well as other needs.

For example, among one family's concerns is their dependency on Aid for Families with Dependent Children (AFDC) for support. The mother cannot get even an entry level job because she lacks education. She is also concerned about her four-year-old who lacks skills for school readiness. Their *needs* are a General Equivalency Diploma (GED) and employable skills for the mother, childcare while she attends classes, and preschool for the four-year-old.

In an advisory session, the mother sets goals:

- identify people she can depend on for encouragement and support when she needs a boost
- find someone to drive her to class
- locate a babysitter for the four-year-old
- list family strengths she can rely on

- write about a time when she succeeded in moving away from an unpleasant situation
- prepare an action plan

Based on the research, the Center uses the following as the dimensions of a strong, healthy family:

- communication styles that encourage give and take
- encouragement of individuals to reach their goals
- commitment to family, a feeling of closeness and attachment
- religious orientation or spiritual wholeness
- social connectedness rather than isolation or separation
- ability to adapt to new, unusual, and difficult situations
- expressing appreciation for small and large efforts
- clear roles and carrying out of responsibilities
- time together

As soon as the parents feel comfortable, the teachers encourage them to discuss how their family can build a sense of trust, play and humor, respect for privacy; share leisure time, build family rituals and traditions; cope with stress and crisis; solve problems together; listen to each other.

The emphasis on communicating is reflected in the Center's environment that encourages reading, writing, talking, and sharing:

- tables for group discussions
- listening centers for tape recorders and literature cassettes
- a message center equipped with paper for students to write to each other
- places to publish on bulletin boards, newsletters, as greeting cards
- puppets, dolls, masks, costumes, and props for role playing and acting out. (Children and parents are encouraged to role play the basic feelings of "mad," "sad," "glad," and "afraid.")
- displays of family receipt books, picture albums, birth certificates, antique clothing, uniforms
- exhibits of family trees, genograms (structure and function of

family members like Dad—Henry; works at Kroger Store; provides basic needs).

The teachers find using literature as a basis for discussion keeps the focus on family strengths. They use poems, greeting cards, and short stories such as O. Henry's "The Gift of the Magi," Truman Capote's "A Christmas Memory," Arna Bontemps' "A Summer Tragedy." The following is a sample of their approach:

Arna Bontemps was a writer out of the Harlem Renaissance Era. He wrote both from the heart and from experience. His story details a particular day in the lives of Jeff and Jennie Patton, who—confronted by starvation and poverty—have run out of hope. He is lame, crippled by a devastating stroke; she is blind.

The Pattons' five grown children had all died within a two-year period. How is it possible that two people, consumed by crises, can demonstrate strength?

The readers and listeners (this is a good story for reading aloud) readily identify the terms of endearment that pass between the two. They recognize the support given by both as they feel compelled to make the most painful decision of their lives.

The pride and dignity, which helped the couple survive earlier tragedies, bolster them as they follow the only escape they think honorable.

The Center has also identified several high interest/easy reading novels like Robert Newton Peck's *A Day No Pigs Will Die* (Dell, 1979) that lend themselves to the program's goals.

A Day No Pigs Will Die, the story of a twelve-year-old boy who becomes a man in one short year, chronicles the months leading up to Rob's father's death. The strengths of the family permeate every chapter and are easily identified by students, who relate closely with a family that lacks education, money, and opportunity, but one that demonstrates caring, love, affirmation and support, reciprocal teaching and learning communication, and above all—understanding.

The strategy for discussing the novel begins by focusing on students' prior knowledge and experience with the language, situations, type of characters, historical and geographical setting. The teachers make connections between the responses and the text.

To connect their writing to their reading, students:

1. Construct a learning log in which they connect facts with feelings.
2. Write dialogue journals where teachers and students converse on paper.
3. Use the class-generated list of healthy traits of families, compare the strengths to those of the family in the novel.
4. Write family memories where similar strengths aided members of their families.

As the Louisville staff designed activities emphasizing a family focus, they also had to keep in mind the need of most of the adults for a collection of skills necessary to receive a GED or other educational credential. One of the skills was the ability to construct, read, and interpret scales, tables, charts, and graphs. The instructors cleverly found a way to combine the acquisition of skills with their goal to increase positive interactions between parents and children: Parents log their parent/child interactions for a predetermined time. After logs are complete, they graph interactions, comparing positive with negative incidents.

The Louisville staff found the content for their language study most often came from real life. They designed activities to help their students become creative and powerful users of language and to realize these exercises were only the beginning of a richer life.

(From *A Strengths Model for Learning in a Family Literacy Program*, copies of which are available by contacting Meta W. Potts, Director of Adult Learning Services, National Center for Family Literacy, 401 South Fourth Avenue, Louisville, Kentucky 40202–3449. Telephone: 502–584–1133.)

CONNECTIONS: LIBRARY-BASED READING PROJECTS

Despite Robert Frost's legacy about good fences making good neighbors, when a fruitful idea to encourage reading comes along, it tends to flow through New England like maple syrup. The Connections program, funded by the Vermont Council on the Humanities, was developed by a group of adult education tutors and librarians and is headed by Sally Anderson, director of the Vermont Reading Project. These humanities programs, often cosponsored by schools, Headstart groups, daycare providers, and continuing education leaders, have spread through the Northeast. We tuned into a good one in New Hampshire.

A library-based reading program, Connections invites people who are new to books to join for the enjoyment of reading and talking about themes and ideas, like friendship and home, topics relevant to their lives. In addition to strengthening reading skills bound to build their self-esteem, the idea is to help adult new readers, and others who might be unfamiliar with libraries and discussion groups, feel comfortable and find pleasure in a world of books and ideas.

Each Connections series, based on children's books related by a common theme, provides a rich source of material for discussion at levels everyone can read and understand. Participants read independently or with their tutor, joining in the dialogue when they feel the urge. To encourage home libraries and family reading, participants get to keep the books used in the programs.

Held in school and public libraries with only student participation, no lectures, the basic philosophy is that everyone, including people new to books, can engage in reading for the love of it when they're introduced to excellent literature that makes sense in their own lives and when they are given a chance to think and talk about their ideas with others. The emphasis is not on reading as a skill, but as a gateway to ideas, interaction, and to full membership in the community.

Director of the New Hampshire program Christie Sarles says that Connections supports the journey from functional to thoughtful literacy and promotes lifelong family reading.

The following is a sample theme used in the program. For more information contact: Christie Sarles, Director, New Hampshire State Library, 20 Park Street, Concord, NH 03301, telephone: 603–271–2866; or Sally Anderson, Vermont Reading Project, P.O. Box 441, Chester, Vermont 05143.

COURAGE

Courage Close To Home:

Lionni, Leo. *Frederick*. Pantheon, 1973.
Mathis, Sharon Bell. *Sidewalk Story*. Puffin, 1986.
Stolz, Mary. *The Bully of Barkham Street*. Harper, 1963.

Courage On Your Own:

Bauer, Marion Dane. *On My Honor*. Dell, 1987.
Gardiner, John Reynolds. *Stone Fox*. Harper, 1980.
Steig, William. *Brave Irene*. Sunburst Books, 1988.

Courage In Other Worlds

Alexander, Lloyd. *The King's Fountain*. Dutton, 1989.
Babbitt, Natalie. *Tuck Everlasting*. Farrar, Straus, 1975.
Sendak, Maurice. *Where the Wild Things Are*. Harper & Row, 1963; new ed., HarperCollins, 1988.

Questions for Discussion:

What do we mean when we say "courage"?
Does courage imply the absence of fear?
What is a hero? What is heroic action?
Can courage be displayed by ordinary people in everyday actions?
How is courage connected to personal conviction and making choices?
Is courage always exercised for good ends? Is it always met with admiration?

WRITING ACROSS THE DISCIPLINES IN HIGHER EDUCATION

With seed money from a Johnson Wax Grant, Millikin University, Decatur, Illinois, engaged William Zinsser, author of *Writing to Learn* (Harper & Row, 1988), to kick off a series of writing workshops for all faculty members from the business school to the science labs. As a guide, using Zinsser's text with the subtitle "How To Write—And Think—Clearly About Any Subject At All," the project began under the direction of Dr. Terry Shepherd, an English teacher who also directed the Student Writing Center. However, after a period of three years, the Millikin faculty proudly reports, the role of project director now rotates to professors across the disciplines.

In the spring of 1992, The Writing in the Disciplines Program, published Volume One of *Millikin University Journal of Writing*. Director James V. Rauff says the journal's purpose is to encompass the entire landscape of university writing: essays, interviews, poetry, pedagogy, personal journal extracts, reports, and letters. A sample of the articles include "Reflective Science Writing: An Excerpt, A Tree's Regeneration"; "Writing in the Field of Accounting"; "Professional Writing in Commercial Art"; "Poetry in the Chemistry Lab," from both student and faculty contributors.

For those of you working with younger children in whole language classrooms, the *Millikin Journal* offers hope that when these kids are ready for college, they will find teachers who appreciate their philosophy and share their urge to write about absolutely everything.

For more information, contact: James Rauff, Director, Writing in the Disciplines, 1184 W. Main St., Millikin University, Decatur, Illinois, 62522.

What Teacher Educators Are Doing and Thinking about Whole Language

Most whole language teachers and librarians in the Metropolitan New York area have a twinkle in their eye, when they talk about the courses and the support they received from The Bank Street College For Education and Columbia Teachers College.

Take Mary Cunneen from Islip, New York, who taught fifth and sixth grade before she left to raise her family. Hating basal readers even back then, Cunneen accepted a first-grade opening at the Maud S. Sherwood Elementary School a few years ago, in spite of the thought of those readers giving her a stomachache. Then she learned it was a whole language school. Even though she had done some innovative work in a private school while her children were growing up, she had another abdominal attack.

Fortunately, that summer she found a two-week, whole language workshop, two first-grade colleagues who had had whole language training took her under their wing, and she followed their lead . . . until January, when, this time, she had a panic attack. These kids were going to have a reading test in May. Out came the basals. Well, what do you know, her kids could read them. Putting the readers back in the closet for good, she signed up for a writing workshop at Columbia and became a permanent whole language champion.

Wherever I went, whomever I talked to, two teacher educators' names turned up, Lucy Caukins at Columbia Teachers College and Moritza Macdonald at the Bank Street College of Education. When I finally spoke to Macdonald, I understood why. Having trained teachers at the University of Chicago, when I had an opportunity to talk to her, I felt as if we were singing a duet.

218

Macdonald, the director of Pre-Service Education, who also teaches Curriculum for Elementary Teachers at Bank Street, points to the major dilemma for teachers who want to implement whole language practices into their classroom. Too many administrators and people doing the assessment have not adjusted their thinking and practices to support the new ideas teachers are acquiring.

If a teacher uses whole language practices, like creative spelling for writing stories and predicting words in reading, but the children in the second grade are given reading tests based on phonics and material that has nothing to do with the kids' interest or knowledge, everyone loses, especially the children. Until whole communities share the same values and perspective—focusing on the child's developmental process—Macdonald says there will be problems.

Macdonald educates teachers, but what she also wants to do is to work with administrators until they are able and willing to support the teachers' new ways of doing and looking at things, as well as equip the administrators to explain the new approaches to parents in language they understand. If the principal can show mothers and fathers stories dictated by kids, letters they have written to thank the man for the trip to the museum, the parents are more apt to understand why their children no longer bring home workbook sheets.

Another of Macdonald's concerns arises when enthusiastic whole language teachers forget that children learn in many different ways and that educators should not totally throw out techniques that have worked for some, just because it is the "old way." Isolated pieces we used to have, now are all rolled into one. Phonics helps some children, especially ESL kids. Working with Asian children who could not pronounce their buddy, Scott's, name because Chinese ends in soft syllables and they simply didn't hear the sharp English endings like Scott's "tt"s, Macdonald gave them a phonics lesson. Then she read *The Hungry Caterpillar* by Eric Carle (Putnam, 1981) emphasizing the words with sharp consonant endings. Phonics certainly isn't the only way, but it should be one of the many approaches a teacher tries when children are having difficulty.

Children can't edit their writing until they have acquired knowledge about punctuation, spelling, and structure. Macdonald tells her teachers, "Sometimes you have to stop to do some straight teaching of skills (mini-lessons) for a specific purpose, not from a grammar workbook, but from the kids' writing, or their needs. Direct instruction is especially important for children learning a new language."

Macdonald shares the concerns I have when teachers tell me about going to conferences to hear the "whole language experts" and feeling as if they aren't in what they call "the inner circle" because they think you can not be a whole language teacher under the umbrella if you do anything that smacks of traditional teaching.

Teachers who occasionally break words into syllables and give a spelling lesson aren't drummed out of the corp at Bank Street, even though whole language is the foundation of their teacher-education program that focuses on the child's development and her acquisition of language. A major goal is to validate people's thinking about their own ideas—as teachers in training—so they will be able to pass it on to their students. "You can't give what you don't have." For example, Macdonald encourages her teachers to write when the children write.

She recently visited one of her teachers who told the children that, while they wrote, she would write a letter to her daughter at college who was homesick. Her purpose was to show where writing fits into our regular lives, as her students didn't often see people writing at home. Intrigued, the kids asked if they could read something she told her daughter. Parents' sending comfort in a letter was a fascinating idea for them.

"New teachers, however, have to land in a system where they are going to be allowed to try what they've learned," Macdonald says. Reinforcement from their Bank Street experience will come when they work with children, as her former student/teachers now do at PS 87 (see pp. 170–176), but there are not yet enough schools where the entire community will back and bless their efforts.

One of the New York schools where they will find a supportive community is the learner-centered Manhattan New School, an alternative public school directed by Shelley Harwayne, a Columbia TC professor. There are 150 kids, and a long waiting list, in K-3 (next year they will add a fourth grade); seven full-time and five part-time teachers.

The director describes the school as an oxymoron, a simple school in a complicated community, but the atmosphere is right. "I care about the kids," she said. "The kids care about each other and their community. High school seniors volunteer to work here. Parents doing writing workshops in the school understand why they don't receive the traditional stuff that has always gone home. We are trying to put literature at the heart of the students' lives. Our teachers, children, parents, read and write and play—a part of the process in two of life's greatest pleasures."

Since it is a public school, I asked what she did about the second-grade reading test, the scourge of innovative educators' existence.

I would also call Harwayne an oxymoron, a practical/creative person. "Oh, a week before the test, we explain to the kids how to fill in blanks, but it doesn't influence our teaching," she said. "Our children know authors, but that knowledge isn't tested, and the standardized reading scores say nothing about them loving to read and write. Our special-ed kids read along with kindergartners; music teachers sing while we read Robertson Davidson's *Walking Spirits*; families ask us to come for dinner. You can't test this stuff with a standarized test."

From the first moment I heard about the whole language philosophy, it grabbed me by the back of the neck. Finally, all of the things I had been thinking, trying, and believing all my unorthodox, professional life came together. At seven years old, Mrs. Funk, a wise woman, made me the teacher of a Sunday School class in a tiny village in Southern Illinois , maybe to keep me from squirming, I don't remember, but I do remember how much I *loved* teaching.

The thrill of working with students to gain knowledge and skills never stopped, but many systems, rules, tests, goals would discourage me, drive me away for awhile, even though, not being able to stay away, I always came back. Like, in the beginning, when I had a former coach for a principal, who called me into his office to compliment me on the outstanding job I was doing at Bowen High School in Chicago, with surely the brightest high school senior English class ever assembled. He said I had such good posture and so much energy, I was a wonderful role model for the students. My posture? Those kids were reading and *comprehending* Joyce's *Portrait of an Artist*, for pity's sake. The next year I was called on the carpet by his successor, a former woodshop teacher, for teaching *Catcher in the Rye*, with all those dirty words, and for explicitly explaining Jake's wound in *The Sun Also Rises*—neither of which would raise his school's SAT scores. Long ago my exasperation faded into regret for all of us that those well-intentioned administrators had not gone to a Harwayne school where, when they were young she would have tried to put literature at the heart of their lives.

Knowing I would be sending my graduate students at the University of Chicago into similar situations, I often felt as if I were betraying them, who were also eager to change the world as teachers. Today, armed with a new philosophy about language, learning, literature, and literacy, I think we are less apt to be Don Quixotes dreaming the impossible dream.

Teaching writing at the New School for Social Research in New York City to people with a meaningful purpose—they want to write a novel—has proven the whole language philosophy to me. I hope it works for you.

A book like this is never finished, finally just abandoned. There is always another good book, a teacher doing something wonderful, a new idea to try. Maybe next time we do a workshop together, it will be face to face.

INDEX